MIND
MEDICINE

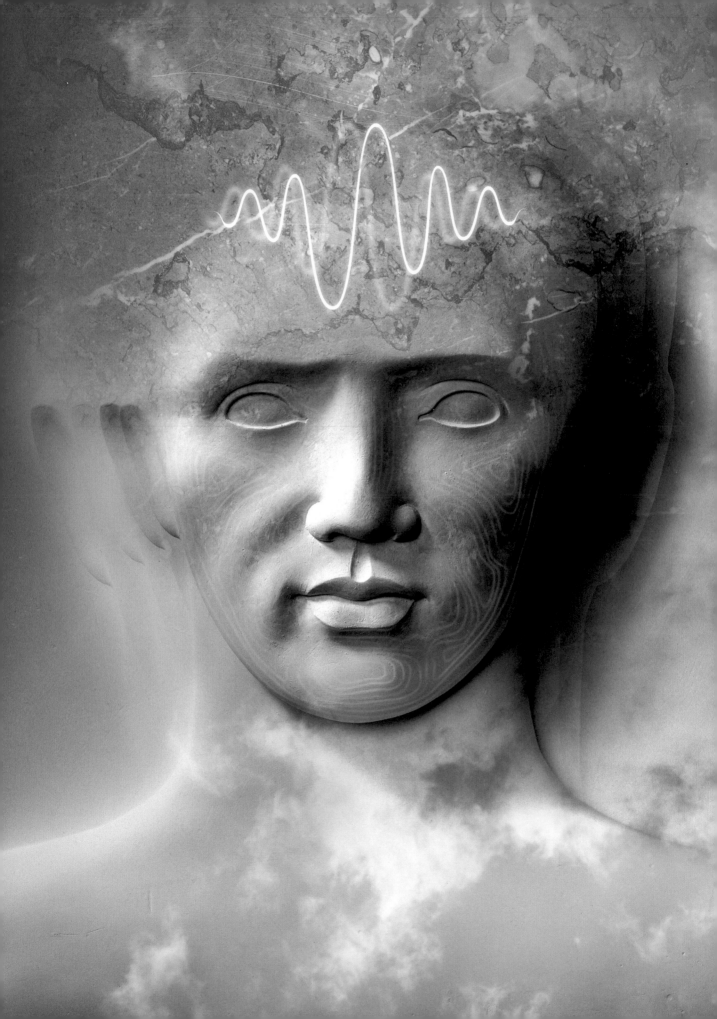

MIND
MEDICINE

❛ MindPower is not a secret I can whisper in your ear. There is not a remedy or pill you can take to enhance your spiritual abilities. But what I can do is show you how the more you understand about yourself, the closer you will come to developing your own MindPower and healing potential. ❜

© Element Books Limited 1999
Text © Uri Geller 1999

First published in Great Britain in 1999 by
ELEMENT BOOKS LIMITED
Shaftesbury, Dorset, SP7 8BP

Published in the USA in 1999 by
ELEMENT BOOKS INC
160 North Washington Street, Boston,
MA 02114

Published in Australia in 1999 by
ELEMENT BOOKS
and distributed by Penguin Australia Ltd
487 Maroondah Highway, Ringwood,
Victoria 3134

Designed and created with
The Bridgewater Book Company Limited

ELEMENT BOOKS LIMITED
Senior Commissioning Editor Caro Ness
Editorial Director Sue Hook
Project Manager Shirley Patton
Editor Jo Richardson
Group Production Director Clare Armstrong
Production Controller Fiona Harrison

THE BRIDGEWATER BOOK COMPANY
Art Director Terry Jeavons
Designer Alistair Plumb
Editorial Director Fiona Biggs
Managing Editor Anne Townley
Project Editor Lorraine Turner
Picture Research Liz Eddison
Photographer Walter Gardiner Photography
Three-dimensional models Mark Jamieson
Illustrators Lorraine Harrison, Rhian Nest James,
Catherine McIntyre, Tony Simpson

An important note to our readers
The information contained within *Mind Medicine* is intended for
educational purposes only and should not be used to replace
medical advice. It is not intended for the treatment, cure
diagnosis or mitigation of a disease or condition. If you have
any medical conditions or are taking any prescription or non-
prescription medications, see your physician before altering or
discontinuing the use of medications. Persons with potentially
serious medical conditions should seek professional care. No
therapeutic or medical claims have been implied or made.

To my little friend Jonathan
1988 An angel on earth
1998 An angel in heaven

Printed and bound in Great Britain by Butler and Tanner Limited

British Library Cataloguing in Publication data available

Library of Congress Cataloging in Publication data available

ISBN 1 86204 447 5

We would like to thank the following for use of pictures:
Art Directors & Trip p. 25, 73, 94r, 172–173, 174–175, 174, 177b;

Bridgeman Art Library pp/Musée d l'Assistance Publique, Hopitaux
de Paris, France 31/City of Bristol Museum & Art Gallery, Avon, UK
83t/ British Library, London, UK 30c/Christies Images 47tc/Musee
Conde, Chantilly, France 83c/Galleria degli Uffizi, Florence, Italy
83b/Guildhall Library, Corporation of London UK 32b, 33b/Holborne
Museum & Crafts Study Centre. Bath, Avon, UK35/Lascaux Caves,
Dordogne, France 40/National Gallery, London,
UK 124, 167t/Oriental Museum, Durham University, UK
47tr/Wallraf-Richartz Museum, Cologne, Germany 47tl;

Corbis p. 194–195;

Liz Eddison pp. 28t, 57l;

Uri Geller pp. 7, 9, 22, 23

Hulton Getty pp. 30l, 89l, 89r, 111b, 156–157, 192–193;

The Image Bank pp. 95b, 125;

Guy Ryecart pp. 1, 3, 13, 54, 55r/
Mark Jamieson 17c, 67, 104l, r, 105l, r, 113l, r;

Science Photo Library pp. 20t, 33t, 48l, 72c, 74, 111t, 130tr;

The Harry Smith Collection p. 36b;

The Stock Market p. 153tr;

Tony Stone Images pp. 17r, 18cr, 26, 27l, 34bl, br, 39, 44l, c, 46–47,
50–51, 56, 57c, 60–61, 65t, 68l, r, 81l, 92bl, br, 94l, 107, 110,
114–115, 116–117,
120, 123, 127t, l, 128, 132, 133, 135r, 137, 142, 145t, b, 146r, 147l,
150t, 151, 152–153, 153bl, 152tr, 154–155, 157, 161, 166, 177r,
180, 181, 185, 187, 191, 199.

CONTENTS

FOREWORD

I really did not know what to expect when I picked up the manuscript of *Mind Medicine*. I had had no contact with Uri Geller in more than 25 years, and when I last saw him, he was a performer of psychic feats who told me he was not interested in healing. He was then young and restless, unable to sit still, and, consequently, also uninterested in meditation. His passion was trying to convince audiences and scientists of the authenticity of his powers of telepathy and psychokinesis and in so doing turn the world on its ear.

The Uri Geller who wrote this book is obviously a different man, one who is thoughtful, mature, and very much interested in healing. I thought I would find in these pages an emphasis on psychic phenomena, with instructions for unleashing the power that Uri uses to bend spoons and keys and turning it on germs and tumors. Instead I found a great deal of very sensible advice for improving general health and wellness and practical guidance for taking advantage of the body/mind connection to access healing. Along the way, this calmer and wiser Uri Geller surveys the history of Western medicine, reviews complementary therapies, explains the actions of endocrine hormones and common pharmaceutical drugs, and gives readers basic instruction in meditation, which he now feels is an essential component of a healthy lifestyle.

Those who enjoy good health will find here many suggestions for maintaining it. Those who are ill will find many specific methods for getting better, including visualizations and numerous self tests to identify beliefs and behaviors that act as obstacles to healing.

Throughout the world people are wanting to take greater charge of their own well-being, to be less dependent on outside experts and authorities, less in need of toxic drugs and invasive medical procedures. *Mind Medicine* helps provide this kind of empowerment by reminding readers of the reality of their own natural healing ability and showing them how to allow it to work for them.

This is not a book of testimonials or miracles that defy rational explanation, nor is it an excuse for Uri Geller to showcase his own remarkable talents. It is a collection of grounded, useful information that I think will help many. I read it with interest and pleasure, not least because it is so revealing of Uri Geller's own growth and development into a man committed to the welfare of others.

ANDREW WEIL, M.D.
Tucson, Arizona
March 1999

> To be able to heal others,
> I have to make sure I live the kind of life in which
> all the ingredients necessary to nourish this power
> are in place. The way I live today is the way
> I have chosen to live because it is a healing
> lifestyle, and I have never felt more
> energetic or healthy in my life.

WHY I WANTED TO WRITE THIS BOOK WITH URI

Uri knew who I was before we even met, picking me out among a crowd of people in London's busy Haymarket. Of course, I knew who he was already – or I thought I did. I quickly came to realize that this was Uri Geller's dilemma – other people's expectations.

If I mentioned his name to friends, their first question was always the same: "Is he real?" I assume they meant, was he a fraud or did he really possess psychic power, and was there really not any trickery involved?

Curiously, no one asked me about his healing power. Over the weeks and months that we worked on this book, it became evident that this aspect of his life was hardly ever talked about. Spoon-bending, clocks stopping and starting, telepathy, yes, but not his healing power.

We had conversations in which we discussed healing, going over the details of each chapter, how the book would look, what it would say. I had no idea that, throughout this time, Uri was continually in touch with ten-year-old Jonathan McCarthy, either telephoning daily or visiting him personally.

Jonathan had fallen ill in June 1997 with an inoperable brain stem tumor. After a course of radiotherapy, a scan the following October showed a remarkable improvement, but by March the tumor had returned. Jonathan died on November 25, 1998.

I remember the date because I was supposed to meet Uri, but he was too upset. When we spoke about Jonathan on the telephone later, all he would say was, "Why? Why do so many young children suffer from these cancers? Is it the world we live in? Are there too many dangers?"

It was only when talking to Uri's wife, Hanna, that I discovered the Geller household was like an airport with the comings and goings of numerous visitors to their home. As well as a group of disabled people who visit every two months and have tea with the Gellers and walk in their gardens, there had been a party of ten Israeli children all suffering from serious illnesses a few Sundays earlier.

Harry Harris told me how Uri visited his 12-year-old son Mark, who was hospitalized with a rare form of brain tumor that had changed this brilliant young schoolboy's personality. "Uri was a tremendous support because he has such a positive attitude. He spent time with Mark who then underwent two years of chemotherapy. This cured the cancer, but Mark's brain damage was severe and the doctors could not repair what had been destroyed."

Mark, who had won prizes in math, science, history, and divinity, was never able to take another exam and now had learning difficulties and no short-term memory. Uri stayed in touch over the years and, when Mark was 20, a place was found in a residential care facility where he made friends and settled down well. On his twenty-first birthday, Uri sent him a bouquet of balloons. Harry recalls: "I cannot forget the look of pleasure on his face when they arrived – he beamed from ear to ear."

I spoke to Ken Barrett whose grandson David, now ten, had surgery two years ago for the removal of a brain tumor. "We are convinced Uri helped him. He laid his hands on David, and meditated while David was being operated on. Everyone was surprised, including his surgeon, when David recovered in a matter of weeks and

*❛ I believe Uri is constantly
in awe of his own power. He sees it as
a precious and priceless gift, and no matter
how many times it has enabled him to perform
the impossible, he is filled with the sheer
wonder of it, as if for the first time. ❜*

LEFT **Uri and Jonathan McCarthy**

was back in school when he was expected to be just getting out of bed and learning to walk again. Uri is now helping my other grandson, Joel, aged nine, who is suffering from a difficult condition caused by lack of sunlight."

When Jamie Patrick was nine, he visited Uri's house. He had just been told he was to have major surgery for a bone disease. His hip was disintegrating and his left leg was very thin and weak. He was in too much pain to walk let alone play football. Uri gave him some healing and a Uri Bear and kept in touch by telephone. When Jamie finally went into the operating room, the doctor discovered an operation was not needed after all. His mother, Paula, said: "I used to be skeptical, but all I know is that a year ago Jamie was dependent on his crutches and was due to have surgery on his withered hip. After seeing Uri, he got better and I was thrilled and relieved."

In fact, there is a very long list of people whose lives are blighted by illness and who have been on the receiving end of Uri Geller's generosity of spirit. Indeed, Uri Geller is Honorary Vice-President of Bristol Children's Hospital and the Royal Berkshire Hospital, both in England, and donates to them and to a children's charity a percentage of the income from his books. All over the world there are children who have received teddy bears, or Uri Bears, which have a crystal energized by Uri around their neck. They also receive his love and compassion – and healing.

There were visits from David and Avril McCarthy, Jonathan's parents, and when Jonathan spent a weekend with Uri and his family, Uri arranged a helicopter ride for him. It was from

ABOVE **Lulu began her collaboration with Uri on this book by asking the simple question: "Why does illness exist?" This led them to look in many different directions, past and present. What Lulu discovered during her research was that she totally shared Uri's belief in MindPower.**

David McCarthy that I learned about Uri's friendship with Jonathan. He told me that, in the final two months when his son's illness became critical, Uri rang him every day and visited frequently.

Uri says, "Healing does not make me a miracle worker. I am an enabler or a catalyst to these children who have their own healing power, and I try to teach them how to believe in themselves and make their own energies work to overcome their disease. I enrich the idea in their minds that it is possible to fight whatever illness they have.

"To me, it's still a mystery. When I lay on hands, I would love to believe I emit a special healing energy, but I don't know that. I do believe that if things are meant to be, they will happen. We can move a little within our individual space but the overall picture cannot be changed. We are like tiny molecules living intelligent lives inside a bottle. The bottle is floating on a river flowing downstream, and although individually we have free will, we cannot stop the flow of the river and we are on an eternal and infinite journey toward our creator.

"Children are so clever and the ones who are dying know, just as Jonathan told me he knew. Yet, he didn't see a death. I had explained there was another life for him somewhere and God needed him, that we would all meet some day whether here on earth or in another place. I told him this was a continuation, a moving on, and wherever he was and wherever I am, we could always talk."

David McCarthy remembers the two of them out walking together one day. "Uri was brilliant with Jonathan. They were best friends and Jonathan always felt happier after seeing him.

They talked on the telephone three or four times a week. Jonathan had told Uri he was concerned about us. 'My mom and dad are trying to save me, but I know I'm going to die and I'm worried about them.' We had believed he was cured. He was to be a shining example.

"When he was first diagnosed, we were told he had two or three months to live. I'm a pharmacist and I realize the value of nutritional therapy and herbal treatments, so I changed his diet and he became stronger. When the tumor was reduced four months later, the doctors said they had never had a result like this at Great Ormond Street Hospital (the world's leading children's hospital in London, England). He was playing football and cricket and swimming, like any other normal healthy boy."

There are no words to describe the depths of David and Avril McCarthy's grief over the loss of their much-loved son who brought them so much happiness.

Uri Geller's sadness is tinged with anger. "At this stage in my life I have an ongoing internal fight because I do question that so many sick children die. I do ask why Jonathan was taken away in spite of all the healing and love we gave him. I would like to believe he was needed in another place, needed to become an angel, to reincarnate into another child. I would like to believe that one of those reasons was the right one, that his was a journey completed."

Uri will not articulate about his power. He has absolute faith in it, and because he trusts it so absolutely, it works. He visits your home and bends a spoon, and when he has gone, you find other metal objects are curling up in front of your eyes. Uri is completely unaware of these incidents, but they do happen all the time. You try to fathom it out; then you try to discover how he can draw a picture just like the one you have just produced without having seen it for even a split second. Measure the picture and the dimensions are the same, as though one was a tracing of the other.

Uri has a big, expansive presence, and when he walks into a room, he can change the atmosphere of that room. It is a personality made for the world of show business, and earlier in his career, his stage performances were always to packed auditoriums. Perhaps a man with psychic abilities, able to generate a force field of energy after minimal concentration, is expected to conduct himself differently and behave as though he possessed the wisdom of the oracle instead of becoming excited at his own feats.

I believe Uri is constantly in awe of his own power. He sees it as a precious and priceless gift, and no matter how many times it has enabled him to perform the impossible, he is filled with the sheer wonder of it, as if for the first time.

When you think about Jonathan and the emotional and physical energy Uri invested in that little boy's short life, you can begin to understand a fraction of the force of our healing power and how seriously Uri Geller uses his gift, not for effect, not for publicity, but to bring healing into another person's life.

Healing can mean many things. It is a way of giving love, compassion, courage, and hope, as well as a way of bringing peace and meaning to a troubled mind when the physical body can no longer cope. This is the healing energy that Uri Geller offered to Jonathan.

So to all those who asked me about Uri, the answer is yes. His power is very real.

INTRODUCTION

I was born with an extraordinary gift – or perhaps I acquired it as a child. Science calls it psychokinesis; headline-writers call it spoon-bending. Everybody calls it strange. Ever since I can remember, I have been able to bend and break metal just by looking at it. Merely by walking onto a stage, speaking on the radio, or appearing on television, I can awaken similar powers in an audience. Bring your car keys to one of my shows and you might end up taking a taxi home.

What can it mean? Why would the powers above us – and I believe fervently in a higher intelligence that guides our lives – bestow something so incomprehensible on me? To anyone seeing it for the first time, metal-bending is profoundly shocking. It is also perfectly trivial. Why does it happen? I am not asking to know the precise physical process by which my MindPower twists a spoon, I am asking for the inner reason. I am asking for the truth.

I do not believe I was given this gift to help the world's silverware manufacturers through economic slumps. What I do believe is that the higher powers require me to bend minds as well as spoons – to turn people's heads around so they look in fresh directions; to make the world see itself in a different way.

The human mind is extraordinarily powerful. I call it MindPower. To maximize its full potential and work properly, the mind must be open, so please read this book with an open mind.

MindPower is not a secret I can whisper in your ear. There is not a remedy or pill you can take to enhance your spiritual abilities. But what I can do is show you how the more you understand about yourself, the closer you will come to developing your own MindPower and healing potential.

There are many levels to self-knowledge, and each one of us who sets out on such a journey of discovery may take a different road. But the motivation that prompts those first steps and carries us along is essentially the same. I set out to explore and explain my own healing power – which means your healing power, too.

Remember, if it helps, that with MindPower I beat a crippling eating disorder called bulimia, and with MindPower I have convinced injured sports stars they can return to peak fitness faster than any doctor believed possible. Ever since my own children were born, I have been anxious to work with sick youngsters, and I have seen how their own raw MindPower can defeat illnesses that have baffled and beaten conventional medicine.

I have spoken to many doctors who practice conventional medicine, yet also believe implicitly in the power of people's minds to enhance their own natural healing process. Alongside scientific methods, such as surgical procedures and laboratory tests, these doctors are encouraging nutritional values and exercise regimes to strengthen the body's immune system, to help counter the weakening side-effects that are the downside of technological progress. I have also spoken to therapists who practice different forms of alternative medicine, and although their philosophies vary, most of them believe what they do is enabled by a natural healing power. I believe we live at a time when some of the most brilliant medicine is available to us and which is a thousand times more effective if it is combined with our own natural healing power. In fact, I think it is extremely dangerous to abandon conventional medicine in favor of an alternative remedy. I listen to my own medical doctor's advice, and he is aware that I also harness my own healing energy, a power we all have within us. I hope you will find the views and approaches of these healthcare experts both thought-provoking and inspiring.

I have tracked back to the past to place us all in the perspective of our modern world. I wanted to see how humanity came to be where we all are today. I dipped into some ancient philosophies, some psychological theories, and paused at some milestones in medical progress. I looked at the old wisdoms and the new, and discovered many different ways of healing.

What I am offering you is a series of significant snapshots so you can decide if you want to explore farther. They are by no means the whole picture, but only elements of an even bigger, grander design.

We have so much today, but without our health we have so little. When our lifestyles begin to work against us, the disruption means that our health suffers because the mind and body crave balance and harmony. I believe we all have the power we need to heal ourselves, to change anything we want, to be anything we want.

Mind Medicine is a book about discovering your MindPower. The mind of every one of us possesses an unimaginable gift and you are about to learn how to use it. Open it now.

‘I do not believe I was given this gift to help the world's silverware manufacturers through economic slumps.’

Uri Geller

I have chosen this time to write a book about healing because I believe humanity has arrived at an extraordinary place. Thanks to the astonishing advances in medical science, life has never been safer and more comfortable in the entire history of humanity.

Yet, in spite of this, people still suffer fears and anxieties over their health. As well as conditions linked to our modern lifestyle, including heart disease, hypertension, and cancer, we have many modern ailments, such as depression, phobias, eating disorders, addictions, and compulsions – illnesses that reflect the state of our minds as well as our bodies. But if the human mind is powerful enough to cause the body harm, it can also heal.

1 | MINDPOWER

THE POWER OF MIND OVER BODY

During the last few thousand years, the power of the mind has played an enormous part in the history of healing. With so little reliable medicine available, the importance placed on the human race's spiritual development often surpassed the search for a cure. Humans needed to possess a strong faith in their spirituality to sustain them when disease caused terrible suffering and death.

This awareness helped people make sense of their world if only, as many believed, to prepare them for the next life. Their lives were shaped by their deeply held beliefs, which many would have died for rather than relinquish.

Few doubted that the mind was capable of having an enormous impact on the body, but unscrupulous charlatans preyed upon the vulnerable people who were sick and dying, and distorted their beliefs. A profusion of magic, disparaging to witches sorcery and spells degraded the ancient healing wisdom that our ancestors knew and trusted. Amid such absurd quackery, where the gullible and desperate paid for useless remedies, people turned away from their natural, intuitive selves and many lost sight of their own healing power.

Matter over mind

As science became more sophisticated, the demands for more authority and status led to the establishment of rigorous standards, which were both commendable and understandable. Evidence-based science reigned supreme, and the medical profession adamantly refused to acknowledge what could not be proven. Whatever was in people's minds was ignored and precedence was given to what was visible and provable. Matter over mind.

During the last 100 years, medical science has raced along with breathtaking speed, and the advanced technology that is modern medicine today has progressed beyond the imaginings of most 19th-century and even some 20th-century doctors. From conception through birth to adulthood, human life can be transformed, genetically determined, or altered, organs transplanted, and longevity pursued through chemical and surgical procedures.

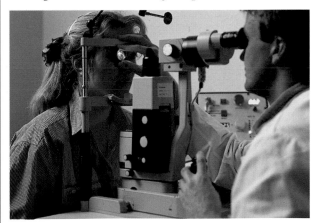

ABOVE **Medical science now uses laser surgery in many surgical procedures, particularly in the treatment of certain eye conditions.**

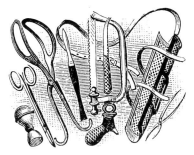

RIGHT **In early medieval England, barbers used surgical instruments to perform operations. Until the 16th century, proper training and regulations were nonexistent.**

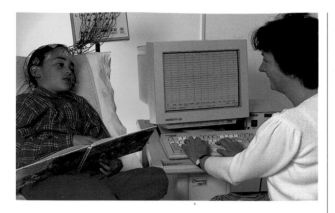

LEFT **By attaching electrodes to the skull, measurements of normal brain waves (alpha waves) can assess the activities of the brain's circuitry.**

BELOW **Nerve cells, or neurons, send out electrical impulses, transmitting information between the brain and different parts of the body.**

MIND–BODY LINKS

Equally impressive as the advances in medical science are the extraordinary revelations surrounding the workings of the mind. Brain waves can be shown on computer screens; the signals carried between neurotransmitters to the brain can be traced and evaluated. Pharmaceutical advances have produced remedies that not only alleviate physical symptoms but are also capable of targeting specific areas of the mind. There are drugs that can inhibit the uptake of certain hormones, heighten happiness, reduce misery, and create calmness. More significantly, doctors are prescribing these medicines for a set of invisible symptoms – emotions and moods.

Today, we can also document the impact of the mind on the physical body, and there is overwhelming evidence of the correlation between the two. Medical science in previous centuries had never been able to do this.

Healing mind and body

The most brilliant medicine in the world, however, cannot cure the body if the patient's state of mind refuses to cooperate, just as a person's state of mind can have a devastating effect on his or her physical health. While science looks for reason and argument, very often faith is what is required.

In the past, different cultures all over the world have combined a spiritual dimension with their approach to healing, but this required belief in an invisible spirit. Now we no longer need a leap of faith to accept that the two are connected. We know the mind-body symbiosis that can lead to disease can also lead to a cure.

Nearly 100 years ago, Sigmund Freud claimed there was a realm of the mind where unconscious thoughts could determine behavior, but fellow members of the medical profession were among his greatest critics because he had come up with a scientifically unprovable theory.

Modern medicine no longer isolates patients into categories of either physiological or mental illness because of the undisputed impact of one upon the other. There is also a growing body of medical practitioners trained in orthodox medicine that is connecting modern lifestyles to the many physical conditions we experience today, and offering complementary therapies, such as homeopathy and acupuncture, alongside general medicine.

Brain and body

The brain is often mistakenly seen as a separate entity to the body, possibly because many of its functions are still a mystery. It is the keeper of people's private thoughts and emotions, which are inaccessible to others, and the search for a scientific explanation of consciousness remains elusive. But the brain certainly does not function in isolation.

The right and left cerebral hemispheres of the brain are responsible for intelligence, speech, and memory. The cerebellum controls balance and coordination, and the brain stem that connects to the top of the spinal cord monitors many of the body's vital functions, such as heartbeat and breathing. The hypothalamus is a part of the brain that regulates body temperature and appetite, and, together with the pituitary gland, controls the release of hormones that are targeted to specific organs.

Whether you read an academic book or a lightweight novel, watch a serious, dramatic movie or a light-hearted comedy, your brain has an appropriate place for processing it. The frontal lobe carries out all our planning and organizing and is responsible for emotions and behavior. The temporal lobe sorts out our memory and our comprehension of the world, including language. The parietal lobe makes sense of the world, dealing with numbers and letters, and the occipital lobe is concerned with vision. The motor cortex controls movement, and the sensory cortex governs sensations.

The right-hand side of the body is controlled by the left-hand side of the brain and vice versa. This means that if the left-hand side of the brain is damaged in any way, the right hand side of the body will be affected. When a brain function fails to be carried out properly, the resulting symptoms can include headache, migraine, and vertigo. Conditions such as neuralgia come from the pain caused by a damaged nerve. Some personality disorders are believed to be caused by an imbalance of the chemicals within the brain.

RIGHT **The human brain, shown in cross section on the right, stores information like a filing cabinet. Its many different compartments receive information along nerve pathways leading from the body's sensory organs.**

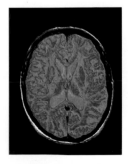

We can benefit from the combination of medical science and the ancient healing wisdom that our ancestors relied upon for centuries.

RIGHT **Medieval doctors believed the ancient principle that disease originated from an imbalance in the four "humors": blood, phlegm, yellow bile, and black bile.**

HOLISTIC HEALING FOR A NEW AGE

I believe the time has come to acknowledge the value of the old wisdoms alongside the new. My enormous respect for the dedicated doctors who practice modern medicine is equaled only by my respect for those who practice alternative and complementary therapies. To ignore one in favor of the other would be to dismiss the achievements of some of our most brilliant minds, just as discarding the wisdom of centuries would be an act of folly.

Our patterns of behavior over the centuries are the same as those of our ancestors – we show predictable responses to life events. Our psyches may be individual to each one of us, but when certain chords are struck, in a similar way, we think and behave almost as if an invisible signal has been sent or received and the only variations come from our cultural backgrounds.

Many serious illnesses, such as cancer, necessitate radical treatments, for example chemotherapy. These chemicals are designed to destroy cancer cells, but inevitably attack the body's normal cells, too. This frequently knocks out the immune system and leaves the patient vulnerable to all kinds of minor infections and viruses that normally would have few ill effects, but can be dangerous without a fully operational immune defense system. Why not counter these side effects with a complementary therapy that will minimize the worst of them? This would not only improve the patient's physical health, but also improve his or her state of mind, which we now know is crucial to recovery.

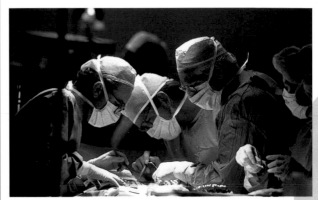

ABOVE **Surgery or medication are the conventional methods of treating illness, but attending to the patient's state of mind is also of vital importance in aiding recovery.**

BELOW **Alternative therapies such as acupuncture, in which fine needles are inserted along the body's energy pathways, can ease the side effects of some serious medical treatments.**

Healing the whole mind

What do the scientists mean by "the mind"? Is it our brain, our emotions, or our spirit? History shows it was our ancestors' faith that gave them hope over lives that often seemed hopeless. This faith springs from the very essence of our being – our spirit. Is modern medicine catching up with the spiritual side of humanity?

We know that if a patient does not believe he will be cured, a cure will not take place. An African witch doctor may agree when a scientist uses physics to explain why a river flows, but he will then tell the scientist that it is because the spirit of the river is making it happen. Taking a medicine to change your mood, increase happiness, or reduce depression will only benefit one part of the mind, the part that reacts mechanically to the altered chemistry. The whole of the mind needs to heal to effect a full recovery.

Many ancient religions that survive to this day contain this element of spirituality in their teachings, believing, as *I* do, in an holistic approach to health. By "holistic" I mean that the whole is greater than the sum of the parts. If only the brain – the mechanical part of the mind – is treated without healing the emotional and spiritual aspects, then recovery will only be temporary. Healing the body means healing the whole mind, and if the mind is in trouble, the body will not heal. Those of us who have been healing ourselves refer to this ability as our sixth sense, because we know its power and value without formal training or prior knowledge.

Science today acknowledges the impact that the mind can have on the body. This means that the emphasis on spirituality over the centuries, alongside the science of these modern times, has brought us to a unique position. As we embark on the 21st century, we can benefit from the combination of medical science and the ancient healing wisdom that our ancestors relied upon.

Treating the whole individual

DR. SOSIE KASSAB, Director of Complementary Cancer Services at the Royal London Homeopathic Hospital, England

❛Mainstream cancer treatment is predominantly cell-oriented, and really just targets the cancer cells. Many people are very apprehensive and fearful at the thought of chemotherapy, but it can cure. It is a question of getting the balance right for individual patients, and because complementary therapies use an holistic approach, very often we can make any side effects more tolerable, which makes chemotherapy more acceptable.

The complementary therapies we use are directed not only to the tumor itself, but to the whole of the individual. When I see a patient, I am not just looking at the tumor and its progression, but at the way it affects that individual, which may be an important factor in the development of the disease.❜

CREATIVE THINKING

In spite of the evidence that there is a marvelously orchestrated interaction between mind and body that plays a vital part in the healing process, many people do not have any confidence in their own resources. The knowledge that we all have the potential to heal ourselves is dismissed as if thousands of years of civilization have numbed our instincts – they have become absorbed into a world in which only the physical exists.

Yet, the greatest scientific inventions of our day have sprung from wildly imaginative ideas, emphasizing the crucial role that creativity has played in humanity's development. It is the essential nature of our adventurous spirit to visualize the unthinkable, to be driven by an unstoppable desire to push out the boundaries and imagine the impossible.

Neglecting this inner part of our being is all the more extraordinary when you consider the immense task the mind completes on a daily basis, silently storing and memorizing more information than we consciously comprehend, coloring our opinions, and enabling us to communicate, converse, and create ideas.

Inner vision

Every book, painting, television program, and movie begins as a tiny seed of an idea, nurtured, developed, and propelled by an inborn knowledge that it will work by someone with the vision to see what has not yet been seen.

No one questions that millions of invisible images hang in the atmosphere and at the press of a button become animated, colored moving pictures, any more than pressing another button introduces the voices of strangers, perhaps sitting in a studio far away, talking to thousands of people they cannot see.

Speaking to one another across vast continents is commonplace through the telephone, and now we can communicate without a direct connection – cellphones bounce our voices off satellites in space. We have come to expect our computers to perform a multitude of functions at great speed without really understanding how the invention of such a tiny microchip makes this possible.

Scientists generally distrust what cannot be explained, yet a physicist needs a vivid imagination to apply his evidence-based knowledge resourcefully. Without that inner vision, how would an experiment ever be expanded upon – how would an ultimate goal ever be reached?

LEFT **The ability of the human mind to think beyond the tangible evidence of what is possible, to imagine the seemingly impossible, has revolutionized our everyday lives beyond the wildest dreams of our ancestors.**

Boundless power

The overwhelming power of the mind to infiltrate and influence every aspect of our lives is gradually being recognized, but, of course, I have known of this extraordinary phenomenon most of my life.

In the past, this psychic power has been abused and corrupted as well as used for positive good. Today, although we know so much more than our ancestors and are aware of the many other functions that the mind performs, we still only know very little.

Technology has invented computers, but no one has yet managed to create an artificial intelligence that even begins to compare with the power of our minds. The human mind can tune into information from the surrounding atmosphere. Science may use physics to explain certain phenomena, but if you can sense a presence or hear an inner voice, why do you need to search for a logical explanation?

Networking

Neurons, or nerve cells, communicate within the brain through electrical pulses facilitated by neurotransmitters, which are the essential fluid chemicals that keep information flowing to and fro. At any given time, thousands of these cells can be engaged, processing thoughts and actions and consigning them to memory.

Gradually a network is formed as the signals link up cells across tiny gaps called synaptic clefts, and each time they do this, a bridge or synaptic junction is formed. This is how our essential wiring is laid down, and the pathways form a map of the brain's network.

As this intricate neural activity continues over the years, the map evolves. Thought patterns governed by emotions and shaped by life experiences define these pathways and the map reflects the people we become, increasing in complexity as our lives progress. But patterns that would seem to have become indelible with time can actually be altered if the will to do so is present.

FOLLOW MY PATH TO MINDPOWER

When I first discovered what I could achieve through the power of my mind, I questioned the source of this power. I had no role models who could advise me. No one had taught me in school that these things were possible. There were no textbooks to lead me through the different stages, no examinations to be passed. I had lots of questions and no answers, but it did not make an enormous difference or stop me from pursuing the endless potential of MindPower. What began when I was a child has remained with me ever since and has become a part of my everyday life.

Although I was constantly curious, I knew instinctively that I should never allow my natural inquisitiveness to block or dilute this energy. This same instinct has served as my guide ever since and given me incredible insights which have reinforced my faith in their wisdom again and again. As a child, I felt an awesome responsibility at being

> *Finding a balance between body and spirit means tapping into the most formidable power of all – your own.*

handed such knowledge, as if I were an adult in a child's body, old before my time.

Comprehending the force of MindPower inevitably led me to develop it and see how far it would take me. I soon learned that its potential is limitless, that I would always be learning. When my personal journey through life has led me down difficult paths, my recovery has added to my experiences which, although occasionally painful, are the surest routes to knowledge.

Tap into your own power

Many people wake up each day in a low frame of mind. They may have many of the material possessions that they believe they need, but they feel jaded and cannot understand why. It is almost as if something is missing. Why are they not happy? This is usually the first question that precedes the search for a greater meaning in life. It comes at a time when we realize that a new possession brings no pleasure any more, and the prospect of a journey of self-discovery is much more exciting.

Finding a balance between body and spirit means tapping into the most formidable power of all – your own. You do not have to spend money or barter for it because it cannot be bought, sold, or exchanged. It is not dependent upon anyone else or anything else.

LEFT **Since his childhood, Uri (right) has been instinctively aware of the phenomenal power of the mind and its limitless potential.**

How I harnessed my MindPower

During the last 20 years, alongside demonstrations of my abilities, I have submitted myself willingly to countless scientific tests under carefully controlled conditions. I was always happy to take part, believing that if the results converted just one cynic, that would be a good enough reason for giving up so much of my time. Now I do not believe that. In my eagerness to defend myself, I did not stop to consider the motives of those who questioned me. Why did I feel compelled to persuade such people to change their opinion of me? Perhaps I cared too much about other people's opinions of me and allowed my egotism to affect my judgment.

ABOVE **The doctors in this Russian hospital were very open-minded about natural healing and very interested to watch me with a patient.**

I already knew the extent of my own healing power because I experienced them myself on a day-to-day basis. Gradually I came to realize that investing precious energy in proving my credibility to other people was simply not necessary. What mattered most was that I believed in myself. I had been dissipating my valuable energy when I could have been using it for more productive purposes. I had to take another look at my values and reassess them. Why was I looking to others for my own worth? I know that true validation has to come from within.

Now I concentrate on using my powers to heal others, and the more I do this, the more I personally benefit from healing. To be able to heal others, I have to make sure I live the kind of life in which all the ingredients necessary to nourish this power are in place. The way I live today is the way I have chosen to live because it is a healing lifestyle, and I have never felt more energetic or healthy in my life.

I learned that we react predictably to situations all through our lives without always questioning our own actions. Defending ourselves is a very natural instinct; so is seeking approval. But it is only when we review our priorities with an open mind that we can understand our real motives for the things we say and do. At that point, we can choose what to select and reject. I learned then that with the courage to believe in yourself comes enormous spiritual strength, which is one of life's greatest rewards.

The twin vocations of medicine and religion have always symbolized humanity's finer qualities: honor and altruism, dignity and respectability – elevating doctors and priests in their communities and providing aspirational goals. The history of healing is brimful with doctors and demons, medicine and magic; ancient adversaries locked in a bitter struggle for supremacy as the true source of healing power. The art of healing was always a divine gift in a world where the conquest of death began at birth. With the prospect of dreadful suffering, people were fatalistic in the face of death and concerned for their spiritual welfare.

2 | DEVILS, DRUGS, DOCTORS, AND DEMONS

WISDOM OF THE AGES

Around 400 BCE, early Greek medicine was already describing conditions such as *dysentaria*, *sepsis*, *arthritis*, *tetanos*, *anthrax*, and *hypochondria*, words that carry the same meaning in today's modern medical vocabulary.

Hippocrates elevated the healing art, separating sickness from philosophy and taking responsibility for healing away from the priests. He declared disease a natural phenomenon and applied treatments based on accurate observation. He created tranquil sanatoria – marble-columned temples of healing set in shady groves under the warmth of the Mediterranean sun – in which patients would be bathed by temple priests and prescribed remedial herbs and a diet while they rested.

Eastern philosophies

Still in 400 BCE, the Chinese practiced acupuncture and applied the complementary principles of yin and yang. The philosophy of I Ching was saying: "The great-souled man meditates on trouble in advance and takes steps to prevent it," emphasizing that prevention was a better option than repression.

In this same century, the Hindu culture was already more than 1000 years old, the Indian civilization even older, and Ayurvedic Hindu medicine based on the "knowledge of life" from the word *veda*, meaning wisdom, was already established.

Even earlier, the ancient Egyptians had been smearing themselves with ointments and fragrances, believing that what was good to smell, breathe in, or even eat was also good for treating and preventing disease. Smells could be good or evil and act as a valuable guide to survival, enabling people to identify medicinal plants and guard against poisons. The bad smell of a decaying wound or a corpse warned people to shun danger and death. The word perfume derives from *per fumum*, by smoke, and sacrificial fires scented with incense were lit in the belief they provided food for the gods.

Ancient holism

Confucius and the beginnings of Taoism described a world in which everything was connected and dependent. Just as each healthy organ in the body depended on all the other organs, for a person to maintain healthy balance everything in the world around that person had to be in healthy balance. Equally, the balanced state of the world depended upon the health of the individuals in that world. This ancient holism decreed nothing could change without changing everything.

RIGHT **Confucius (551–479BCE) was a Chinese philosopher who believed that goodness and benevolence were fundamental for the maintenance of harmony at all levels of society.**

Hippocrates' legacy

In the second century CE, Galen partially revived Hippocrates' enlightened principles, but since very little was known about the anatomy of the human body and dissection was forbidden among the Greeks and the Romans, Galen's lack of knowledge led him to invent elaborate theories that obscured the simpler truths uncovered by Hippocrates.

More than 100 years later, Hippocratic medicine came to the city of Alexandria in Egypt; the city was named after Alexander the Great whose army conquered those lands. Physicians discovered ways of tying a bleeding artery and identified heart valves as devices for protecting the heart from impurities. But the so-called discovery that human arteries contain only air persisted as fact for 500 years longer.

When the Roman empire fell to the barbarians, the high standards established by Hippocrates, applicable today, were lost for 18 centuries as deeply rooted superstitions and dogma swept away his guidelines. Rational medicine deteriorated from logic and reason into a hotchpotch of talismans and magic spells. Healing became largely a matter of superstition and the supernatural, with unreliable potions peddled by quacks and charlatans.

MEDICINE AND MAGIC

Around the world, history shows that people in most of the different ages of humanity had faith in the existence of another dimension and a life beyond the physical. Death was accompanied by rituals and there were usually invisible spirits, both good and evil, to be placated.

Early humans, in their ignorance and fear, drew on the walls of their caves to drive away these evil spirits, and early cultures offered human sacrifices in the hope of appeasing angry gods. Some worshiped rivers, trees, and mountains. Others carved idols and imbued them with sacred powers. The sun, moon, and stars were used as indicators of good or bad fortune.

People relied on primitive philosophies of healing, believing that disease was sent to the sinful by supernatural sources. Ceremony and superstition were employed to drive it out. Humanity's natural spirit of inquisitiveness was suppressed along with intellectual courage.

SICKNESS AND SIN

Medicine reverted to its primitive state when the early Christian teachings decreed that all physical and spiritual salvation was to be found in the Bible. Physical health was subordinated because the Christian church attached more importance to preparing a person for the next life than curing his or her condition in this one. People's minds were filled with sin, death, judgment, and the afterlife.

Sick people called for the local priest when they were ill, but not in the hope of a cure. The remedy was to pray and ask for their sins to be forgiven,

LEFT **The cave paintings of our prehistoric ancestors were not merely decorative but of great symbolic significance, representing and communicating with the spirits that they believed governed their existence.**

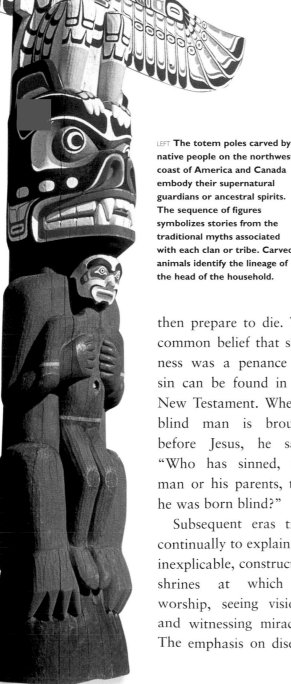

ABOVE **A 15th-century devil conjures further demons from the mouth of Hell. Evil spirits were once believed to cause illness by cutting their victims off from God.**

LEFT **The totem poles carved by native people on the northwest coast of America and Canada embody their supernatural guardians or ancestral spirits. The sequence of figures symbolizes stories from the traditional myths associated with each clan or tribe. Carved animals identify the lineage of the head of the household.**

then prepare to die. The common belief that sickness was a penance for sin can be found in the New Testament. When a blind man is brought before Jesus, he says: "Who has sinned, this man or his parents, that he was born blind?"

Subsequent eras tried continually to explain the inexplicable, constructing shrines at which to worship, seeing visions, and witnessing miracles. The emphasis on disease as divine retribution for the sins of the flesh pervaded many communities.

People would isolate themselves and fast and pray for weeks, deliberately denying themselves food, welcoming the hunger pangs they suffered as penance for their sins. Others would indulge in a frenzy of flagellation, whipping themselves raw, convinced this self-inflicted pain would serve as a punishment and cleanse them of all evil.

Demons and devils

By the fifth century CE, it was believed that wickedness also came from other sources, such as demons and devils that entered the minds and bodies of the innocent, thus corrupting them into sinners. St. Augustine summed up the early Christian concept of disease in this way: "All diseases of Christians are to be ascribed to demons, chiefly do they torment the fresh baptized, yea, even the guiltless new-born infant."

No one doubted the presence of these invisible creatures that "invaded" the bodies of the sick, turning illness into possession. People readily believed their minds could be taken over by demonic forces and that this would, in turn, affect their physical bodies.

LEFT **Frightening gargoyles were carved on churches and cathedrals to remind Christian worshipers of the face of evil, and to inspire them in their vigilance against temptation.**

Sorcery

So strong was the power of suggestion in those dark times, when people were faced with the reality of dreadful suffering, that healing the sick became a matter of sorcery, a battle of good over evil. Life became an obstacle course with hidden devils waiting to lure people into temptation, while only prayer had the power to cast them out.

In the sixth century CE, Pope Gregory the Great related the tale of a nun who ate some lettuce without first making the sign of the cross, thus swallowing a devil that happened to be sitting on the lettuce leaf at the time. The people who cast out such devils were careful to keep their own lips clamped together through such exorcism procedures in case the devil jumped out of the patient's mouth into theirs.

ABOVE **Advances in agriculture encouraged the establishment of permanent settlements. This change in lifestyle began to influence the natural environment, leading to pollution and the spread of disease.**

Demons were charged with having sexual intentions. An incubus, or male demon, was said to prey on young virgins, while a succubus, or female demon, robbed young boys of their innocence. Numerous nuns claimed the devil had deflowered them, even producing bruises as evidence of the assault. It was not unknown for a rich man to employ monks to sit beside his bed through the night in case a devil tried to enter his body while he slept.

Abuse of power

Such faith in the power of priests as healers gave them dominion over people's lives and inevitably led to abuses. The man wielding the power was in supreme control, and all too often sorcery flourished under the guise of spiritual healing. If a witch doctor suggested a person would die in ten days, he surely would. If the local priest or healer told a patient his condition was terminal, then it surely killed him. This worked in reverse as well. In the face of such trust, medicine might well cure a malady. If a person was mad and the "devil" was exorcized, his or her sanity returned.

If the sick did not recover during the worst ravages of pestilential diseases, this was seen as a stubborn denial of faith. Often, as a plague tightened its grip on a diminished town, up to a dozen sufferers would be seized, bound together, and thrown on the floor of a church, where they would lie until either their faith returned and their devils were thus expelled or they died.

THE SPREAD OF DISEASE

Life was always hard. The fear of becoming sick or injured was an understandable terror when the smallest injury and most illnesses frequently proved fatal. The different ages of man experienced varying states of health.

The early hunter-gatherers who led nomadic lives often suffered injuries from their dangerous hunting activities; broken limbs left them maimed, open wounds made them susceptible to gangrene and botulism, and the eating of raw flesh exposed them to various infectious diseases from animals. Over the centuries, humans learned to plant seeds and grow crops.

Early pollution

Having previously made little impact on the places they stayed in temporarily, humans now settled in one place, tending the land they had cultivated. Water sources became polluted from human waste, and with the domesticating of animals, people became exposed to another whole range of diseases passed from the animals with whom they lived in such close proximity.

Unhealthy urbanization

As these tiny hamlets grew into towns and cities, instead of relying on whatever was produced on the land, families began to sell their surplus harvests. The marketplace provided contact with the wider population, as did the storekeepers in the towns who sold on these provisions to those who had other occupations and relied on being able to buy their food. Country dwellers could buy other goods from the proceeds of their toil on the land and improve their standard of living. If their crops failed, they starved. If they or their produce were infected, the disease was passed on.

Gradually, as the populations of these villages spilled over into towns, and the once-isolated communities were now in constant contact with the wider world, the transmission of infectious diseases flourished where once it might have been contained in the small villages.

RIGHT **In the 14th century, the bubonic plague began to travel over land to Europe from the east. The first infected ships arrived in Genoa in 1348, and by 1350 one third of Europe's population had died.**

Moscow

London

Cologne

Paris

Rome

The proliferation of disease

Parasites such as worms led to malnourished bodies, while smallpox and tuberculosis came from cattle, and fatal food poisoning bacteria passed to humans from cats, dogs, mice and rats, chickens, ducks, and geese.

Water sources already contaminated by human waste became worse with the addition of waste from fowl and animals, and gave rise to many diseases such as cholera and typhoid. As industrialization lured increasing numbers of country people to the overcrowded cities, diseases that would have once spread slowly across isolated farms made a more rapid progress in overcrowded tenements. The lice that lived in the seams of people's unwashed clothes thrived in the filth and squalor and led to typhus fever.

Global infection

Many diseases originating in one part of the world were carried by people unwittingly to another. The Crusaders traveled to the East and spread smallpox and scarlet fever. Conquering armies were defeated by the endemic diseases in the lands they intended to colonize, diseases to which the natives were immune. These same colonists, in turn, unwittingly introduced diseases that wiped out native populations unused to the ravages of conditions such as measles and whose immune systems had not built up any resistance.

Leprosy, with its biblical connotations, deformed and destroyed people for hundreds of years. Sufferers were regarded as the living dead, torn from their families and exiled into lazarettos, originating from the monasteries of St. Lazarus where "Christ's Poor," as lepers were called, were incarcerated. Lepers were ordered to wear masks to hide their deformities and carry a bell warning people of their approach. Philip the Fair of France suggested a way of controlling leprosy: "Let us collect in one place all of the lepers and burn them, and so often as more appear, let us burn them also, until the disease is eradicated."

In other parts of the world, humanity's progress was also accompanied by the increase of disease, transmitted from insects, such as fleas, and birds and animals. From Africa to India and China, the rivers that fed the crops also nurtured the parasitic worms that produced elephantiasis and bilharzia, and the mosquitoes that spread malaria and typhus.

ABOVE **A 16th-century barber surgeon removes an arrow. Infection could thrive in open wounds.**

RIGHT **12th-century Crusaders faced the possibility of foreign diseases spreading virulently throughout their retinue.**

Conquering disease

On the battlefield, disease defeated more armies than the actions of war. By the 16th century CE, a barber was likely to be a surgeon as well. Ambroise Paré, whose inspired surgical skills on the

Étude par le peintre Matout

pour son tableau "Ambroise Paré repoussant le fer rouge après une amputation"

Tableau qui décorait l'Amphithéâtre de l'École de Médecine et a été brûlé dans l'incendie du 15 Octobre 1889.

— offert par M. Matout fils — 1903

LEFT The "Father of Modern Surgery," Ambroise Paré, improved the treatment of war injuries such as gunshot wounds and amputated limbs. His writings provided a basis for the future development of surgical techniques.

the greatest killers of all time, sweeping across a defenseless world, leaving a trail of death in its wake – the victims were numbered in millions. Each recurring epidemic devastated communities and entire families were wiped out in days.

No one knew how the plague was transmitted, so no one knew what to avoid to prevent contamination. Bubonic plague is a bacterial disease of rats and is transmitted to humans by their fleas. The fleas leave the dying rodents and infest humans, and their bite transmits the disease bacteria, which cause virulent blood poisoning.

battlefields of France saved countless lives, typified the prevailing approach.

Abandoning the agonizing cauterization that once routinely followed an amputation, he began tying the torn ligatures instead, sparing the patient terrible suffering and probably saving his life as well. But in spite of his evident skill, Paré retained the belief that the outcome for his patients was not in his hands, but in those of a higher authority. Modestly, he would say: "I dressed him, God cured him."

THE BLACK DEATH

Sometimes a combination of animals and insects could lead to disease. Bubonic plague was one of

Persistent parasites

History shows that vermin and parasites, such as rodents and parasitic worms and insects, persisted for centuries, bringing widespread illness and suffering to the population at large. The people who lived in the abject squalor of the Middle Ages were bedeviled with a whole range of parasitic insects – flies, fleas, and lice – but they were not the first people to fall victim in this way. Evidence of ancient nits, the eggs of head lice, which infest human hair and skin, was found in the mummified remains of an Egyptian pharaoh.

Epic epidemic

Neither the medicine nor the hygiene practiced in the Golden Age of Rome were effective against the terrible progress of the plague. Only when Rome fell and travel ceased did the epidemic stop. In the years 68 and 79 CE, there were outbreaks of plague in Rome, then again in 125 CE, and again in 164 CE when it continued for another 16 years to wreak havoc on the population. At its height, it killed 10,000 people in one day.

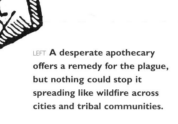

LEFT **A desperate apothecary offers a remedy for the plague, but nothing could stop it spreading like wildfire across cities and tribal communities.**

BELOW **The Thames carried death to 12,400 Londoners in 1665, as foreign ships disgorged plague-infected rats and sick sailors. Insanitary conditions in the surrounding urban sprawl multiplied the disease's devastating effects.**

After the sixth century CE, the plague lay relatively dormant for 800 years. In 1345, the first apothecary shop was opened in London, and, in that same year, bubonic plague had reached epidemic proportions in Asia and Africa. It slowly spread to Greece and Italy, gradually sweeping across Europe with such virulence that it killed almost 20 million people in the first three years of its relentless course through terrified communities. It was to last for the next 300 years.

Defenseless victims

In the face of such a ferocious killer, people were helpless, and inevitably religion offered the only spark of hope. In 1348, Pope Clement VI declared a Holy Year and granted absolution from all sins to the pilgrims traveling to Rome, promising that the souls of those who did succumb to the plague would go straight to heaven without passing first through purgatory. Some carried the plague with them, but once they reached the crowded city, its rapid spread ravaged the population and less than ten percent of those pilgrims ever returned home.

Today, it is hard for us to imagine bodies of the dead and dying blocking the streets or being thrown into mass graves, even into the sea where

THAMESIS

piles of bodies were washed up on the shores. Medieval Europe was a place of indescribable squalor, and the number of flea-ridden rodents multiplied as conditions worsened. The sheer terror that accompanied each fresh outbreak led to wild accusations, and thousands of innocent people were tortured to death, accused of poisoning the wells and spreading the plague.

ABOVE **Today we can identify devastating plague bacteria under a microscope.**

"The Poor Man's Plague"

By the time the disease reached London in 1665, it was called the Poor Man's Plague because the wealthy had left, the courts had closed down, and prisoners died in their cells. Those who fled the towns and boarded the ships to escape found the plague already on board, and entire crews perished at sea. Looters who took advantage of the breakdown in law and order robbed the dead only to die with their spoils in their hands. London's physicians had also deserted, but the apothecaries of the city refused to leave, and continued to dispense remedies, winning admiration and respect from the people for their admirable courage.

The living dead

Dogs and cats, believed to be carriers of the disease, were slaughtered, but no one thought of the rats as being the culprits. The dying were incarcerated in their homes and their doors marked with red crosses. Armed guards prevented anyone from leaving these infected dwellings in an attempt to stop the spread of the disease. In the same way as the lepers, plague victims were considered to be the living dead.

Some of the afflicted frantically offered all their possessions to the church. If this plague was divine retribution and came from the wrath of God, such acts of piety would surely redeem sinners, or so they thought. But bubonic plague made no distinctions when it struck. All too often the churches were abandoned as the corpses of priests and physicians joined all the other powerless victims whose bodies were piling up in the charnel houses.

FLUVIUS

South   Winchester house   Warke

> *Many primitive tribes thought that by eating the raw heart of a lion they would absorb its bravery and physical strength.*

FROM THE ABSURD TO THE PROFOUND

In the 15th century, a belief that witches could conjure up disease fueled a fear that led to the deaths of thousands of innocent women. In those dark Middle Ages, when any number of pestilences could kill indiscriminately, people had no idea how to avoid contamination and escape a gloomy fate.

Confronted by such a mysterious and malevolent presence, fear, ignorance, and bigotry thrived. Pointing an accusing finger at witches and blaming a supernatural force for the sickness and death that surrounded them was just one way of understanding those dreadful events. It was no more obscure than the belief held by many primitive tribes that by eating the raw heart of a lion they would absorb its bravery and physical strength.

Ineffective or deadly "cures"

It is easier to understand the rationale behind the lion's heart notion than some of the more obscure "preventions" and "cures" that prevailed through the ages. Medicines prescribed as tonics consisted of colored water. Pills made from sugar sometimes led to a patient's recovery in spite of their worthlessness. The nastier the ingredients, the more impressive the remedy – some ointments consisted of crushed lice and incinerated toads.

Healing power

The sick were offered the curative powers of pearls, musk, and sarsaparilla. Extraordinary powers were attributed to the execution of criminals; touching the hand of a man on the gallows while it was still warm meant good fortune, and a moss called *usnea*, scraped from the skull of a criminal, was credited with medicinal value. Even today, the slaughter of rhinos in Africa and tigers in India persists in the mistaken but deeply rooted belief that both these creatures possess medicinal and aphrodisiacal powers.

RIGHT **The centuries-old belief that animals such as tigers and rhinos possess medicinal and aphrodisiac properties persists even today.**

Royal healing

In Britain, the King's Touch originated with Edward the Confessor, and this laying on of healing royal hands, known as touching for "the King's evil," became widespread practice among European royalty. Such a healing power was seen as part of the divine right of kings, and the king would touch the sufferers, then bless them and give some gold coins. The King's evil was *scrofula*, or tuberculosis as it is now known.

James I doubted its efficacy, while William III was cynical, blessing people as he laid his hands on them, but adding: "May God give you better health and more sense." In France, Louis XIV touched 1600 people on one Easter Sunday. When Queen Anne of Britain died in 1714, the practice ended and one of the last to be touched was the celebrated English writer, critic, and conversationalist Samuel Johnson, then four years old.

Charles II was one of the busiest royal healers, and in 1684 there were so many people waiting for his touch that the crowds trampled some of their number to death. In a cruel irony, Charles II's faith in his own power was not shared by his physicians when he was lying on his deathbed.

An account of the 14 physicians attending him began with the king suffering a convulsion that left him unconscious, and that was, in all probability, an embolism. He was bled from his right arm, then "cupped" on his shoulder to extract more blood, dosed with emetics and purgatives, before his head was shaved, and a blister raised on his scalp where a powder was sprinkled to "strengthen" his brain. A plaster of pitch and pigeon dung was applied to his feet, and as the days went by, numerous medicinal drinks and enemas were produced and administered containing herbs, flowers, and animal extracts, including 40 drops of human skull. When the king failed to rally, a mixture of julep and ammonia was forced down his throat.

Strange remedies

By the 17th century, those who tended the sick had acquired more knowledge about poisonous substances than those who offered medicinal benefits. Snake venom, opium, and a variety of vegetable substances, including antimony, rock salt, violets, beets, camomile flowers, fennel seed, and cinnamon, were often mixed with human excrement and urine, based on folklore practices handed down from generation to generation. Powders produced from hellebore root and cowslip flowers were administered, as we have already seen in the case of Charles II, to "strengthen the brain."

Over the centuries, herbs and spices were traded across continents and served both as medicines and condiments. Amid the bleeding, purging, and poultices, the unscrupulous offered crocodile dung, powdered Egyptian mummy, and unicorn's horn as remedies. Thousands of ineffective, but inventive, remedies were proffered to the sick or wounded, such as "healing salve" and "sympathetic powder," which were applied to the clothes of victims. Ludicrous, yet effective, was making the sign of a serpent over a patient's head or placing a drop of magical elixir on their lips. Certain medicines were said to work only when a "magic" incantation was recited while the patient drank the especially prepared potion.

ABOVE **The use of plants to treat illness flourished as the 17th century progressed. Thanks to the invention of the printing press, physicians such as John Parkinson (1567–1650) and** Nicholas Culpeper (1616–54) secured their reputations by publishing herbals. Their works soon became essential reference material across the English-speaking world.

The first antidepressant?

In ancient Greece, Hippocrates prescribed hallucinogenic drugs to treat depression and described this as sending people to the "temple of dreams." One of the substances used originated from wild lettuce. The thick stem of the lettuce was cut, and when the emerging white sap was distilled, it became a powerful morphinelike drug. Hippocrates believed the dreams were healing, because they helped to reveal the problems of the spirit.

*' The mind is only too happy
to accept the absurd if it blocks
out an intolerable reality. '*

ABOVE **Folk superstitions surrounding black cats (signifying good luck) and breaking mirrors or walking underneath ladders (bad luck) still survive.**

In our sophisticated and scientifically literate world, some of the bizarre practices that cluttered up the processes of healing sound amusing, even ridiculous. But to people who are desperately ill, maybe suffering agonizing pain and terrified of dying, the mind is only too happy to accept the absurd if it blocks out an intolerable reality.

A return to logic

For hundreds of years, hysteria and hallucinations, often the result of eating medicinal substances, increased people's suggestibility, creating a fertile breeding ground for every quack and conjuror to make a fortune from the misery of sickness. Not until the 19th century did logic and common sense prevail and better standards of practice were laid down, paving the way for the medical profession as we know it today – taking up the principles decreed by Hippocrates in ancient Greece.

We are vastly better educated today than our ancestors and have abandoned some of the more ridiculous superstitions of bygone ages. We know, for instance, that an emerald tied around a woman's ankle does not assure easy childbirth. We no longer whip a flooding river to control the evil spirits as did the Egyptians. Neither do we dissolve pearls in wine to ward off ill health, nor burn witches.

Nevertheless, many of us do suspend belief in the face of reason and avoid walking under ladders, opening umbrellas indoors, or breaking a mirror in case of bad luck. Is this the same as discarding the facts, or an example of not bothering to look for them? Aristotle claimed women had fewer teeth than men, which was accepted as fact until someone was inspired to count them and prove him wrong.

We can blame ignorance and lack of education and information for many of our ancestors' beliefs and behaviors, but today we can only blame ourselves. There is so much knowledge available to us all, yet we pick and choose the areas of that knowledge much more carefully than we realize, and reject what we know very little about. We worry about ill health at a time when we should be enjoying health excellence. I have wondered about this curious irony for a long time.

MAKE A COMMITMENT

To discover your MindPower, to strengthen and improve the health of your mind and body, and to find the courage to discard whatever has no value. Read on and share my thoughts.

I believe that healing is one of humanity's most glorious gifts, and the strength of will that fuels this remarkable power has the capacity to restore physical and mental health. The human mind is a powerhouse of energy, but amid the frenetic pace of our modern world, many people have never tuned into their personal power – their MindPower.

Yet, healing from within is an ability that lies dormant inside us all, a sleeping colossus waiting to unleash its formidable curative force. Everyone can harness their own power and become healthier in mind and body, change their lives for the better, and keep that power working.

3 | MIND MEDICINE

KNOWING YOUR OWN MIND

To understand how the force of MindPower can be harnessed for healing, you first need to understand yourself on many different levels. If MindPower describes an invisible force for healing within our minds, how would you describe your own mind? Today, the mind represents many different things to each one of us.

In the opening chapter, I looked at mind–body links and how one impacts on the other, and particularly so when it comes to our health. A hundred years ago, new psychological theories could only speculate and surmise, but now advanced medical knowledge means that these connections can be demonstrated with scientific evidence. But this scientific proof still perceives two elements – the mind and the body – and to explain farther how

MindPower works, I have to elaborate on the extraordinary complexity within our minds. Yet, the reality is also extraordinarily simple.

Think of energy: It is everywhere in our world, and if we could see it, we would not be able to see anything else. Then divide the mind into energy bodies. One is emotional, another is mental, and another spiritual. Then allow for the fact that two-thirds of our thoughts are hidden from our conscious awareness and we are left with one-third of ourselves actually knowing what we are doing. Then add the fact that this mental energy – the mechanical processes we call the brain – has been operating on the same program that Stone Age man used, and you will realize we are getting the same signals and reacting the same way as he did but in vastly different circumstances.

The power of invisible energy

- We all accept the invisible power that is locked inside a fossil fuel such as coal. It is only when we put a flame to these coals that we see the physical evidence of the ancient energy they release.

- Clear Air Turbulence, known as CAT, can violently shake aircraft, but pilots cannot avoid it because it is impossible to see.

- In extreme climates, tornadoes and hurricanes scoop up debris and spin it with such force that a spiral of wind becomes visible. But even in this case, what you see is the debris circulating within that spiral, not the invisible energy of the wind itself.

- Thoughts and feelings also generate energy which, although we cannot see it, is just as real.

BALANCED HEALING

If we are faced with fear, the brain floods our bodies with adrenalin. This is because our ancient ancestors back in the Stone Age had to either fight with or flee from any threat to their well-being in their struggle for survival. But modern humans, civilized, socialized, and educated, have other options. We may use persuasion, manipulation, or intellectual supremacy over our opponents, but all that surplus adrenalin speeding around our systems has nowhere to go.

Stone Age people would have been fine. After expending all the energy that the extra adrenalin delivered in their fight or flight, the natural healing processes of their bodies would have restored the balance that they needed to remain in good health. But today, we rarely correct such imbalances.

Treating the whole self

Conventional modern medicine is allopathic, which means that when our physical body is suffering from an illness, treatment is aimed at individual symptoms that are experienced physically. In contrast, holistic medicine takes the mind-body links into account before deciding on a remedy. It is like taking a step back to get a broader view of a person instead of isolating individual parts of the body for healing.

ABOVE **Faced with fear, Stone Agers used up the energy produced by the adrenalin rush in fighting or fleeing.**

If I have a headache, I might take an aspirin for instant relief, but if I continue to suffer from headaches I need to ask myself why I have them, because otherwise that aspirin is just treating a symptom. The pain may go temporarily, but without discovering the cause of my problem I have not healed myself, only awarded myself a brief respite from the pain. There is nothing wrong with taking an aspirin and buying time. We live in a modern, fast-paced world, and if we have commitments, an aspirin provides an expedient solution.

However, if the cause of my headaches does not come from my physical body, the logical assumption is that the origin lies within my mind, and if so, what should I do about it? But healing the mind? That is something much deeper and more significant, because true self-healing treats the whole of you, which includes all your four energy bodies – your physical body as well as your mental, emotional, and spiritual bodies. Removing pain and finding out why you have become ill is only part of the healing process. As with Stone Age humans, natural healing restores balance to your entire system, taking you back to where you were before any symptoms of illness or pain even emerged, back to the place where you were whole. This, then, is the truest meaning of holistic spiritual healing, where all the parts of you have healed to restore the whole person. This is MindPower – the key to balanced healing.

HOW MINDPOWER HEALS

Today, the word "healing" usually means that an illness has been cured and the patient has recovered. Such a recovery implies that the patient is back to full health, which strictly speaking would be correct, since healing is essentially a process of transformation. But for true healing to have taken place, all traces of damage from all the physical and emotional symptoms of an illness would have to have been repaired.

Treating your mental energy body

Your brain represents your mental energy body and is influenced by your emotional energy. Mental activity is considered an important factor when it comes to living longer, and if you also have an active imagination, you are less likely to suffer from senile dementia. Like all our muscles, the right kind of stretching and exercising can maintain suppleness and agility. If your thoughts are about things that interest you, they will make you feel alert and enthusiastic, and you will send similar messages to the rest of your system.

Brain power can actually increase with age, and any mental activity that is challenging and stimulating actually increases the brain circuitry.

When you break your leg, once the bones have mended your doctor will say that you have recovered. When you suffer from an infection, a course of antibiotics will knock out the bacteria. If you are unhappy, an antidepressant will lift your mood and alter your state of mind, and insomniacs can take sleeping tablets for a full night's sleep. Your physical symptoms will have been alleviated and some of the ones originating in your mental and emotional energy bodies will also have been addressed. But spiritual healing is about a total recovery in which all the energy bodies are fully restored. They are returned to the place where they were before any symptoms of illness emerged.

Energy healing

Michael van Straten, a practicing naturopath for 35 years, and well-known British broadcaster and writer on health matters:

❝The treatment I offer is aimed at healing different energy bodies. The physical is initially treated by orthodox medicine, and I would send the patient to a doctor who I know is happy to work alongside my natural treatments.

The mental energy body needs massage, aromatherapy, and relaxation exercises, which are all functional therapies designed to remove the tension that is a causal factor of its condition. The emotional energy body will be involved in therapies such as yoga and meditation. The patient will be more likely to continue a therapy if it is one that appeals to them, and this is important.

Naturopaths believe we have another role which is to teach our patients about caring for their health as much as to help them when they have problems. Basically, it is the treatment of illness and the promotion of good health through the use of therapies that promote the body's own healing abilities and the avoidance of anything that interferes with that process. This includes diet, exercise, manipulation, herbal medicines, homeopathy, yoga – anything that enhances the body's defense mechanisms, avoiding surgery, pharmaceutical drugs, and suppressive osteopathy, if possible.

Many Western people are uncomfortable with the word "spiritual," but healing the other energy bodies makes it easier for them to acknowledge and embrace their own spirituality.❞

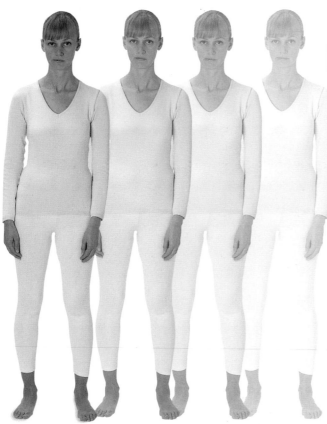

ABOVE **True healing lies in restoring the whole person, which means rebalancing the four energy bodies – physical, mental, emotional, and spiritual – that impact on each other.**

The four energy bodies

When you are ill, your mind or body produces symptoms that are the signals to alert you to the fact that the normal processes within your entire system are changing. It makes little difference whether you have physical or mental symptoms, because none of them operate in isolation, so if the physical starts to break down, it has an effect on the mental, and vice versa.

This change is your illness, and your spiritual, mental, and emotional energies combine to exert pressure on your physical body. For instance, if you have been sleeping badly, over-working, and suffering from anxiety, your mental and emotional energies will give frantic signals to your physical energy and you will develop a headache. This puts pressure on the natural harmony of your different systems, and

taking an aspirin only sorts out the physical energy, leaving the other energies in disarray. If you continue to ignore these warning signals for long enough, this imbalance becomes your normal situation.

TREATING THE ENERGY BODIES

Self-healing begins with identifying the cause of your symptoms and establishing in which of your four body energies they started. You can then select an appropriate remedy that targets the specific energy body. For instance, if you cannot sleep because your mind is racing, the cause may originate in your mental energy body as a consequence of working too hard. The relentless demand on your mental energy to keep thinking and thinking has set off an imbalance and, try as you might, you cannot shut off your thoughts at night. If you select a therapy to help you heal this damage, you can rebalance and restore your mental energy.

However, only *you* can work on your spiritual energy. Healing three parts of you may be fine for a while, but if your spirit is not healed, the cause of the problems will not go away. Ultimately, you need to treat all your body energies to become completely healed.

Which therapy?

The chart on the opposite page is a concise guide to just a few of the many complementary therapies available today, and indicates which specific energy body or bodies each therapy targets. For more information about these complementary therapies, turn to pages 208–10. Conventional or modern medicine, which includes any of the medications listed in the quick-reference guide on pages 210–16, together with surgical procedures, act on your physical energy body. This is where you are first alerted to any symptoms, whether you experience an itch, ache, numbness, or a painful throbbing.

Healing therapies for the four energy bodies

HEALING	PHYSICAL	MENTAL	EMOTIONAL	SPIRITUAL
Osteopathy	✓	✓	✓	✓
Color therapy (including chakras)	✓	✓	✓	✓
Flower essences	✓	✓	✓	
Psychotherapy/hypnotherapy		✓	✓	✓
Reiki		✓	✓	
Meditation		✓	✓	✓
Crystal and gem therapy		✓	✓	✓
Aromatherapy		✓	✓	
Acupuncture	✓			
Acupressure	✓			
Reflexology	✓			
Shiatsu	✓			
Homeopathy	✓			✓
Feng shui	✓	✓	✓	✓

PHYSICAL ENERGY BODY

Osteopathy, color therapy, flower essences, acupuncture, acupressure, reflexology, shiatsu massage, homeopathy, feng shui, vitamins and minerals, herbs (swallowed), nutrition, exercise

MENTAL ENERGY BODY

Osteopathy, color therapy, flower essences, psychotherapy/ hypnotherapy, reiki, meditation, crystal and gem therapy, aromatherapy, feng shui

EMOTIONAL ENERGY BODY

Osteopathy, color therapy, flower essences, psychotherapy/ hypnotherapy, reiki, meditation, crystal and therapy, aromatherapy, feng shui

SPIRITUAL ENERGY BODY

Osteopathy, color therapy, psychotherapy/hypnotherapy, meditation, crystal and gem therapy, homeopathy, feng shui

BELOW **The realignment of the skeletal structure by therapies such as osteopathy can have profound effects on all four energy bodies.**

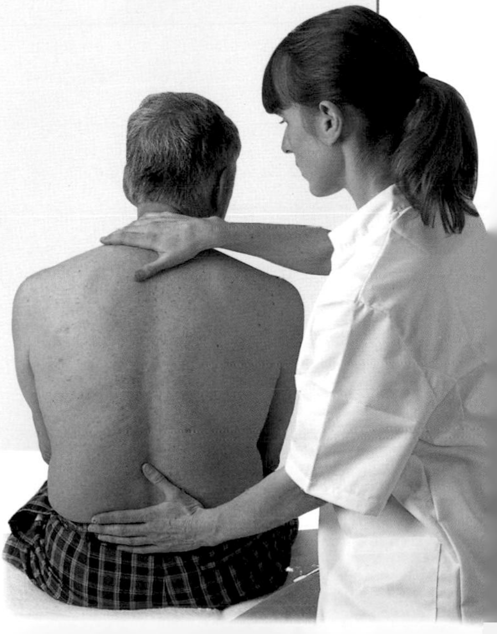

OPENING UP YOUR UNCONSCIOUS MIND

When we have been working extremely hard and hanging on counting the days until our vacation, by the time we are due to leave we are exhausted. We spend the first few days uncoiling all the stress that has wound up our system, and by the time our holiday is over we will be wonderfully relaxed and refreshed. But then we return to work. This is the place where all the stress began, so it is only a matter of days before we have forgotten the recuperative effects of our vacation. In fact, within a couple of days, it feels as though the vacation never happened. This is largely because the root cause of our troubles had not been addressed, so going away did not solve the problem because it was always there awaiting our return.

So it is with our minds. We already use one-third of our brains consciously. We collect all the knowledge humanity has gathered over the centuries and we use it in our everyday lives. We believe we have most things worked out. We know how the left brain works differently to the right, which parts listen to music and which parts add up sums, where we store memories, and where we regulate hunger, appetite, sleep patterns, and body temperature. But we generally have no conscious awareness of the other two-thirds of the brain which we call our unconscious mind, but because it is very powerful and has absolute knowledge of how we are and how we work, it continues to run things very efficiently, even though we may not have consciously realized this yet.

❝ You can combine your modern knowledge of today's world with the ancient wisdom that lies deep within us all. ❞

ABOVE **Journeying into your unconscious mind can often reveal a great deal of knowledge about yourself and may explain how and why you function.**

ABOVE **Self-discovery means opening up and exploring every avenue of your inner world without constraint, free of mental and physical barriers.**

Gaining access to this part of your mind means you can combine your modern knowledge of today's world with the ancient wisdom that lies deep within us all. This is where you heed your instincts, where there are no physical or mental barriers, and where your faith becomes your guide. By bringing them together, you will discover how and why you become ill. The more you tap into this power, the more you will learn.

Losing control

Today, we are constantly being urged to strive harder, to take control and empower ourselves. Once I would have agreed with that, but now I believe the opposite is true and that we should strive for less of both. Control means constraint, and I want you to open up every possible path, not block any off. Control implies keeping a tight rein on thoughts and emotions; it represents the antithesis of freedom.

Self-empowerment makes me think of one person snatching power from another, so one person's gain becomes someone else's loss. Why search for something outside ourselves when we already possess it within ourselves? Throughout this book I have included a series of meditations and exercises to encourage and support you on your journey of self-discovery. These can lead you to create optimum health for yourself in every sense of the word. MindPower is the key to balanced healing through a greater understanding of the wider causes of illness.

TOUCHING YOUR SPIRIT

Within your mind, the difference between mental energy and emotional energy is that one registers your thoughts and the other registers your emotions. Mental energy says "I think" and emotional energy says "I feel." Your spiritual energy body simply says "I believe."

The spirit has faith in its infinite wisdom and the mental energy, the brain, provides the mechanism for generating thoughts. Your emotions spring from your personal environment, performing all kinds of juggling tricks with your perceptions according to your own life experiences, coloring and shaping your opinions and attitudes and guiding or distorting your thoughts. As I have said before, all three of these energy bodies impact on your physical body and have a great effect on your wellbeing.

MENTAL ENERGY — **I THINK**

EMOTIONAL ENERGY — **I FEEL**

SPIRITUAL ENERGY — **I BELIEVE**

ABOVE RIGHT **Having an unshakable belief in your own spirituality –
that inner voice that is the core of your being – could lift you to
a vantage point of true wisdom.**

Discovering your spiritual energy is impossible
to value because it is a prize beyond worth. It can
be elusive, because although you may be aware of
its existence, you have probably become so locked
into certain beliefs and ways of behaving that they
have become normal for you. Abandoning them
and going down entirely new paths is essential, but
after such a long time your mind and body may
have forgotten how to think and act any other way.
So are you ignoring the signals you are being sent?

The core of your being

We all hear expressions such as "follow your heart"
and "go with the flow," as though we need those
phrases to explain the inexplicable. Have you ever
sensed that something just "felt right" and called it
a hunch? Or, have you ever suspected that someone
was untrustworthy without having any specific
reason for thinking this other than a feeling? When
events turn out unpredictably, how many times
have you shrugged your shoulders and said "What
will be, will be," comforting yourself with the belief
that, although it may not be clear to you right now,
there is a reason for everything that happens?

Physically, the human body is built along the
same lines. What we all think is shaped by our
emotions that are, in turn, colored by all the
different people, events, and experiences in our
lives. But what creates our individuality is our
unique essence, the core of our being. This is our
spiritual energy body.

SPIRITUAL HANG GLIDING

If your spiritual energy is guiding you, then follow
it. The person you are suspicious about may one
day give you good reason to be glad you followed
your instincts. You formed an opinion without any
hard evidence, but so what? Life is not a court of
law. People can fake everything, particularly
sincerity. Trusting your inner voice means you will
always receive the greatest wisdom.

Be true to yourself

I learned from the concept of spiritual hang-gliding
that we all know, at some very deep level, when we
are taking the wrong direction, making the wrong
move or saying the wrong thing. We may pretend
to ourselves that we are not aware, but this of
course is self-deception. If our actions or words are
so out of balance that we have to deny them, surely
that speaks for itself? Only by being truly and
totally honest with yourself can you come close to
touching your spirit.

MAKE A COMMITMENT
Never to give up on your health, and resolve to keep
improving physically and mentally, emotionally
and spiritually day by day. Read on, and I will show you
ways of getting in touch with your own healing power.

The spiritual dimension

Michael van Straten, a practicing naturopath for 35 years, and well-known British broadcaster and writer on health matters.

❛The Dalai Lama says whether you say Hail Mary or speak to Buddha, the spiritual aspect of ourselves is a great comfort once it is discovered. It gives shape and meaning to life. Everyone has a spiritual aspect to themselves whether they believe in a specific religion or not. At their bleakest moments, even the devout atheist will find someone to speak to, a god of their own.❜

ABOVE AND LEFT **Everyone experiences the divine in a different way. Spiritual inspiration can come from many sources, from the contemplative Indian mystic, Buddha (left), to the wild, dancing Hindu deity, Shiva.**

The power of prayer

Larry Dossey, M.D.

Author of Healing Words, The Power of Prayer, and The Practice of Medicine.

❛Without doubt, science has been toxic to spiritual sensitivity, and in medicine we are taught that we are just a collection of chemicals and we will simply be finished when we die. This is destructive and has caused immense suffering, and is a regrettable effect of modern science. It is ironic, but quite wonderful, that science is at long last producing evidence for a spiritual realm.

I practiced medicine for 20 years, did not belong to any religion, and certainly never prayed for my patients, so discovering scientific evidence showing the healing power of prayer was unsettling. Now I believe if you want the best chance of recovery, you choose prayer.

The most significant study of the effect of prayer on illness was carried out in December 1998 at the California Pacific Medical Center. The findings show fantastic, statistically significant differences, which means you cannot ascribe them to chance. Had such results been seen for a new drug, they would have been hailed as a therapeutic breakthrough.

Prayer is a form of healing, and preventative prayer is one of its most overlooked uses. Many wait until they have a crisis before invoking a prayer. I believe its greatest value is not to make diseases go away, but to provide a sense of connectedness with something greater than the individual self. It is the most majestic function of prayer and brings meaning and significance into our lives and if we use it practically to cure cancer or heart disease, that is a wonderful, added benefit.❜

THE JOURNEY TO YOUR INNER WORLD

Once you have made the decision to develop your MindPower, you need to know two things. The first is that the greater your ability to relax and meditate, the sharper your concentration will become.

The second is that once you have begun to explore your inner world, you will never want to go back. You might well look over your shoulder with some astonishment when you realize how much you did not know. You might also reflect with some pride that you had no idea how much you really did know. But you did not use it, and that is what I want to change.

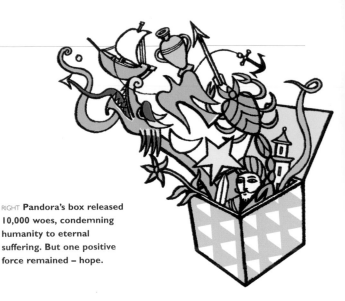

RIGHT **Pandora's box released 10,000 woes, condemning humanity to eternal suffering. But one positive force remained – hope.**

Opening Pandora's Box

When I first set out to discover why illness existed, I likened my quest to opening Pandora's mythical box, because once I began exploring the many extraordinary ways in which our minds influence our bodies, it showed me how we often create our own ill health. Why on earth would we do that?

LEFT **MindPower is a universal force which will reveal new dimensions in your life. Facing your fears can be surprisingly healing.**

One find led to another and another. I had to dig deeper and deeper, never sure what would lie beneath the next layer and the next, but unable to turn away, however disconcerting the revelations might have been. Your search will be similar. But the one factor that linked all my discoveries was that whatever was causing ill health, each one of us possessed the power to make a dramatic impact on our own lives, and we could do this through healing.

It does not make any difference whether you follow a particular religion or whether you believe in the presence of a superior, universal force. What does matter is that you think your life is precious enough to protect by learning how to harness such a power. All we have to do is learn how to listen to the guidance we are sent and trust its wisdom.

This is the force I call MindPower, and my promise to you is that the more you discover about yourself, the more you will be able to direct this power to get the best out of your life. I call this an unforgettable journey because everything you learn will always stay with you. This means enjoying the best health you can – one of the most precious gifts in the world.

As you progress on this journey, it might take you to many places that you have found uncomfortable – places you might have found difficult and places you may have been too fearful to explore. But my promise to you will remain constant from the start and through every stage of your journey. However, I cannot promise that you will reach your destination, because this is a never-ending journey. The more you discover, the more you will want to explore and the easier the journey becomes. Eventually you will find the courage and confidence to trust and believe in yourself and your own powers. If you use them wisely, you will become untouchable. Discovering the power of your mind is to discover your spirit and your healing powers.

The art of self-protection

There are numerous factors that contribute to ill health, and the farther you travel on this journey, the more you will find your health improving as you learn to protect yourself, drawing on you powerful inner energies as I have always done. But I would like to reassure you that this kind of protection is not about an endless list of self-denial in which you have to give up pleasures, forgo favorite foods, and live an ascetic life. It is about being aware of your own mind and body, so that whatever life events may occur, your energy bodies will be balanced enough to deal with them without absorbing their damaging effects.

My promise to you is that the more you discover about yourself, the more you will be able to direct your MindPower to get the best out of life.

Stress can come from the most unlikely sources, and the slightest hurt can be just as difficult to bear as a more obviously, unhappy situation in which most people would expect to feel miserable.

Self-protection is being able to feel compassion and sorrow, and yet not absorbing these destructive emotions to such an extent that they damage you. Self-protection is also about enjoying a life that is full of laughter and love. It also means liking yourself enough to feel comfortable about who you are, wherever you are and whoever you are with, never feeling the need to alter to fit in. You need to be able to look back with pride at worthwhile accomplishments. Happiness and love, both giving and receiving, are vital to the healing process, and later in the book I will show you how they can also protect you from ill health.

LEFT **The power of positive thoughts and actions leads to fulfillment and happiness and defends the body against illness by keeping it balanced.**

THE VALUE OF MEDITATION

I believe the fundamental principle of self-healing can be found through meditation. It is a means of stopping – a way of taking time out of your life to be still and peaceful for a few minutes so that you have a chance to listen to your inner voice. Anyone can meditate, and meditation can take place anywhere at any time. The more you practice, the more you will understand its value.

You will discover very quickly that it becomes a place to go when you need to calm yourself, think through a problem, generate ideas, or wind down after a very active day. It will give you whatever you believe you need, providing a secure foundation that will help you feel more confident about your own abilities and from which you can draw strength. It is the chance to become whatever you were always meant to be with no practical, financial, or logical barriers to stand in your way. If you meditate daily, what begins as a fantasy can become a reality.

Look upon meditation time as giving yourself a special treat. Taking ten minutes out of your day to explore your inner world and discover your own power is the most valuable gift you can ever award yourself.

In some countries, people grow up without ever spending any time on their own in their entire lives. They are born into large families where everyone shares the same sleeping area, often living and working together throughout the day. The concept of being alone is alien to them. Personal space is a precious commodity to be treasured.

Contemplation before meditation

Over several centuries, meditation from the East has evolved and been adopted by the West, sometimes referred to as contemplation. I prefer to combine both – meditation for the still space it gives you and contemplation for the puzzles that can be solved within that space.

BELOW **Meditation allows you to create a still, personal space independent of the physical situation you may be in. In this tranquil place, you are able to draw on the power of your inner world to help you in whatever way you need.**

As you progress through the book, you will find some questions you can take into each meditation. After meditating, I suggest you write down your first thoughts as soon as you can after you have finished. This is part of a self-monitoring exercise, and if you come back to those thoughts days, weeks, even months later, you will see how much you have learned and come to trust your inner voice. This is how you will know that you are discovering your own MindPower.

LEARNING TO MEDITATE

One of the misconceptions about meditation is the idea that you must always empty your mind of all thoughts while you sit motionless with your eyes closed and wait in the silence for something magical to happen. During a normal, busy day, you probably have thousands of different thoughts streaming through your mind continuously. In fact, they flow at a speed much faster than speech, and you may often wish you could capture them, perhaps dictate them onto tape or write them down, because later, when you try to return to a specific thought, you cannot always recall it.

When you first try to meditate and sit quietly, far from your mind becoming a blank, the opposite happens. You become immediately aware of your thoughts that, try as you might, take you in all sorts of directions. Have you ever begun with one particular thought and seconds later found yourself thinking about something completely different and totally unrelated? It is only when you track back that you realize how one thought has led to another with such a smooth transition that you barely noticed it.

Breaking down barriers

As soon as you set out to meditate, stopping your normal activities to make that space for yourself has exactly that effect. Within that space you now have a chance to notice the endless stream of thoughts that run through your mind, whereas before you probably gave them a fleeting second of attention before they and you moved on. Let them flow and go wherever they take you. Eventually, you will discover that if you remove all physical boundaries and all mental and emotional barriers, you will then be guided purely by your spiritual energy. This is how meditation helps you find the route for your journey of self-discovery.

Please persevere with meditation, and do not go into it with preconceived ideas because you will be disappointed; expect anything and nothing. This tranquil, contemplative state is the most powerful and effective natural gift that we all possess. The more you use it, the more dramatic the results.

> *If you remove all physical boundaries and all mental and emotional barriers, you will then be guided purely by your spiritual energy.*

MEDITATION METHODS

There are many different methods of meditation and these can be explored through any of the excellent books that specialize on particular approaches (*see* Further Reading, page 221). I recommend that everyone should try to meditate daily for ten minutes, and I have suggested a number of meditations throughout this book. If you do not feel comfortable with a particular meditation, you may prefer to select something different. You can also combine one or two of the meditations, or you can add as many other meditations as you wish, choosing whatever you feel is right for you. We all have individual paths to follow and only you can know whether or not you have picked the one that leads you along the most direct route. It is not important *how* you meditate. It is only important *that* you meditate.

Try to find a time to meditate that really suits you. Some people treat this meditation time as an energy boost and spend ten minutes after lunch on "refueling." Many say they cannot get through the day without these still spaces. Avoid meditation at times when you are likely to be feeling very tired and sleepy, unless, of course, your purpose is to wind down from your day and enjoy a good night's sleep. The important thing is to relax and allow the process to happen.

Where to meditate

You can meditate in whatever position or situation you feel most comfortable. Unless you are following a specific system that requires you to adopt certain positions, I recommend a comfortable chair, perhaps with your feet up, or lying on your bed. Check that you really are completely comfortable. You may want to put a pillow under your head if you are lying down, and if you are cold, cover yourself with a blanket. Try to avoid interruptions. If you have a telephone answering machine, remember to turn down the volume of the ringer and switch off the television and radio. When you become used to meditating, such precautions will eventually be unnecessary because you will naturally tune out any sounds.

I know people who have become so accustomed to meditation that they can slip in and out of their meditative state in seconds. One person I know meditates so effortlessly now that he takes advantage of his long journey home from work and meditates sitting on the bus. I have seen people meditating on train journeys and on airplanes. I know people who find time between business meetings, sitting quietly waiting for an appointment, or even on a park bench.

LEFT **To prepare for meditation, mentally conjure up all the parts of your body, starting from your head or your toes. As you come across any pockets of tension, gradually loosen and relax those areas with each out-breath.**

You can also meditate in a small group, if you can find one or two like-minded people to join you. Many people find that a guided meditation works the most effectively for them, which means that someone takes you through a meditation, and this, of course, allows you to relax completely and just focus on his or her voice.

Breathing in meditation

There is a proverb that says, "Life is in the breath, and he who only half breathes half lives." We are able to survive without any food for a few weeks, without sleep and water for a few days, but without breath for only a few minutes. And yet, we carry out this vital process without even thinking about it. However, I would like to recommend a special method of deep breathing to use when you are meditating. But please approach this method of breathing with caution. If you become dizzy or breathless at any time during the exercise, you should stop immediately and revert to your normal breathing pattern.

Deep breathing exercise

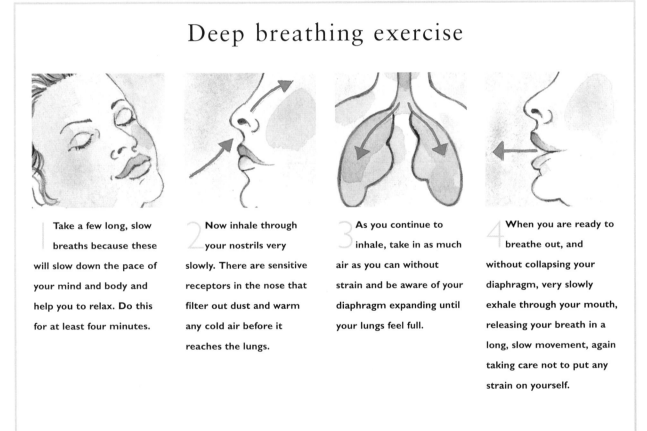

1 Take a few long, slow breaths because these will slow down the pace of your mind and body and help you to relax. Do this for at least four minutes.

2 Now inhale through your nostrils very slowly. There are sensitive receptors in the nose that filter out dust and warm any cold air before it reaches the lungs.

3 As you continue to inhale, take in as much air as you can without strain and be aware of your diaphragm expanding until your lungs feel full.

4 When you are ready to breathe out, and without collapsing your diaphragm, very slowly exhale through your mouth, releasing your breath in a long, slow movement, again taking care not to put any strain on yourself.

5 Repeat this breathing exercise, increasing the number of repeats at a rate that feels comfortable for you. Ideally, four repeats will be sufficient – it may take you many weeks or just a few days to build up to this. You decide what is right for you.

GET IN TOUCH WITH MY MINDPOWER

Touch the palms of your hands with mine, then close your eyes and concentrate, looking deep inside your own mind. You already have your own power and my hand could act as a catalyst to help you harness this inner energy. Touch my palm with yours and trigger your own force for healing.

Hand

Place your hands on mine: Close your eyes for one minute and visualize thousands of tiny lights twinkling and glittering.

Now, using the power of your imagination, as you continue to focus on these lights, you will see their shapes become more defined as you gradually turn them into masses of brilliant stars.

Still using the power of your mind, gradually merge them all together so they form a single, bright, white light.

You have now created a positive force by drawing on your own inner power.

> **MAKE A COMMITMENT**
>
> Create a different lifestyle for yourself. Treat yourself to the freedom of living life without any "oughts" or "shoulds." Decide how you want to be and think and feel, then make a plan to achieve this.

RIGHT **Before you read on, take time to connect with your inner power. Follow the instructions above, using my hand as a catalyst for your own positive energy.**

I pray twice a day for one minute at 11am and 11pm (UK time) and I ask you to join me during that time to send out positive thoughts.

Heart

Concentrate on the image of this heart for at least 60 seconds. Think of someone who would benefit from receiving love straight from your heart.

Now send out your positive healing energy and pure love to the person who is in your thoughts, even if you do not know where that individual happens to be.

LEFT **Focus on the positive energies of love, joy, and happiness and feel their warmth emanating from your heart to surround the person in your thoughts.**

ABOVE **Focus on this circle of friends to strengthen your bonds with those you care about. Think of a prayer that will benefit their lives.**

Circle of friends

The circle of friends is in the heart of my home, situated on a table in the room we use regularly, so it is at the centre of most of the events in my life. Focus on this circle for 60 seconds. Now say a prayer for all the people whose lives are linked to yours. This prayer can be anything you want it to be and the words can be the ones you have chosen because they hold the most meaning for you. This is how you can use your MindPower to connect with your own circle of friends.

MEDITATION WITH COLORS

Healing with color works by tuning into the energy vibration of each color according to your needs. The way color affects us all in our everyday lives can be significant, and the clothes we select and the shades we choose to decorate our homes – even the flowers we grow – reflect the state of our world whether we realize it or not. Becoming more sensitive to color means finding out more about yourself. After all, many people claim to have a favorite color but do they know why are they attracted to it? Do the colors we dislike trigger unpleasant memories?

The healing spectrum

When white light passes through a prism it refracts, breaking down from its original single color, and emerging instead in the colors of the rainbow. White light is actually a combination of many colors, each one with its own special energy and complementary color.

When you meditate, you can call light to yourself and the color of that light can be whatever you want it to be. You can wrap this colored light around yourself or send it to different parts of the body as healing light. When you close your eyes, focus on the back of your eyelids and look at the color you see there, or fill that area with the color of your choice. Many believe that, in self-healing, certain colors work best for certain parts of the mind and body. The only way to know what color you need is to listen to your inner voice and go with whatever it tells you.

Red

Red is the most dominant color, situated at the hot end of the spectrum, vibrant and strong, energizing and stimulating. It can help to fight infection, destroy bacteria, and reduce inflammation. Its powerful effect works well when the physical system slows down, raising body temperature, improving circulation, and combating conditions such as anemia. Red light creates a sense of warmth and comfort.

Orange

Orange is a more assertive color than red and symbolizes femininity because it is the energy of creation, bringing freedom of movement and dispersing heaviness. Its healing powers affect mental, emotional, and physical energy bodies. It can change negative energy into positive, so it is used to help with conditions such as depression.

Yellow

Yellow is related to the intellect and can stimulate mental activity, bringing detachment and objectivity to judgment. Healing with yellow can be used to treat obsessions and addictions, because it helps to rationalize feelings and actions that have become habitual. Its healing properties do just that – they heal. Where skin is damaged, yellow repairs and improves, so many skin problems and rheumatic conditions benefit from its use.

Green

Green is a mediator, situated midway in the spectrum, neither hot like red, orange, and yellow, nor cold like blue, violet, and indigo. Its specific energy

represents balance and cleansing. It unites the intellectual left brain hemisphere with the intuitive right brain hemisphere, and balances negative and positive energies. When the mind is befuddled by a clutter of jumbled thoughts, green clears the chaos. Green heals the mental and emotional energy bodies so a muddled mind becomes sharp and focused. Its cool comfort works well with conditions linked to nervous tension, such as migraines and indigestion.

Blue

Blue is the traditional healing color because it conveys calm and tranquillity while stimulating all the body energies and strengthening the immune defence system. Blue heals most particularly where there is inflammation and where the body energies are out of tune; it permeates every cell and fiber of the physical body, as well as reaching into the emotional and mental energy bodies with its calm, recuperative energy.

Indigo

Indigo signifies flexibility and release, targeting the physical, mental, and emotional energy bodies. It heals by soothing where there was uncertainty and encouraging where there was reluctance. By helping to discard thoughts,

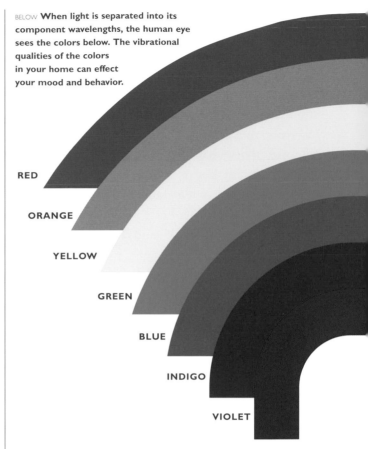

BELOW **When light is separated into its component wavelengths, the human eye sees the colors below. The vibrational qualities of the colors in your home can effect your mood and behavior.**

RED

ORANGE

YELLOW

GREEN

BLUE

INDIGO

VIOLET

emotions, and actions that have become harmful, it brings freedom to all four energies. This makes it helpful in conditions in which there is inertia, such as benign cysts or tinnitus.

Violet

Violet enhances the power of the spiritual energy body by stimulating the imagination and generating greater awareness and spiritual insights. In healing, it restores self-esteem, controls uncertainty and insecurity, and strengthens the emotional energy body. Its considerable power is of use wherever there is a weakness, and it invigorates and rejuvenates the entire system.

LEFT **The colors of the earth are naturally clear and strong. They have effects on animals just as they do on humans,** indicating if a plant is nutritious or poisonous, or attracting insects to carry their pollen to another plant.

MAKING SENSE OF YOUR VISION

During meditation, when your thoughts run in all directions, remember that this is completely natural and trust your inner wisdom to sift through the tangle of seemingly unconnected thoughts. Gradually patterns will begin to emerge. As you remain calm and peaceful, you will discover that what seems like an uncontrolled process actually begins to have meaning for you.

You may not understand the significance of these patterns at once, but I recommend you just relax and enjoy the shapes and colors, drifting and floating wherever your thoughts take you. You are traveling on a journey where there are no barriers. You can go anywhere you want to because anything is possible.

Meditation will eventually become as much a part of your daily routine as brushing your teeth, and you will find yourself looking forward to this precious personal time. The value of setting aside this space for yourself will be revealed to you. The things that once confused you will begin to make sense, and the people or situations that made you unhappy will be less important and no longer have the capacity to upset you. Meditation will help you find a natural balance and put your life into perspective.

The revitalizing force

Free from worry and anxiety, you may well begin to find other outlets for your energies, and discover ways of spending your time that are more enjoyable or bring you greater satisfaction. Insights will emerge and perhaps surprise you. Often such revelations have a dazzling simplicity about them and

Just listening to your inner voice is to use the power of your own mind, and allow that force to revitalize you.

Elemental power

You can use the four powerful elements of earth, water, air, and fire in your meditations. Surround yourself with these elements in the same way as I have described how to use colored lights (see pages 56–57).

EARTH
Earth represents our world and supports all the living systems within it that require light, air, and water.

AIR
Air represents the vital, universal invisible life force or energy.

WATER
Water sustains, refreshes, and cleanses.

FIRE
Fire is a great purifier and regenerator.

Soothing sound exercise

LEFT **Soothing music will help to lead you from a mentally and emotionally drained state to a calm inner world where you can regenerate your energies.**

We all have days that leave us feeling wrung out and exhausted, when everything that could go wrong did go wrong. The idea of meditating at this time is probably the last thing you will want to do, but relaxing contemplation is exactly what you need to heal yourself. You also need a different atmosphere to break that mood, and this is when I suggest you try meditating with your favorite music in the background.

This state of mind drains the system, runs down your mental and emotional energy levels, and leaves you at a very low ebb. It can make you irritable, and the checks and balances that would normally prevent you from taking out your mood on other people have closed down. This is extreme tiredness, a state of mind past sleep because the last remnants of your mental and emotional energy are still churning around even though your physical energy is running out.

Try to find a piece of music that will play for the same length of time as you plan to meditate, and if it will play for longer, even better. You need to be taken out of your day and guided gently into your inner world where you can restore your energies.

1 **Focus on the music and listen to each note, visualizing each one hanging in the air.**

2 **Imagine the sounds as illuminated colors, bathing you in a calming, soothing balm. See these colors playing on your emotional energy, smoothing its rough edges and softening the stresses locked into your mental energy.**

3 **Sense the music playing on your physical body, removing the tensions of your day. The more you do this, the more this music will affect you. Whenever you hear it, you will be able to summon up this calm atmosphere, taking you to the heart of your inner world.**

you will begin to see your life not as a complex of problems but as a natural progression in a direction that feels completely right for you.

This inner knowledge will become your invisible armor, protecting and guiding you. Meditation will unlock the door to your inner world and reveal the enormous potential you have within you – to hear the unspoken and see the invisible. Just listening to your inner voice is to use the power of your own mind, and allow that force to revitalize you.

ENTERING YOUR DREAM WORLD

Have you ever found yourself daydreaming? Perhaps you have been with friends and, without realizing it, have tuned out of the conversation and drifted off into your own reverie? Or, perhaps you have stared into the flames of a fire and found your thoughts wandering off, or looked up at the clouds and imagined they represented shapes and images.

What happens at such times is that your unconscious mind takes over and continues with you on this journey in your mind while you consciously opt out and abandon awareness for a while. Dipping in and out of your conscious mind into the realms of your unconscious can happen without you realizing it, and certainly without you actively having to initiate the process.

It happens when we wake up in the morning and before we fall asleep at night. There is a layer of consciousness between sleep and wakefulness. When we are dropping off to sleep, this is called the hypnogogic layer; when we are awakening, it is the hypnopompic. Several other layers of consciousness with different degrees of depth lie in those layers.

In a trance

Hypnotherapists induce a trance state within these layers and obviously the depth of the trance depends upon the layer you sink into. You may even be aware of these layers. Have you ever heard someone calling you or perhaps the telephone ringing just as you were dropping off to sleep? Were you jolted out of your state of mind, realizing that you were no longer awake but not actually asleep yet? Equally, this can happen in the morning before you have achieved full consciousness but have left the sleep state behind.

These layers are believed to enhance our creativity. Mozart is reported to have heard most of his music in this state. It is probably the last chance most of us have to dream. As soon as we are awake, our dream will begin to fade. Within perhaps 40 seconds, the memory will have vanished and for another ten seconds we might possibly retain an awareness of that dream. A minute later it has disappeared, or so it seems, but what has really happened is that the dream, which contains significant personal details, has returned to our unconscious minds.

Hypnotic trances

JOHN BUTLER, psychologist and hypnotherapist:

❝Hypnosis uses the power of suggestion and trance and involves deep relaxation that is also beneficial to the patient. Initially, a variety of procedures can be used to induce a trance condition, but it is the interactive nature of the communication between the hypnotherapist and the patient that really determines its effectiveness. The patient is usually encouraged to enter a state of deep relaxation through a series of repeated suggestions and visualizations. Eventually, their conscious mind moves aside and is temporarily out of its control position.

The induction of a trance can take a few seconds or half an hour or more, and this variation depends very much on the subject's rapport with their hypnotherapist and their belief in hypnosis' potential. We know several different levels of trance exist, but exactly how many levels there are is still a big area of debate. Different degrees of hypnosis are recognized, but there is no consensus of opinion that we are all capable of experiencing the same number of levels. We do know that people generally go into deeper levels of trance with an increasing number of sessions.❞

Occasionally, something during the day will trigger a thought and "break your dream." This means that a key phrase or word has accessed thoughts in your unconscious mind, which is also your dream world.

All I ask is that you create a small space in your daily routine because I want to guide you to that place where healing begins. I want you to enter your dream world.

USING AFFIRMATIONS

Repeating Affirmations to yourself constantly reminds you of where you are and where you want to be. Anyone who has ever suffered from "over-thinking" will recognize the value of repeating something positive to stop his or her mind running on with pointless thoughts. Positive Affirmations also fill the spaces where negative phrases might have become a habit.

I have included a powerful Affirmation after each meditation throughout the book. Select one that best fits with the particular stage you have reached in your journey of self-discovery and repeat it three times each day for a week.

> ❝ *All I ask is that you create a small space in your daily routine because I want to guide you to that place where healing begins. I want you to enter your dream world.* ❞

LEFT **Entering your dream world activates your unconscious mind, which stores more information about you than you can remember. Your unconscious can help you to develop your creativity and intuition.**

WRITING YOUR OWN PRESCRIPTION

Here I have compiled some lists for you to make and recommended some diaries for you to keep that will offer you great insights into your own mind. You can complete all the lists or just a few, and keep as many diaries or as few as you choose. These exercises have to fit into your life. They are intended to be treated as a pleasure, not regarded as a burden.

The written exercises in this book are far more effective than people at first imagine. Transferring mental energy into physical energy by converting thoughts onto a page is to give them a physical shape and make them very real to our conscious mind.

This process is an important feature of the new you, because you will see how much you have moved forward. You may have thought nothing very much was happening, but the responses in your lists will show you how much progress you have made. You will see the gradual changes and notice the subtle difference in the way you feel about yourself, your life, and your health.

RIGHT **Producing lists enables you to assess your progress and acts as a prompter for releasing unconscious thoughts.**

Making lists

I recommend that each time you complete one of these lists, put it somewhere safe and then return to it a month later and check out your answers. You may be pleasantly surprised.

Notching-up-success list

List everything you have done that has succeeded at some time in your life. The purpose of this is to acknowledge your abilities and encourage you to generate the energy to accomplish more. These successes can cover work, relationships, and leisure. Success can mean different things to each of us, so choose any area where your success has meaning for you.

Like-yourself list

List all your positive qualities, in other words, all the things you like about yourself. The more you acknowledge these qualities, the more you will recognize your own value. The greater your sense of self-esteem, the more your creative energy will flow.

Spoil-yourself list

Make a list of all the things you would love to do just for your own pleasure, no matter how large or small, that would enhance your life. This will help you to see whether you sublimate your own needs for others, and whether you would cherish some personal space and value yourself enough to believe you deserve it.

Dream-the-impossible list

Make a list of some of the things you would love to do, however far-fetched or impossible they might seem, as though there were no barriers getting in your way, either physical, financial, or logistical. Do not restrict yourself to plans that are feasible, but open your mind and really let your imagination soar. This will help you to unlock your natural creativity and is one of the most enjoyable lists to produce because, if you really let yourself go, you will not only be astonished at the places to which your mind can take you to, but just how much fun you will have on the journey.

Stumbling-blocks list

List those things you believe are preventing you from achieving what you want. You may feel others bring you down or get in your way. You may identify parts of yourself that are resistant to change. This list only works if you are very honest with yourself, and as soon as you do this, those things that have limited you will begin to disappear. This list shows how much you have come to understand and accept about yourself, which is the first step toward letting go of those blocks that have been holding you back.

Clearing-out-the-negatives list

Make two lists opposite each other on a page. One is a list of negative beliefs and the other a list of positive ones. You may find there are more negatives than positives, but this does not matter. Read through the list and see how you can make a negative message into a positive one just by changing some of the wording.

Reading your own mind

These diaries are again part of the regular stock-taking process, providing you with an encouraging insight into and record of your progress.

Daily diary

Twice a day, make two small entries in your diary recording your state of mind or mood from the first moment you open your eyes in the morning and again just before you go to sleep at night.

Job diary

Note down the jobs you have set yourself to complete that week. These can be large or small jobs, from spring-cleaning the entire house to making a telephone call you have been putting off. Tick off each job when you have done it.

Daily dream diary

Keep paper and a pen beside your bed. You will need to write down your dream the second you wake up before the memory quickly fades away. When you read through this diary at the end of a week, you will probably find your dreams form a recognizable pattern that gives you a greater understanding of yourself, because these dreams have emerged from a selection of your unconscious thoughts.

MAKING A BOOKING

Once you have made the decision to improve your health, you have taken the first major step on this journey. Now I want you to make a booking and decide on a date to set off. This can be days, weeks, or months ahead; you can allow yourself whatever time you believe you need to contemplate starting this journey. But whatever you choose, write the date down and repeat it to yourself several times, reminding yourself regularly that what this date represents is Day One of the new you.

Even if the date you have set yourself for this journey is weeks ahead, there is no reason why you should put off meditating until that time. In fact, I recommend you begin now, taking it slowly and only spending a few minutes to begin with, gradually building up to ten minutes or more. Do not forget to include focusing on the date you have set in your meditation. This is part of a psyching-up process and has a crucial role in strengthening your motivation.

This is important: I want to emphasize that I am not offering you overnight success on a plate or a quick-fix miracle that will change your life. This book is about discovering a profound and deeply significant part of yourself that can have far-reaching effects on your life. The rewards it will bring are enormous, but it may take you some time and perseverance before they are revealed to you. After all, how could such a prize be that easy to win?

Commit to yourself

Having set a date, make a commitment to yourself – you have decided you want to be healthier in mind and body and you are going to make every effort to find out what is holding you back. Try to

LEFT **Make a date to begin the journey to the new you. This will give you time to focus on how that journey will begin with daily meditation.**

RIGHT **Your road to self-discovery will open up new ways of thinking, and you will begin to see the world as a place of endless opportunity.**

set aside a few minutes each day for some of the written exercises that can be completed on a daily or weekly basis. They can be combined with the meditations or completed separately. There are no strict rules about how often you must do them, only that you do them. They do matter and are designed to help you gradually build up your awareness and, ultimately, your MindPower.

Remember, you are answerable only to yourself. If you miss out on meditation or some exercises, you have no one to apologize to and no need to think of an excuse. You are running your own program now. I would suggest that if for any reason a day or two does go by when you have not followed your program, do not be hard on yourself over the issue, but simply return to it the next day or as soon as you can, and promise yourself that you will try to keep to the program in future.

To those who feel their lives are just too action-packed to do this, I suggest that there is always time if you want to find it, even if it means getting up a little earlier in the morning or going to bed slightly later. You can find time. You can do anything if you really want to do it.

As you progress, another important element is the sense of achievement you will experience having set out to do something and seen it through. This will prove that you can achieve what you set out to do and it will prove it to the very person who often doubts it the most – yourself.

Your reward

The exercises are deceptively simple and will prompt many different avenues of thought that can be contemplated when you meditate. You will get used to devoting this space to yourself each day because it will have the effect of grounding you, leaving you balanced and centered. You will find yourself beginning to look forward to these times – their accumulative impact is enormous.

Realistically, you cannot change the world you live in, but you can change the way you react to its everyday stresses and strains. As you learn to understand your own emotions, you will see very clearly the way they motivate you or hold you back, and how they can either enhance or damage your equilibrium. You will also gain a wider knowledge of your own place in the world and how you fit into it. Perhaps you will discover answers to questions that you have not yet asked.

Your guide to exploring your inner world

- Tune in to your MindPower. Remember, before you meditate, contemplate.

- Take some thoughts into your meditation. Ask yourself what changes you want to make today. Then ask your MindPower if those changes feel like they are the right changes for you. Trust your inner judgment.

- Remind yourself what the positive effects of meditation will be.

- Select one Affirmation for that week that you feel is particularly appropriate and repeat it three times each day.

The Greek God Zeus devised a punishment for his enemy by offering a gift that was, in reality, a curse. He warned the beautiful Pandora that if the sealed box she carried was ever opened it would be catastrophic. She could not resist, and all the evils inside flew out of the opened box and have continued to afflict the world ever since. Hope alone remained. The message was that mankind's natural inquisitiveness would always be its downfall. If someone fell sick, then they must have sinned. Today we know better. Exploration leads to greater knowledge, and self-knowledge can release your inner power so you can learn to heal yourself.

4 | INSIDE PANDORA'S BOX

WHY DOES ILLNESS EXIST?

Following a five-day bout of flu, a friend was complaining about the futility of illness. "I went to bed suffering from a pounding head, aches and pains in all my limbs, a high fever, and a sore throat and head cold. I was very bored, worried about the amount of work I would have to catch up on, and thoroughly miserable. Explain it to me Uri, because that bout of flu wiped out nearly a week of my life and I just cannot see the point of it."

The point is there is no one point. There are, however, several signposts that come from and lead to different destinations. The individual routes we have chosen to take in life are tailor-made to fit our own distinctive life patterns and partially explain why some of us are dogged by ill health while others are hardly ever affected. It sometimes seems the choice of who gets what is merely a matter of good or bad luck, but in reality poor health is not down to such a haphazard selection process. Only by looking a little more deeply does a significant pattern emerge that helps to explain why we get ill and what actually happens.

Not one answer but many

When I first tried to discover how or why illness happens, I realized very quickly that my search was like unpeeling the layers of an onion. Each time I formulated a plausible theory, based on my own and other people's careful observations, I then found another very different but equally acceptable explanation underlying that finely constructed thinking.

I never came close to a definitive answer because I now know that to suggest that ill health is down to either this or that particular cause is inaccurate. I could go on theorizing to the end of time without finding a conclusive answer, because the more layers I stripped away, the more was revealed to me. What it showed me was how very complicated we all are, and how differently each individual reacts to certain circumstances. Illness invades people's lives for a wide range of different reasons and some of us are affected occasionally, others catch anything and everything, while some people can truly boast that they are never ill. But then, trying to pinpoint a specific cause and effect for something as multi-faceted and intricate as the human mind is bound to be an impossible task in any case.

LEFT **Finding out why you are ill can be like peeling off the layers of an onion, each layer showing you another dimension to explore. We are all dynamic, constantly changing beings, and each one of us will find a different way to maintain a healthy balance in our lives.**

WHAT CAUSES ILL HEALTH?

If poor health prevents you from getting full enjoyment out of life, what can be done to improve the situation? There may not be simple, individual answers to explain the causes of your ill health, but there are broad areas where you can certainly lay the blame for letting illness into your life.

ABOVE **Some working environments are deceptively unsafe. The effects of modern office technology such as computers and photocopiers, plus air pollution from cars and factories, can all undermine the body's immune system.**

LEFT **Illness can be a form of protection, providing a temporary refuge from having to deal with life's problems.**

Emotional demands

Your emotional environment reflects the effect of everyday stresses and strains, many of which are unavoidable. It is the extent to which you allow them to dictate your state of mind that is crucial – emotional turbulence is sure to undermine your physical health.

Then there are people whose emotional needs are so specific and demanding that they can only be met by creating ill health. There are also people who really do need to be ill, but not all the time, just occasionally. They find that being ill protects them from their lives, and if things are going badly, it produces a perfect alibi and alters the way others think about them. Being ill gets them sympathy, compassion, and solicitude, all of which involve lots of attention.

Others need their illness just to survive. They may have ignored their instincts or refused to slow down, or perhaps absorbed all the stress that their situation has created, and as a result have jeopardized their immune system's effectiveness. Illness becomes nature's way of forcing them to stop. In such cases, illness can lead to improving a person's health.

Environmental factors

Your physical environment can be damaging, too. From the moment you step outside your front door each day, the very air you breathe exposes you to a cocktail of toxic chemicals from car emissions, while in the average office, staff suffer from viruses circulated by air-conditioning systems, as well as emissions from equipment such as computers and photocopiers. Your body's ability to cope is weakened insidiously day by day.

What causes cancer?

DR. SOSIE KASSAB, Director of Complementary
Cancer Services at the Royal London Homeopathic Hospital, England

Cancer is a major medical challenge and no one knows why it starts or stops. It is an enigmatic process and stress may play a part, but I would not put it more strongly than that. The causes of cancer are far from understood, and there is far more to it than stress. Some people suffer horrendous stresses in their lives and do not get cancer, so it is very much different for each individual.

I strongly believe there are multiple causes for cancer, and while some people may have a genetic susceptibility, there are an enormous number of other factors that have to be considered as well. The disturbing thing is we do not know who will be affected or what the ultimate trigger is that makes one person develop it and another not. Perhaps it comes from a combination of triggers and causes, and on top of an individual's susceptibility.

The risk of cancer is increasing and that risk rises with age, so as our population lives longer, we see an increased incidence. I think this is because as we get older our bodies do not function so effectively. When a tumor grows, the immune defense system normally suppresses that growth. But when the body is not balanced, this may increase that person's susceptibility to the disease since the cells do not regenerate as perfectly as they should.

I have seen tumors disappear, and although we do not really understand the mechanism that makes this happen, we know some people improve and others do not. It is a mystery, and all we can do is move forward as positively as possible with whatever treatment we think is appropriate.

I am sure there is some inner healing power and some people are better at tapping into it than others, and it takes different forms for different people. I do not know whether it is spiritual or emotional, or a combination of the two.

PROFESSOR KAROL SIKORA, Professor of Clinical
Oncology at Hammersmith Hospital, London, England

Cancer is one of the biggest challenges of this century and it will increase over the next. The next 20 years will bring us the golden age of drug discovery, and from this new treatments will almost certainly be devised. These treatments will be given systemically, that is either by mouth or by injection, and go right around the body targeting cancer cells where they are hiding.

The causes of cancer are well known. Of the 10 million new patients in the world that got cancer last year, 3 million cases were due to tobacco-related causes, 3 million due to diet, and 1.5 million to infection. The fact that infection is a cause of cancer often surprises people, but the relationships between hepatitis B and hepatoma, human papilloma virus and cervical cancer, and helicobacter pylorii and stomach cancer are well worked out.

> *Both mind and body have their own self-healing systems and the potential ability to regenerate . . . we are all capable of healing ourselves.*

MIND VERSUS BODY

Our mind and body are very familiar to each other because they have been working together for a long time. Imagine them like any couple who are close, whether married to one another or colleagues at work, who practically know what the other person is going to say before they even speak. They understand each other, and the more time they spend together, the more they learn and the greater their knowledge.

They know each other so well they also know which buttons to press to get the reaction they seek. When they fall out, they do it fully armed with the kind of information that is targeted to hurt and destroy. Some of the bitterest family feuds and closest business partnerships have delved into this resource, and in doing so have become spectacularly vicious enemies.

It is the same with the mind and body, and if they fall out, it can be disastrous. But it is also not a fair fight. We operate using only one-third of our conscious mind, and the two-thirds that represent the unconscious mind are in possession of the lion's share of information. This means you have no idea what kind of ammunition is being used against you because your opponent is keeping all the secrets hidden.

Such a rich source of personal knowledge means that once the mind and body begin to work against each other, the results can produce mental, emotional, and physical chaos. In the face of anarchy and confusion, the mind sinks into a negative state and the body follows, shutting down the mechanisms that keep it buoyant, relinquishing the struggle to fight off ill health.

Finding your way back

It is a difficult place to climb out of because the deeper you sink, the steeper the walls that surround you. Both mind and body have their own self-healing systems and the potential ability to regenerate when necessary. This means that none of us need look to others when we are at our most desperate, because we are all capable of healing ourselves. The attitude and approach we use to tackle the worst moments in life depend on the amount of belief we have in our own power.

Sometimes a situation can be so bad that you cannot find a way out and every road you try is blocked. That fact alone could be significant. All those routes may be denied to you because they will never lead you to the solution that actually lies within your own grasp. Perhaps this situation has been designed to ignite the spiritual sparks that

LEFT **Body and mind work in harmony to maintain health. If the two begin to pull in different directions, the antagonism can result in physical symptoms.**

have been deadened, buried deeply beneath the surface of consciousness for so long that their impact has been dulled. When your emotional and mental world is out of tune with your physical body, harnessing these inner powers can lead to amazing results. If the mind can produce an extreme stressful state, it can also reverse that process.

Have you considered that your inner wisdom is already influencing you and that, deep down, the paths you have chosen are the wrong paths for you to take? Your inner voice is warning and guiding you, but because you have shut it off, the only way it can protect you is by blocking your route.

Self-healing can restore the essential balance that has been lost in the emotional confusion and send beams of subtle, restorative energy into the system, helping you to find the way back to your spiritual home. Yes, back – you may think you have never been there, but I promise you that you have.

Personality and illness

The kind of personality you have can often determine the type of occupation, partner, and lifestyle you choose. Just as the mind influences the body, your personality type often influences the illnesses you attract. The partner you choose, the occupation you follow, and the lifestyle you adopt can offer clues as to the way you respond to the everyday stresses and strains of life.

People under pressure to succeed, high-achievers, and workaholics often develop high blood pressure and heart problems. Introverted people catch colds and flu far more often than outgoing types. Great socializers who probably come into contact with more viruses and infections because they meet so many people in their daily lives actually catch fewer infections than those who lead more isolated lives. Your particular personality type can have a bearing on whether you develop asthma or arthritis, eczema, hay fever, or migraine.

People under a strain or leading unhappy lives are more prone to disease, but someone in the right job but with the wrong approach is also likely to suffer a higher incidence of health problems. For instance, the stereotypical accountant who deals with precision and figures likes his world to be orderly and everything in its designated place. But if he carries this attitude of mind to extremes and becomes obsessive about orderliness and controlling events, the job he is so good at may actually in the end work against him and cause him to suffer from any number of debilitating stress-related conditions.

However, regardless of personality type, it has been shown that people who meditate regularly and use relaxation techniques in their day-to-day lives dramatically improve their chances of recovering from all types of illnesses.

NATURAL MECHANICS

Natural healing does exist. If this were not true, the human race would have died out centuries ago, but the body's capacity to heal itself has been evident for aeons.

In the ancient world, the structure of the human anatomy was little more than an educated guess. In battle, the wounded were studied in the hope of enlightenment. In cultures where it was permitted, human and animal corpses were dissected in the pursuit of anatomical knowledge. Medicinal herbs were administered alongside special "magical" incantations, and equal faith was placed in both. When a wound was dressed, the patient was given a poison to eat or drink in the belief that it would purge the system internally and purify the wound. Although evidence exists of skilled bone settings carried out thousands of years ago for broken or fractured limbs, very few other remedies were effective, and some probably made the patient worse.

Today, we know that there are implicit, life-saving procedures that restore the human mind and body. Looking back at our own history, we can see clearly that when patients recovered, it was usually because they had survived an absurd medical treatment by harnessing their own natural healing power.

Programed to heal

Every part of the physical human body is an efficient machine with built-in mechanical reactions. It is also a complex network of self-regulating systems that act as internal healers, programed to repel and defend as well as repair. Look at the way nature deals with a simple cut. Blood loss is instantly limited because the arteries constrict and a clotting system operates, while a microscopic army rushes in with supplies to clean up and

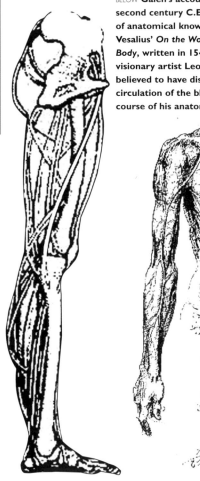

BELOW **Galen's account of anatomy, dated second century C.E., was the only source of anatomical knowledge until Andreas Vesalius'** On the Working of the Human Body, **written in 1543. However, the visionary artist Leonardo da Vinci is believed to have discovered the circulation of the blood in the course of his anatomical studies.**

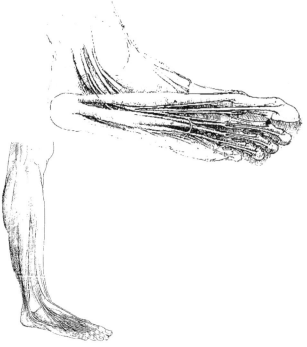

rebuild the damaged tissue and defend it from invading bacteria.

The mind also has the power to repair damage and it does this by regulating the body's physical responses. In fact, the power of our minds is effective on several different levels because the activity of every organ in the body is controlled by the nerves that ultimately connect to the brain. These represent our emotional wiring system, and the messages they transmit from the brain to various parts of the body trigger our physical reactions to heat, cold, or pain, just as the body reacts to emotions such as anger, fear, and anxiety.

Extreme fear can cause paralysis to our limbs or flood the body with adrenalin, set the heart racing, dry the mouth, produce excessive sweating, cause vomiting and diarrhea, and even block pain. Extreme anxiety can produce trembling, agitation, insomnia, nausea, fainting, and panic attacks.

Often the very worst injuries shock and numb the senses to such a degree that pain only sets in much later. When a limb has been amputated, patients often complain of "phantom" pain that continues in the nonexistent limb, because the brain has not severed the neurotransmitters that transfer such messages.

A vital sign

We need to experience pain – the signals the brain sends are vital for our survival. Imagine burning your hand or breaking your arm without realizing it and what the effect would be. Pain is also an important symptom of internal problems – often the only one. The invisible discomforts of stomachache, earache, or pains in the chest sound the warning bells that alert us to the fact that our system has a malfunction, whether it is an infection or a serious disorder. Without the pain, we would continue in ignorance and the condition might become worse, perhaps even fatal.

Pain thresholds

The amount of pain we can tolerate varies enormously, because our individual pain receptors are governed by our emotions. Some people experience pain more intensely than others because their "pain barrier" is pitched higher or lower and affects their tolerance. A classic example is the ability of Eastern yogis to walk barefoot over hot coals, demonstrating the power of the mind over matter.

We only have to delve into medical history to shudder at the thought of amputations or complicated surgery without the benefit of anaesthetic drugs, or wonder how people survived the agony of infected wounds or decaying teeth. Yet, what is unimaginable in this century undeniably affects our perception of the pain our ancestors suffered, whose expectations were in tune with their time and therefore reflected their levels of tolerance.

ABOVE **In Sri Lanka, a man walks across hot coals. He tunes out the messages sent by his nerve pathways and does not perceive the severe heat as pain.**

Any disharmony in a person's life usually means the balance of their emotions is precarious, and this is echoed in the fragility of their immune system.

THE IMMUNE DEFENSE SYSTEM

The linchpin between mind and body is the immune defense system, and when harmony exists between the two, the immune system is at its peak, carrying out its protective and defensive functions from a position of strength. We all have our own immune defense system, which acts like a guardian angel sweeping the length and breadth of the body on a search and destroy mission. Its purpose is to flush out anything that can harm us, and repel any foreign body that tries to invade such as viruses, bacteria, fungi, and even cancer cells.

It does this by stimulating the body's own natural defense mechanisms to leap into action and attack, eliminating whatever threatens the body's state of health. The degree of immunity each person has can be measured at those times when a virus, such as flu or a cold, is going around. Just by noting the people who succumb to the infection and the ones it passes by will give you an indication of how such immunity works and how successfully each person's immune system is functioning. It explains how some people can come into contact with all kinds of infections and yet survive an entire winter without a single day's illness, while others in the same circumstances seem to catch everything.

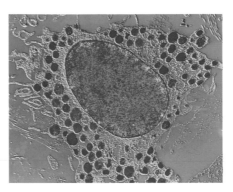

The nucleus of a mast cell forms part of the defensive army of the body's immune system. Mast cells contain antibodies that destroy or neutralize toxins.

The invisible barrier

Very often, those most vulnerable have less immunity, which means their systems are not protecting or defending them to their fullest extent. We are all exposed to numerous infections on a daily basis, and it is our immunity to them that enables us to fight them off. When immunity is high, it forms an invisible barrier like drops of water being splashed onto an oily surface, where the infections touch down briefly only to slither off because there is nothing to adhere to or support them. When people are unable to ward off infections, it is because their weakened immune system is giving up and simply does not have enough energy to withstand the invasion, let alone fight back. One of the surest ways to deplete these immune energies is through stress.

The stress effect

Stress covers a multitude of different mind states and emotions, and can be caused by one factor or several. But whatever the origins, destructive, negative stress can have a corrosive effect on the state of your health.

Bad stress takes time to accumulate in the body and might begin with such mild symptoms that no one is alerted to the potential damage. Over a period of time, however, its insidious effects set in until the sufferer becomes accustomed to living with a stressed state of mind and it becomes their normal mode of living. From the moment they wake up each morning until last thing at night, their thoughts are muddled. This kind of confusion can be likened to the brain working on overdrive. As each new day dawns, the stressed person's only goal is to get through it without anything terrible happening, and without cracking up completely.

Any disharmony in people's lives usually means that the balance of their emotions is precarious, and this is echoed in the fragile condition of their immune system. The destructive effects of the stress this causes can be enormous and can spread out to affect every area of our lives, creating havoc and limiting our potential to achieve fulfillment and happiness.

Maintaining a strong immune system to safeguard our health means avoiding such stress, but, of course, that is not always as simple as it sounds. Often the very moments when our emotions are in turmoil are also the times when we need to summon up all the strength of our mental energy. The times when this precious energy is most needed can also be the moments when we are least able to deliver.

Nourishing your natural defenses

LORD COLWYN, *practicing dentist for over 30 years, President of an All-Party Parliamentary Group for Alternative and Complementary Medicine; President of the Natural Medicine Society in Britain:*

❝I believe in enabling the body to maintain and build an efficient immune system, because this is what actually fights the things that go wrong. This means that nutrition has to be balanced and people should make sure they have all the amounts of minerals and vitamins they need.

Anything that is an antioxidant is anticancer and antiheart disease, and helps to maintain the immune system, which is important because antibiotics and most pharmaceutical products will depress the immune system.

There is a variance of opinion on vitamin C and vitamin E, but we do know that these two vitamins are antioxidants and that they remove dangerous byproducts from the body. The breakdown of fats causes the formation of free radicals, which are unstable molecules and believed to be the basic cause of most disease.

Minerals such as selenium and zinc race around the body in a scavenging operation, scoop up these free radicals, and get rid of them. The body has its own natural mechanisms to dispose of such things, but when you are surrounded by the destructive effects of electric lighting, traffic fumes, and a poor diet, your immune system is constantly under pressure and needs a bit of help. ❞

LEFT **Antioxidants, found mainly in fresh fruit and vegetables, can help protect against certain cancers and heart disease as well as maintain the body's natural defense system.**

SELF-HEALING
Meditation for Clarity

Take a few minutes before you settle down to meditate and read the following questions, which you can then take into the meditation. Reading these questions is more important than answering them because they are contemplations. Afterward, write down your thoughts.

Contemplations

→ Do you experience a set of mild symptoms that come and go from time to time without any obvious explanation?

→ When you have an important occasion coming up, do you worry in case you become ill on the day and cannot attend or cope with it?

→ When you were ill as a child, did your mother insist on sending you to school saying that if you became worse the teacher would send you home?

→ Has anyone accused you of being a hypochondriac – or of faking or imagining you are ill?

→ When you were ill as a child, did your mother comfort you and give you treats to compensate for having to be in bed?

→ Do you think other people in general expect too much from you?

→ Is your bedroom a sanctuary, a place to escape to when someone has hurt your feelings, just as much as a place to retire when you are physically ill?

Meditation

If you are ill, your mind and body become uncomfortable so you are ill at ease. In other words, you are "dis-eased," and the immune system is your main defense against this. You can meditate to open your mind and clear any blocks that affect the way you think, feel, and behave. Your spiritual journey is unique. Even if you are the only person on the planet to choose that direction, you will find the courage to follow where your heart leads you.

Relax, breathe deeply, and meditate

Close your eyes and visualize your immune system as a silken thread linking all the parts of your body so every organ, every nerve, and every cell is connected. Give this vital cord a color and watch that color thread itself through your whole body, connecting the energy between your physical, mental, and emotional bodies.

Somehow, and for reasons you will probably discover in the future, there are breaks in this essential link and these tiny chinks in your defensive armory are enough to make you vulnerable to passing infections. If you have been predisposed to particular conditions in the past, they will return time and time again.

As your inner eye travels along the entire length of your immune system, notice that as well as breaks there are also blocks preventing energy from flowing freely, keeping some of it out and locking some in. Remind yourself that your intelligence, which represents your conscious thinking, can only do so much and may not fully understand your spiritual needs.

Imagine you are talking to your spirit. Ask your spirit if your hands can become healing hands. Ask your spirit where to explore and touch, where your healing hands can best clear the blockages and repair the broken links in your immune system. Then let your spirit respond by guiding you.

Visualize your hands as though they are illuminated and glowing with a healing light as they move over the different parts of your body. Sense where they need to touch with this healing power and then surround that part of you with this healing light before moving on to the next. That healing light's power comes from its energy. Keeping your eyes closed and again allowing your senses to direct you, move your hands physically over the parts of your body as your spirit guides you. These are the parts that need to be healed.

Just as you did before, pause at each part of your body directed you to, call in

SELF-HEALING
Meditation for Clarity

Record your first thoughts

As soon as you can, write down your thoughts on the contemplations you took with you into your meditation. Try to be as spontaneous as possible and do not worry about the way you phrase your responses or how they look. Ideally, allow your thoughts to tumble out of your mind and lie on the paper just where they fall naturally. Keep these notes for later and come back to them from time to time. You may find that each time you read them, they reveal something fresh and new that helps you to understand more about yourself.

What your responses reveal
Mostly "yes" answers

You are reflecting disappointment in the way others see you, as well as with some areas of your life. Perhaps you feel ignored, that your efforts have gone unnoticed by other people and your talents are left unrewarded. You believe no one takes you seriously or trusts your judgement. You find this frustrating and it sends waves of negative feedback into your system, and your dilemma is how to convince other people.

But convince them of what? Your importance, your value? The other aspect of your deep frustration is that you are not sure yourself and then you search around looking for solutions, but because you never look in the right place, you do not find the answers you want. When that happens, you become very negative and suspect everyone else is right and you are wrong. Your confidence plummets and you become ill. This is the only way you know how to get others to comfort you.

 Ask yourself this: Do other people sense your confidence, or do other people just mirror your dissatisfaction?

Mostly "no" answers

You are very balanced in your outlook, and with so little emotional turmoil, you should be very healthy. You have a sense of your identity and your worth and are comfortable about your place in the world and how you fit in with others. You can accept a different view easily without it affecting your confidence. When someone disagrees with you, it does not make you doubt your opinion, yet if their argument is valid, you can be flexible and adapt. Your immune system defends your health, unimpeded by emotional chaos, and your health and vitality should be thriving because your life is so balanced. If they are not, perhaps you need to reflect on your responses.

 Consider this: It may have taken a lifetime to create your world as it is now, but the natural power of healing will be with you for even longer.

Half "yes," half "no" answers

Although you need to take stock, there is nothing desperately wrong that needs to be remedied instantly.

You are learning lessons through experiences, and they are proving of immense value. If ever you feel despondent, look back at the last year and see how far you have come so that you can banish negativity. If you suffer from aches and pains, explore them from a different perspective. You may find a deeper significance in the messages your body is sending you.

 Tell yourself this: I may make mistakes, but I will always try never to make the same mistake twice.

 ### Affirmation

I am now taking full responsibility for my thoughts, emotions, and actions, not because I have been told to and not because I feel I ought to, but because I want to and because I can.

RESTORING THE MIND-BODY BALANCE

The more you know about yourself, the greater your power to bring balance and harmony to your mind and body. Greater insight means greater wisdom – knowing your flaws, your strengths, your passions, and your needs. It is this knowledge that can help you to enhance your positive characteristics to create more confidence and a sense of your own worth, all of which creates better health.

In ancient Greece, Hippocrates believed individuals could exert tremendous influence over the progress of their own disease and recommended meditation to help them relax mentally. A few hundred years later, the Roman physician Galen observed that cancer occurred in more patients who were depressed than those who were happy.

Just as an anxious state of mind can bring on a physical illness, peace of mind and contentment can reduce the risk of disease. People who are relaxed and unstressed will be able to influence their own blood pressure as well as slow their heart rate.

Losing our minds

When people set out on a journey of self-discovery, they expect to discover insights that will make them want to change themselves. But I do not want anyone to change. This is altering the essence of who we are. It is like exchanging our soul for someone else's.

I have a different purpose. I want you to discover the parts of your mind that you have temporarily lost, perhaps buried deep inside your unconscious mind for so long that you have forgotten their existence. If you are not fully aware of all your senses, how can you be complete? It is like telling someone your name, but leaving half the word out. How would anyone know what to call you if such a vital piece of information were missing?

I want to show you other aspects of yourself and help you get in touch with them. This is why I say

that finding out more about yourself does not necessarily mean you have to make drastic changes. Often it is a question of bringing out another side of yourself that has been hidden. I believe we are all composed of many facets, but sometimes we impose a limit and only allow one or two aspects of ourselves to come to the surface.

Letting in the light

A restricted self-image leads to a restricted life. Taking a narrow view narrows our horizons, and without enough space to move or stretch, new ideas are constrained in such a claustrophobic space that the thinking process adapts and becomes accustomed to its cramped conditions. The spectrum of colors that makes up our characters becomes dimmed and the darker aspects of our nature take precedence, squeezing out the lighter shades and filling up the spaces with one dense color. The mind becomes one dimensional. Imagine living in a large mansion with dozens of

ABOVE **Searching for your path in life can seem like facing a maze with no way out. Changing your thought processes could free you from this introspective image.**

spacious rooms in which each enormous window offered a magnificent view. Then imagine living in such a place with all the windows boarded up. Not only would it be like spending your life in a dark cupboard, but why would you choose to do it anyway, particularly with such wonderful options available? Rediscovering the brilliance within the mind throws light on dark thoughts, bringing variety and diversity to everything you do and say and think. Awareness brings a wider vision and a greater breadth of knowledge. As your eyes are opened, the new images now in front of you will penetrate all your senses, touching the deep and extraordinary powers that have been lying there dormant.

Obscuring the view

Many people have become so used to seeing themselves in a particular light that a distorted image has become their reality. They have no idea how multifaceted they really are because the dark shade that obscures their inner vision has damaged their sight. Their lack of belief in themselves is reflected in their state of mind, and the longer they exist with this distorted view of themselves, the more this view is perpetuated, spreading out and affecting all the other areas of their lives.

They have filled their minds with this darkened image of themselves to the extent that it has blocked out any new ideas or suggestions. There is nowhere for a chink of light to pierce this gloom, no room for any more enlightened thoughts.

The concept of free will in their lives or of being in possession of any kind of power is alien to everything they have come to believe about themselves. It does not enter their conscious mind because it is so far away from their reality that they do not bother to give it consideration. Being regarded as a person whose views carry authority or weight is a notion too far-fetched even to think about, the sort of thing that only happens to other people. The blocking mechanism kicks in, the shutters come down, and the vision is closed off.

LEFT **Your outlook on life is influenced by your willingness to open your eyes to the outside world. Shutting yourself away as a protection from life's hardships, literally or metaphorically, can also deprive you of life's beauty.**

COMING TO OUR SENSES

Why do people cling to the things that make them unhappy and unhealthy? Is this a fact of modern life, or has humanity always had this streak of timidity that has prevented us moving forward? Why do so many of us not realize we have so many choices?

People generally feel far more comfortable with what they know than with what might be. It may not make you happy, but at least you know where you are, and within its safe parameters it becomes more tolerable than uncertainty. Tackling your problems means confronting the things that may terrify you. Staying exactly the same becomes a reliable option. But let me ask you this question – is the place where you are really where you want to be?

When people are described as being half out of their mind, most of us assume this means they are frantic with worry and anguish, but to me this phrase means they are people who have locked up a part of themselves and are only using half of their minds. When they "recover their senses" they are back to being themselves again. But are they? Does this mean they have now developed greater insights into themselves, having unlocked all those parts of their minds that they had shut away? I suspect it means they have resumed the kind of behavior that makes them safer to others. They

ABOVE **People who stand out in a crowd and express their feelings are often more healthy than** those who repress themselves for the sake of "fitting in" with other people.

will not be coming up with any outlandish views, and their behavior will not break any of the social rules that we all live by.

Living by the rules

Being "socially aware" is a natural progression we all make from infancy and childhood through to our adult lives. We know how to behave in a civilized way. For instance, we will not walk down the street without any clothes on because we are all concerned about what others think of us. Being normal and knowing the rules is both important and reassuring.

But being "normal" can be damaging. I hear a great many people say they feel bewildered, as though they have lost their identity. They complain they no longer know where they fit in. Just giving voice to these feelings of isolation means that they have taken the first step toward healing themselves, mentally and physically.

Their troubled mind has prompted them to question, and only by finding out who they are and where they really belong will they find contentment. Only by discovering their true selves will they enjoy peace of mind.

When 99 people share the same opinion but you, number 100, take a different view, it does not automatically mean you are wrong. It simply means there is a possibility that those 99 are right, but not necessarily that they are. A probability is not a fact.

THE NEED TO BELONG

The need to belong to a particular group of people is one of the most fundamental of human needs. Have you ever wondered why our whole society is organized into groups? From the day we start school as children, we are divided into classrooms, and from that time onward we join clubs, work for companies, organize associations, sit on committees, and belong to political parties. Political leaders gather a group of senior political advisors around them.

But when a particular individual cannot find a group with which they can identify, they become social outcasts. History is filled with such people who have lived on the edge of society, sometimes because their beliefs set them apart from their neighbors, or they had been rejected because they were different in some way, whether in their appearance or outlook.

Challenging the status quo

Some took pride in their differences, perhaps set up their own group and became its leader, becoming absorbed into this new community they created for themselves. These were the people with the courage to challenge the rules and rewrite them. Their refusal to show unquestioning compliance may have caused them all kinds of difficulties, even cost some of them their lives. But being different can also suggest being unsuitable, unacceptable, and unlovable. The rejected often have no choice but to wear the label they have been given as though it has always fitted.

ABOVE, LEFT AND BELOW **Religious reformer Martin Luther (1483–1546) (top), patriot and martyr Joan of Arc (c.1412–31) (center), and astronomer and mathematician Galileo (1564–1642) (below) were condemned for their beliefs in their own time. They have been celebrated since for their courage and insight.**

BELONGING TO YOURSELF

Today, we are motivated by the same forces that drove our ancestors, either to rebel or comply. The person we present to the outside world is not necessarily the person we feel like inside at the core of our being, and such conflicting images can be so confusing that we lose sight of our true identity. We may try to merge into one group or another, never really fitting into any one of them very well. On the outside, it seems as if things are fine, but inside our heads it can be chaos. The goalposts have been moved so far apart that there is very little we recognize any longer.

Some people stick with one idea, cling to it tightly, and defend it against any suggestions that things could be otherwise. Blocked in and locked up, every ounce of energy is negatively concentrated on maintaining the status quo, and this negativity fills the mind and seeps into the body. Some people find such compromise anathema, and although the first twinges of doubt are deeply disturbing and their natural compulsion is to turn and run, they persevere.

Guided by your inner voice

If you asked the people who refused to compromise at the time why, they might not be able to tell you. Later on, as their discovery of themselves revealed more, they might explain that their deepest instincts reminded them that hiding from the truth was not a real escape route at all. But by listening and trusting their inner voice, they boosted their self-belief. What they had done was to begin to explore their own potential with a renewed confidence in its power.

Being alone can mean being lonely, but it can also mean being complete in yourself, content with your own company. It can signify that your mind and body are synchronized, running along the same track. You may not belong to a group of like-minded people, but you do belong to yourself.

Lasting impressions

Often one of the last things we learn in life is the effect we have on others. Sit in front of a mirror and gaze steadily into your own eyes. Look at yourself as if for the first time, as though you were seeing yourself through someone else's eyes. Imagine you had never met this person before and ask yourself what impression you would get. Would you find this person attractive, strange, compassionate, or hard? Would you be drawn to his or her energy because it feels welcoming and approaching, or is this person sending out a signal that warns others not to invade his or her personal space?

As you study your own image, change your expression, relax your shoulders, smile at yourself with your eyes, and observe the ways in which it changes your reflection. If you like those changes and feel they reflect the real, inner you, practice them. Practice them regularly and they will not be changes but the positive, outward-going part of your natural self.

ABOVE **How do others see you? Look in the mirror as if seeing yourself for the first time.**

SELF-HEALING
Meditation for Protection

Take the following questions into your meditation to contemplate and then write down your spontaneous reactions afterward.

Contemplations

→ If you could change your physical appearance, do you think you would be happier and more successful?

→ When you are hurt or angry, do you seem to suffer physical symptoms such as indigestion or headaches?

→ Do your friends appear to have more interesting social lives than you, with more invitations and a wider circle of friends, and you cannot understand why them and not you?

→ Do you worry about the state of the world and easily get upset when disasters are shown on world news?

→ Do you ever wish you had chosen a different career and envy those you suspect are completely happy in their work?

Meditation

If your energies are vibrating at so many different levels that they are not connecting, this creates a wayward, directionless energy field. In this situation, your thoughts are heading off along one path while your emotions are feeling their way along another. Your physical energy, reacting to the detrimental effects of this disharmony, caves in because it is has no idea in which direction to go. The chaos could make you ill.

Relax, breathe deeply, and meditate

Think of the various parts of your body that have been affected by illness and go through them one by one. Talk to each one in turn. Tell each body part that you are going to remove all the stress and tension that has been constricting it so it will once again be able to function properly.

Create an image of this tension. See it as a strident, overbright mass of color that resonates loudly and disturbs and disrupts everything it comes into contact with. Imagine this rampaging, destructive color now flowing through your entire mind and body, filling every part of your being with its awful heaviness. Experience that sensation as vividly as you can and pause for a few minutes so you will always be able to remind yourself at any time of the unpleasantness of harboring so much stress. Notice how restricting it is. Stretch out your fingers as if you are about to play the piano and notice how awkward your joints feel. Hold your arms out on each side of you as though you are going to raise them high above your head and note how this stress has stiffened your limbs and stopped your energy from flowing freely.

SELF-HEALING
Meditation for Protection

Now talk to this tension and tell it gently but firmly it is time to leave your mind and body. Watch the unnatural brightness of this color start to drain out of you. As it gathers in a cloud above your head, notice how your own natural coloring has returned, flooding your whole mind and body with glowing health. When the last pocket of tension has left your body, capture all the released tension and gently and firmly send the bright-colored cloud away. See it float into the distance and over the horizon until it vanishes from your view.

Now you can heal all the parts of your body. Go through each one and visualize it as though it had been sleeping. Tell it you are going to energize it so it will be fully alive and healthy again. Tell it you can provide this energy. Imagine you are reaching for the switch that turns on a light. Until you touch it, the lightbulb is dark. It is not broken beyond repair. It simply needs an injection of the right sort of energy and then it will illuminate the room.

Go through all the parts of your body you sense need reenergizing; pause, focus your attention on each body part in turn, and flood it with healing light. When you have completed this, reflect on the new sensation of health now flooding through your mind and body and savor it.

Promise yourself that you will maintain this effect and defend your mind and body against the invasion of stress and tension. Promise yourself that you will constantly safeguard your health.

Record your first thoughts

When you have finished meditating, have a pen and paper beside you so you do not forget to write down your first thoughts on the contemplations.

What your responses reveal

Mostly "yes" answers

You need to rethink the way you allow life to affect you. You make negative comparisons and draw negative conclusions, and holding all this inside you does not stop the negative signals you send from reaching others. Clinging to hard knots of resentment can prevent the flow of healthy energy and make you ill.

Consider this: Only by experiencing negativity can we learn how to discard it.

Mostly "no" answers

You are very laid back about yourself and your place in the world, almost to the point of being disconnected from everyone and everything. Contributing a little more and becoming involved with people and events outside your own existence should bring you a greater awareness of your potential.

Consider this: Static energy allows space for complacency, and then apathy and boredom move in and your whole system seizes up.

Half "yes," half "no" answers

You are probably addressing some of the problems you have surrounding your emotional reactions and have already found you can bring a lot of compassion and understanding to others.

Consider this: We are dynamic beings and need to keep moving forward because activity generates energy.

Affirmation

I will not hide behind possibilities or let probabilities hold me back. I will savor every moment as an incredible opportunity.

Questioning the established doctrines of medicine has always provoked criticism. Toward the end of the l9th century, one of my distant relatives, Sigmund Freud, did exactly that with his new provocative and challenging theory of psychological analysis. He was the first person in his field to give credence to the power of the mind and suggest that thoughts could determine the way people behaved.

At that time, conventional treatment for mentally disturbed patients consisted of confinement in asylums, often accompanied by additional restriction in chains. To be out of your mind meant you also had to be out of sight.

5 | INVISIBLE MEDICINE FOR THE MIND

DISCOVERING PSYCHOLOGY

Freud's new modern theory identified a series of defense mechanisms employed as avoidance tactics, such as repression and denial, transference and projection. But his emphasis on sexual drives and the gratification of pleasure supported his notion that man possessed a very basic, instinctual nature, with few redeeming qualities, and the process of learning social behavior only provided a facade.

Not surprisingly, he offended the middle-class Viennese society in which he launched his ideas. Much later in his life, the unrepentant Freud likened the events of that time to throwing a pebble in a pond and watching the ensuing ripples spread farther and farther out.

Sigmund Freud qualified as a doctor in 1881, and his interest in psychiatry led him to develop theories that were to have universal implications. The advent of World War I brought to his attention the plight of many wounded soldiers who were suffering dreadful nightmares following their appalling experiences in the trenches. Today, we recognize this condition as post traumatic stress disorder.

Buried memories

Freud's belief was that these troubled men had repressed their dreadful memories, pushing them down to a part of the mind where there was not a conscious awareness. Although he was not the first man to identify the existence of the unconscious mind, he was the first to give it an important status. He considered it a realm of the mind that had its own wishful impulses, its own mode of expression and particular mechanisms. It was Freud's belief that the human mind cannot tolerate such painful memories, however deeply buried. To relieve the mental pressure the soldiers were under, their minds released these thoughts as dreams, but because they were so bad, those dreams emerged as nightmares.

The new psychological analysis, initially implausible and incomprehensible to its critics, provided an infinitely more productive and compassionate therapy than anything that took place in the horrendous lunatic asylums of those days.

ABOVE **Freud's belief that the unconscious mind held repressed memories was given credence by the many World War I soldiers who suffered nightmares. Today this condition is known as Post Traumatic Stress Syndrome.**

Regression therapy for phobics

JOHN BUTLER, psychologist, psychotherapist, and hypnotherapist. John Butler tutors medical students at King's College, in London, England, and set up the first formal hypnotherapy courses for nurses as part of their training, validated by the University of Manchester, also in England. These were designed to incorporate hypnotherapy into specialties such as emergency treatment, palliative nursing care, and obstetrics, as well as the treatment of certain phobias. It can also replace anaesthetic drugs in surgical procedures.

❛Various techniques are used to extinguish phobias. One approach is through regression therapy in which the phobic is taken back through their memory using hypnosis until they discover an event or reason for their phobias. This can produce extraordinary results. The unconscious mind has the capacity to retain the memory of an emotion, which means that regressing back into childhood can prove effective in understanding fears that had been unexplained.

To an adult phobic, revealing the origin of their fear in early childhood also shows them they will never again be that vulnerable. Encouraging them to look at that fear in the present day in their conscious mind is to disempower it and stop it from ever being so destructive again. For someone who has suffered without knowing why, it is like opening a window and allowing cool, fresh air to blow away ancient dusty cobwebs. ❜

UNCONSCIOUS INFLUENCES ON BEHAVIOR

Freud also believed that what happened in our childhood was retained in our unconscious minds and our individual personalities developed from those experiences, explaining why we behave and experience life the way we do.

He defined three levels of awareness: conscious, preconscious, and unconscious. The first is what we are already aware of, the second is what we can remember if we want to, and the third is that level of unconsciousness we cannot recall under normal circumstances, but which can direct our actions and is often the force behind our behavior. He believed we are all motivated by these forces but are largely unaware of them. Instead, we choose to rationalize, delude, or justify our actions because we prefer not to see our real motivation.

Evidence of an invisible force

During the next 40 years, Freud developed many other theories on personality that offered insights into human behavior and still form the basis of many therapies today. But he was constantly

LEFT **Discarding the emotional "baggage" you have carried with you since early childhood helps to move your life forward.**

criticized because he could not offer scientific evidence that his theories were any more than that – just theories.

Proving that an invisible force directed different parts of the mind and led to thinking and behavior patterns was impossible. Yet, Freud never doubted his original firmly held belief in the power of the unconscious mind and the important and influential role it played in directing man's behavior. Using the evidence of his own ears and eyes led Freud to trust his instincts that something else was going on inside the mind. Just because it was not visible did not reduce the havoc it created.

The fact that both Freud and his contemporary, Carl Jung, were medically qualified lent weight to their theories, and enabled them to produce persuasive arguments that carried implications for everyone. Even so, those ripples of criticism spread far and wide. Even today, we live in a scientifically literate society that still tends to distrust anything that is not tangible. If you cannot see it, hear it, feel, or touch it, then it does not exist.

My own powers have been validated at the prestigious Stanford Research Institute, in California, and written up in *Nature*, the most important scientific magazine in the world, yet many scientists are still skeptical. They know about invisible energy but my powers elude them because they cannot capture them.

Diagnosing the emotions

Medical science has come full circle and doctors today prescribe medicines for the mind. These include antidepressants, medications which secrete extra hormones into the brain to make the patient feel happier, and tranquillizers, which relax the body's muscles to alleviate tension. There are also many hormones available that are believed to slow down the aging process, and others which help people sleep or reduce the effects of jet lag. There is also a range of beta-blockers with a mechanism to literally "block" the function of the body that is causing problems, one of which is designed to deal with anxiety. The irony is that doctors diagnose these problems from a set of invisible symptoms – symptoms based on the patient's emotions and feelings.

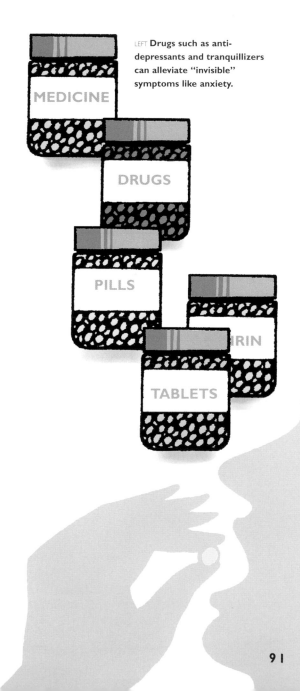

LEFT **Drugs such as antidepressants and tranquillizers can alleviate "invisible" symptoms like anxiety.**

MEDICINE

DRUGS

PILLS

IRIN

TABLETS

ONE THEORY AFTER ANOTHER

Carl Jung's theories added another realm of the mind – the "collective unconscious" – which he claimed stored inherited memories of the past, such as dreams, myths, and legends, and which were passed down from one generation to the next. Jung used the word "psyche" in broader terms than Freud, seeing it as encompassing not just the mind but also the spirit or soul.

What Freud called the libido, Jung called psychic energy, but both saw this as a life force that flows between two opposite points, creating tension and energy. Freud's rather pragmatic and cynical view saw humans motivated by the pursuit of pleasure and the avoidance of pain. Jung believed the soul of man had infinitely more depth and was directed by emotions as well as logic. This life force constantly needed to regulate itself to maintain each person's equilibrium.

RIGHT **Carl Jung (1875–1961),** unlike Freud, regarded neurosis as a potentially positive experience, focusing the individual on an aspect of his or her personality in need of attention.

Selective memory

Humans remember things. What kind of things they remember and how much they retain is determined by the way their mind perceives those memories. Just as enjoyable occasions are recalled with pleasure, there is an understandable reluctance to recall unhappy moments and times of deep despair.

We select the memories that we like, and those past experiences that we prefer not to dwell upon are sometimes pushed down into the unconscious part of the mind. This is where a vast amount of information is stored but not necessarily accessed.

❛Many present-day conditions, including eating disorders and phobias, are often long-held fears that have been ignored for too long and grown out of proportion within the mind.❜

Neurosis – negative or positive?

Jung described neurosis as a particular kind of psychic disturbance that interfered with the health of the person suffering from it, and that consequently disrupted the individual's life. He believed this conflict arose through a complex process in which there was a splitting off between parts of the mind, and when this happened, awareness went from consciousness into an independent but unconscious existence.

Freud claimed that the defense mechanisms he had described originated from conscious thoughts and feelings being lodged or hidden in the unconscious part of the mind. But ignoring these emotions or pretending they did not exist did not mean that they simply evaporated. Freud believed that they would emerge later as an anxiety or neurosis.

Jung saw the same tendencies, but he insisted that this was not a negative trend. Instead, he felt it could actually enhance personal growth. Neurosis was, he said, like a commanding voice drawing your attention to a side of the personality that had been neglected.

"I have no ready-made philosophy of life to hand out. I do not know what to say to the patient when he asks me: 'What do you advise?' I only know one thing: When my conscious mind no longer sees any possible road ahead and consequently gets stuck, my unconscious psyche will react to the unbearable standstill."

Jung considered that imagination and intuition were vital for a balanced personality. "Man likes to believe he is master of his soul," he wrote, "but without mastery over emotions and feelings, we are still wandering in a wilderness in which only logical facts contain meaning."

Repressed emotions

This emotional baggage is locked away and never referred to until it seems, in the conscious mind, that it never existed. But the unconscious mind continues to log everything that we think, feel, and experience. Occasionally, in the present day, an incident might trigger a long-repressed memory, and however fleetingly this memory is recalled, the effect can be enormous. Sometimes it can be just too big to tolerate, and the mind pushes it away in another direction.

Holding the lid down firmly on a pan of boiling water does not prevent it from boiling over. At first only the steam escapes, but later the lid will blow and the contents will spill everywhere. Many present-day conditions, including eating disorders and phobias, are often long-held fears that have been ignored for too long and grown out of proportion within the mind.

Distorted perceptions

Distorted thoughts produce distorted perceptions. A person suffering from anorexia cannot look in the mirror and see anything but an overweight body. The phobic can logically acknowledge that the thing they fear so dreadfully will never actually harm them, yet the fear they experience is so real it disrupts their lives.

COMMON PSYCHOLOGICAL PRINCIPLES

Fritz Perls, a Berlin-born psychiatrist, broke away from Freudian theory and founded Gestalt psychology based on his belief in the fundamental integrity of human nature. No matter how damaged a person might have been, the drive toward self-enlightenment remained. Perls described this as healing. He saw this as a creative process of continuous adjustment taking place within the mind to maintain balance in an ever-changing world. He didn't see any gap between the mind and body and adopted an holistic approach – the sum of the whole is greater than the sum of the parts.

Many other theories have been developed since those early days. Some have been gentler, some more confrontational, some weird and way out, but whatever the route, the destination and the underlying principles have always been similar. There is always emphasis on the links between mind and body and the impact of one upon the other, as well as the need for balance and adjustment throughout life.

What is also recognized is the uniqueness of each person and the presence of their spirit or soul as a separate entity to the physical workings of the brain and the mechanics of the body. This is the part of us all that retains the ancient wisdoms of our ancestors and the instinctive powers that enable us to adjust and alter when the balance of our psyche is upset. In short, the power to heal ourselves.

THE SIXTH SENSE

Instinct and intuition are valuable elements of our psyche. Just as we all carry the genes of our ancestors, so we all inherit thoughts and patterns of behavior that alert us to situations, warn us of dangers, attract us to certain people, and draw us into situations we will enjoy.

Files of experience

This enormous storehouse of human memories is passed down from one generation to the next and contains many of the ancient wisdoms that have a valid role in our modern lives. Tapping into this sixth sense does not deplete any of our other senses. If anything, the opposite occurs, and the more we use this sixth sense, the more intensely it develops.

The unconscious mind catalogues everything we see, hear, touch, smell, taste, and think, from birth to adulthood, filing this information throughout our lives. Some people believe that everything a baby learns has to begin from scratch, as though a tiny baby were a blank canvas and the colors and pictures to be painted would all be entirely new.

Others attribute "unlearned behavior" to infants of all species. For example, a baby under three months will grip hard when a finger is placed in its fist; a kitten will wash its face with its paw after licking that paw first; a puppy will use its tail to signal its state of mind, wagging it with pleasure or hiding it between its legs when miserable. These creatures are born with this knowledge embedded in their DNA code, which sets the pattern of their being.

ABOVE AND LEFT **Every animal, from human beings to dogs and cats, inherits a genetic blueprint of instinctual behavior.**

RIGHT **A new born baby grips its father's finger, a reflex common to all babies. She will also instinctively feed by suckling. This "unlearned behavior" characterizes all species.**

❛Sixth sense is also healing power, when the touch of one person ignites the healing power of the other. It is also about healing yourself.❜

Power and energy

What, then, is sixth sense to me? I believe it represents a deep wisdom that we all inherit from our forebears and which, once harnessed, can effectively give every one of us much greater knowledge and insight into our lives. I believe that with such awareness comes healthier minds and bodies.

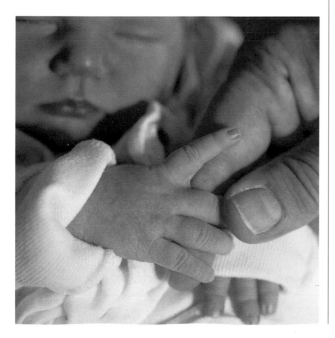

ABOVE **Sixth sense is an invisible yet formidable universal force, embodying the wisdoms** inherited from our ancestors down the ages and affording us an invaluable insight into our lives.

Some of us learn how to tap into this energy earlier than others; some come upon it through trial and error. Others cannot explain it but trust it totally. Its power is formidable and this frightens those who have not yet reached the point of understanding the potency of such an invisible force.

Most of us are aware of auras and often refer to the atmosphere in a room, or tune into other people's vibrations by getting on someone's wavelength. These are all invisible, yet potent, energies that our sixth sense picks up on. Sixth sense is about a special energy that transcends all the normal barriers and can move through matter, space, and time. Telepathy, premonitions, a sense that for no special reason a situation was right or wrong, a sudden realization, or a flash of comprehension are all inspired conclusions of sixth sense. Sixth sense explains the inexplicable.

Sixth sense is also healing power, when the touch of one person ignites the healing power of the other. It is also about healing yourself.

SELF-HEALING
Explore your state of mind

As with the other meditations in the book, the following questions should be taken into your meditation to be contemplated. They are about moods and lifestyles, gifts, and wishes. Wait until you are meditating regularly and have become comfortable with the process before embarking on this exploration. Select only one section at any one time, returning to the next ones later and so on as you progress through your healing. As before, think about them first, meditate, then write down your thoughts afterward.

Tuning into your thoughts and feelings

These contemplations are designed to focus attention on your state of mind so you can identify and recognize your own feelings. They will also make you think about your ambitions and hopes. It is often the case that people who are existing in a state of gloom cannot find anything they enjoy doing. This can also happen to people whose lives are enjoyable. If you asked them to name something they really wanted, they might not be able to because their lives are already so full. Others tend not to ask themselves why some people always manage to make them feel guilty or sad.

Living with these thoughts and perceptions daily is your normality, so however you feel right now is normal for you. But if you awaken with lightness in your heart, whether you are greeted by thunderstorms, snow, sleet, or sunshine, you will find something good to look forward to in your day. If you awaken each morning to a joyless world, the view from your window will never be very exciting. But you can feel better. You can achieve health excellence.

Section one

Your mood

→ Are you uncomfortable among friends, unable to be completely relaxed and enjoy yourself because you are constantly aware of how different you are to the rest of the group?

→ Do you often leave situations feeling that, although everything seemed fine on the surface, inwardly you have a sense of regret and wish you had handled things differently?

→ Do you feel exhausted when you first wake up in the morning, and does this fatigue gradually evaporate as you get on with your day?

→ Do minor ailments constantly keep you away from work or force you to cancel social engagements?

Your lifestyle

→ Do you make a point of checking the labels on food products and avoiding chemical additives, opting for as healthy a diet as possible?

→ Do you enjoy your job, but wish it left you more free time for a social life?

→ Do you find punctuality is a problem, and you are late for work and last to arrive at a party?

→ Do you have a regular routine each week and always know exactly what you will be doing?

Your wishes

→ Do you envy your best friend and wish you could change lives with them because they have all the qualities you would like to have?

→ Do you wish the state of your health did not hold you back from enjoying your life?

→ Do you wish you could turn the clock back ten years and train for a different occupation?

→ Do you daydream about winning a fortune because you believe it would change your life?

Section two

Your mood

→ Are you surprised when someone pays you a compliment?

→ Do you blame yourself when things go wrong and believe all your problems are of your own making?

→ Does your level of confidence depend on what you are wearing that day? If you do not feel comfortable with your appearance, you will not feel comfortable about yourself?

→ Do you ever accept invitations when you really do not feel like going out?

→ Would it upset you if a good friend turned to someone other than you for help?

Your lifestyle

→ How much time do you have to spend on personal hobbies?

→ Do you wait for others to organize outings even· though you always enjoy going along to them?

→ Do you wish you could find a hobby that seriously interested you, because you have never yet found something that excites your passion?

→ When you were a child, did you envisage a different sort of life for yourself?

Your wishes

→ Would you love to wear an outfit that attracted attention when you walked into a room?

→ Would you love to change your physical appearance, but have never dared?

→ Would you like to be wealthy enough to indulge yourself so whenever you felt low you could go out and spend some money?

→ Would you love to have been cleverer and had an occupation that would make people admire and envy you?

SELF-HEALING
Explore your state of mind

Section three

Your mood

→ Do other people's problems swamp you at times and make you feel guilty?

→ Do you feel bored for long periods of time?

→ Do you find it difficult to concentrate and forget things easily?

→ Do you disapprove of friends whose lives involve a lot of socializing?

Your lifestyle

→ How would you feel if you knew you would be doing the same job and living in the same place with the same partner in 20 years from now?

→ Does your fatigue begin to build at the start of the week so that you are just getting through the days rather than enjoying them?

→ Do you find it depressing to read newspapers because they are full of bad news?

→ Do you always double-check when you leave home to make sure you have locked the doors and windows properly?

Your wishes

→ Have you made plans for the moment when you can retire from work, such as moving to a country cottage or living somewhere sunny?

→ Would you accept without hesitation a trip around the world if you won it?

→ Would you love to get yourself fit and healthy enough to run in a marathon?

→ If you won a fortune, how much of it would you give away and who would you give it to?

Section four

Your mood

→ Does bad weather make you feel gloomy?

→ Do you find it difficult to sympathize with people when you believe they make their own problems?

→ Do you find your mind is in overdrive when you go to bed at night even though you feel tired?

→ If you stumbled slightly and everyone laughed, would you feel angry or would you join in?

Your lifestyle

→ Although you know what changes would improve your life, do problems always seem to crop up which get in the way?

→ Would you like to have more responsibility at work instead of always having a boss over you?

→ Do you hesitate before inviting people to your home because you never feel it looks the way you would like it to?

→ Do you often return items you have bought because you realize you have made a mistake?

Your wishes

→ If someone handed you the chance of a perfect day, how would you spend it?

→ Do you nurture a dream of making a parachute jump or climbing a mountain without ever believing you could achieve either?

→ Do you wish you could wave a magic wand and treat friends and family to a wonderful vacation?

→ Do you dream of the day when you can leave your job and tell your unpleasant boss what you really think?

moment. It can change from day to day because you are changing. I have showed you how to use music in your meditation (see page 59), but to add a new dimension, you can tune into your sense of smell instead by lighting scented candles. Again, choose a scent that best fits your mood on the day. Make yourself as comfortable as you need to be and try to avoid outer distractions. Your meditation world is intended to help you focus inwardly. Above all, visualize positive images to create positive patterns.

Inner imagery

Healing your unseen emotional and mental energies is often considered very complex but it can actually be very simple. Just as you and your mood affect the way you see your outer world, so you can shape the way you see your inner world. You can visualize all the parts of your body and give them colors and shapes. You can pay special attention to the areas where you have specific problems and fill them with healing light, surround them with healing energy, or create light that enters your entire body and fills it with luminescence.

Pick the colors for your imagery by sensing the ones with which you have the most empathy at that

Visual healing

Use your most imaginative fantasies for visual imagery in your meditations because they will make you feel better. The more you make them the way you would love them to be, the more enjoyment you will have in creating them. In this way, their effect will stay with you long after you have finished meditating, which is a healthy effect because the mood you are in changes the way you see life as a whole. It reflects your state of mind, representing your emotional and mental energy, and if the weight of your mood is heavy enough, it will bear down on your physical body too. This, of course, leads to mind-body illnesses.

The links between the mind and body are seamless, and when there is balance between the two, the entire system works effortlessly and naturally. Thoughts, emotions, and impulses are passed from the mind to the body and are reflected in the state of the body's health. When someone feels good about themselves and their life, the energy that flows from their mind to their body sends encouraging, positive signals and the body reacts accordingly. A healthy psyche leads to a healthy body. Equally, someone in a discontented or depressed state of mind can have a dismal effect on their own physical health. When the mind is in bad shape, the body suffers in the same way.

6 | MIND–BODY SYMBIOSIS

PSYCHOSOMATIC ILLNESS

To stop our negative thoughts and feelings causing problems for our body, we need to look inside ourselves for an explanation. Why has this illness happened and what particular situation did it stem from? Having discovered the cause and effect of psychosomatic illness, we can now take steps to make sure we do not allow ourselves to become vulnerable.

There is a very fine line between the point where physical illness begins and negative emotional energy causes those physical symptoms. While there are numerous physical conditions that are directly linked to an emotional source, there are many conditions for which there is no direct mental link. We know that a patient in a poor emotional state can actually make their illness worse, but in many cases the cause and effect is blurred.

> *There is a very fine line between the point where physical illness begins and negative emotional energy causes those physical symptoms.*

RIGHT **If your mind is in a constant state of anxiety, this turmoil can in turn be inflicted on your body, manifesting itself in ill-health.**

Emotional damage

If a condition has persistently occurred, then questions do have to be asked because there is obviously a cause which needs to be eliminated. Ultimately, I believe the best way to create good health is through prevention.

Of course there are cases where people deliberately create illness or block their own healing power. They are probably not consciously aware of the damage they are doing to themselves and they cannot stop. The origins of their illness take on more significance because only by looking deeper into their own mind will an explanation emerge for what appears to be contradictory behavior.

How do emotions become converted into a physical illness? That they do is proof of the enormous power of the mind and the control it can exercise over our bodies, but even acknowledging this does not prevent this process from happening. So, first let us look at the way it works so we can then begin to dismantle the process.

CREATING A HEALTHY ENVIRONMENT

Problems create all kinds of energy. They can stimulate people into positive action, produce exciting
challenges, and lead to a terrific sense of achievement, often just from the fact that an attempt to
challenge the situation has been made. The opposite of rising to such a challenge is when you allow
a problem to overwhelm you. This happens when
you begin to believe you are helpless, unable to
deal with anything.

Victim mentality

If you have persuaded yourself that events around
you are determined by others, you are also
accepting that you have become a victim of your
problems and worries, and that any decisions
which could affect your life are reached by other
people. Eventually, victim-mode becomes so
entrenched that you find it hard to remember any

*" Whatever has happened to you
has taught you something, even though
you may not yet know what it is yet. But I
can promise you this – you will. "*

other kind of state of mind. This is how you see
yourself, and you no longer think for yourself
because you now believe your thoughts and opinions have no value.

What has happened is that you have abandoned
self-belief. Ignoring the power of your own mind
to evaluate situations, form opinions, or make
decisions is to hand over responsibility and
become childlike, as though you never had the
ability to think for yourself. This is a complete
rejection of your own intelligence – you cannot
trust or believe what you think. Now you defer to
others, persuading yourself they must know better.
Quite simply, you have lost faith in yourself.

If you look around you, you will recognize the
people whose negative thoughts are manifesting
themselves in negative responses from their bodies
because everything about them is diminished.
Their body language speaks volumes. They are
diffident and apologetic, as if merely existing was
something they should be sorry about. They carry
themselves in a way that indicates they wish they
were invisible.

Anyone feeling victimized in life is psychologically
disposed to being unhappy and to suffer emotional
problems that will hold them back. If you are
trapped in this syndrome, whatever you set out to
achieve is programed to fail. Each failure confirms
your inadequacy, and this spiral of negativity sets in
and spreads throughout your physical body.

LEFT **Self-protective body
language could indicate that
your mind is distorting the
size of a problem. By
changing your posture, you**
**release the negativity.
Sitting up straight and
facing the world
immediately makes you
look and feel stronger.**

Lowering your defenses

As well as becoming prone to all kinds of stress-related conditions, you are in such a low physical and mental state that you will be much more susceptible to infections, vulnerable to every stray virus or bacteria that a stronger immune system would have beaten off.

Your mental and emotional energy is working at full strength but it is being used to exert a negative influence on your life. It is within everyone's ability to switch their thoughts into a different program and reverse this process in favor of a more positive approach.

Turning negative into positive

As soon as you begin to turn those negative mind–body links into positive, uplifting thoughts, you will start to feel the difference in the way your body feels. Once you decide you deserve a healthier body and mind, you will be taking a vital step toward rebuilding your depleted system.

When we heal ourselves in these situations, we are actually recharging a tired system that has been starved of vibrant, invigorating energies. But healing can also take you by surprise. Sometimes the astonishing difference it can make to the way you think and feel about life contrasts so sharply with the person you were that you are taken aback.

It is difficult to be analytical about a situation when you are in the middle of it. It is even harder when your natural emotions run amok and color your opinions, tap into your deepest insecurities, and test your confidence – even determine the way you behave and the things you say at such times. You might feel angry with yourself for sinking into a downward spiral that drained you physically, but the state of mind you are in determines the way you view life. The same situation can appear completely different, depending upon your own mood.

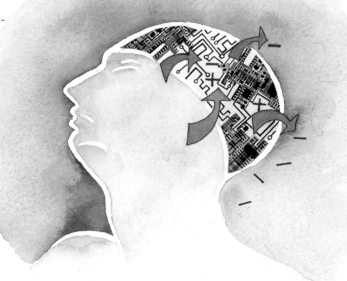

Positive thinking

We are not computers but human beings, and the essence of ourselves is not a silicon chip but a spirit that has more power and more influence than we can imagine. We know that we can change anything we want to if we want to badly enough. So why allow your brain to control you when it should serve you? If our brain program no longer suits our needs, we can redesign it or replace it by switching negatives for positives. This will cancel out conditioned reflexes.

Whenever you find you are repeating a negative thought, just add a positive one each time. Eventually, the positive ones will totally replace the negatives and literally push them out of your mind. If your actions are negative, you can alter them by the same method, by adding positive ones every time.

Do not waste time looking back at the way you were. Do no beat yourself up over your lack of logic or common sense. Whatever has happened to you has taught you something, even though you may not yet know what it is yet. But I can promise you this – you will.

EMOTIONS THAT MAKE YOU ILL

Guilt, anger, boredom, and fear – these four emotions are the most destructive to your well-being and need to be recognized and dealt with.

Guilt

If something you are doing is making you feel guilty, you have two options. Either stop doing whatever is causing the guilt, or simply give up the guilt. If it is something that happened in the past, tell yourself you will never repeat it and move on with your life.

This particular form of self-torture stems from an overzealous conscience. We feel guilty when we do not match up to other people's expectations, and we feel guilty when we are subjected to emotional-blackmail tactics from those we love. Guilt hits at the very core of our self-esteem and can create unbearable pressure if we allow it to. Putting this damaging, commonplace emotion into perspective is one of the most healing things we can do for ourselves.

Anger

Uncontrolled anger coupled with frustration can be profoundly physically destructive and can create excessive levels of acidity in the stomach and raise blood pressure, as well as triggering heart attacks and strokes.

Anger is normal and natural and should be expressed, because denying it can cause additional harm. But when it is a constant, continuing state of mind, it actually becomes an extreme form of stress and the long-term effects of this emotional state have been known to lead to a variety of serious illnesses, including cancer and heart disease.

It is incredibly important to tackle anger, and if you have a short fuse and become infuriated within seconds, you certainly need to find a way to block this extreme overreaction, because its emotional impact on you is destructive in many ways. Each angry outburst will leave you feeling very tense and wound up, your thoughts in a complete jumble, and unable to deal with anything in a proper way.

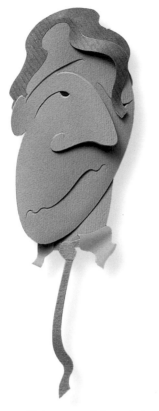

Boredom

Inactivity is incredibly stressful and depletes physical and mental energy, making the sufferer even less likely to spring into action. It is also a kind of fatigue with your life, perhaps your work or lack of it, or simply being occupied in an area that brings you no satisfaction or pride in achievement. Bored people have no way of imagining a better future, because their state of mind prevents them from being stimulated or excited by the prospect of anything. They cannot see farther than filling each day with the same monotonous routine. Suggest a hobby and this will be viewed negatively. Suggest an outing and the reaction will be the same.

Bored people have to find their own motivation and recover their zest for life through making an effort, not relying on the efforts of other people. Once they have expressed a desire to help themselves, you can assist by encouraging a gentle return to real life, perhaps a one-day-at-a-time program of activities that will stretch instead of sedate their mind.

Fear

This underpins so many aspects of our lives and lies at the root of the worst scenarios we ever imagine. It holds people back, distorts reality, and creates symptoms of illness and enormous emotional distress causing apprehension, anxiety, insomnia, and phobic terror. The fear of failure stops people from taking risks, trying out something new, and testing themselves. Denying so many aspects of life through fear is emotionally constricting and worsens conditions such as eczema, asthma, and chronic indigestion. Fear, like so many other feelings, stems from lack of belief in ourselves and our abilities and has to be overcome if life is ever to be normal.

I recommend a meditation in which people can visualize the best possible outcome of whatever frightens them, and gradually what seemed unthinkable slowly becomes a distinct possibility. Renewing self-esteem means facing up to and challenging your fear, since ultimately this is the most effective way of dealing with it.

Other damaging emotions

Lying in-between these destructive emotions are many other damaging states of mind that, if left unchecked, will inevitably undermine your health. We all experience them from time to time, which is absolutely natural because life is unpredictable and deals us blows as well as gifts. It is only when we hold onto negative emotions longer than necessary, or allow our imaginations to work against us so we experience them when there is no real need, that they cause us problems.

These include frustration and disappointment, hurt and loneliness, hostility, resentment, rejection, and despair. If you recognize any one of them, why not treat it as an early-warning signal that you are in danger of sliding toward a more severe state of stress?

Your inner voice will alert you to the meaning these signals have for you. If you are sensitive to their approach, it follows that your intuition will also be able to guide you and help you block out the worst of their effects without diminishing your sensitivity. This is important because your thoughts and feelings reflect the essence of your spirit. When they are under threat, they need protection not oblivion.

> *Your inner voice will alert you to the meaning these signals have for you.*

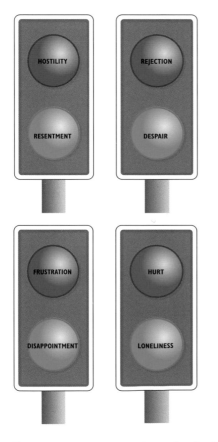

ABOVE **Negative emotions can be early-warning signals that changes are needed, and denying their existence will not limit their damaging effects.**

Are you bullied by fear?

While it is normal for fear to be part of our lives, it is not normal when it is the dominating force. Every time we cross the road, fly in an aeroplane, or swim in the sea, we are taking a risk. But it is a calculated risk and we cannot allow fear to overwhelm us to the point where we would never step onto the street or get our feet wet.

We cling to fear even though it repels us, as though ignoring such a power is somehow tempting fate. Consequently, letting go of fear is very frightening. Dealing with fear means facing up to it and challenging it. Fear is like any coward that bullies and threatens. As soon as we stand up to it, it becomes less powerful. The more we understand it, the less it threatens us. Pretending it does not exist gives it strength. Acknowledging it puts it into perspective. The more you know about your fear, the more easily you can learn to put it to one side. The longer it sits on the sidelines, the more balance you bring into your life. Promise yourself that you will not allow fear to cause you any mental or physical health problems. Promise yourself that you will use MindPower to rid yourself of this highly damaging emotion.

SELF-HEALING
Sending pain away

Sometimes a very deep hurt can overwhelm you. Each time you force yourself to think about something else, your thoughts keep returning to the same subject. When you go to bed at night, as soon as you close your eyes, you see an image of the person who caused you this pain in your head. It prevents you from switching off just when you need your rest, and if it persists for any length of time, your sleep patterns become disrupted and you suffer from chronic tiredness, barely able to summon up the healing energy you need for yourself. This is the time to take positive action, using your MindPower.

Imaginary figures

Lie in bed and with your eyes closed picture two air balloons hovering in the sky. Put whoever has upset you into one and then see yourself in another. As the balloons soar higher and higher, use your MindPower to help you draw an imaginary figure-of-eight in the air as you float high above the ground. Starting with the first balloon, take your imaginary pencil and make a circle around it and continue with this unbroken line and cross over to the other side and make another circle around your balloon. The center of the figure-of-eight should cross over and separate your balloon from that of your antagonist. This is the first figure-of-eight and the two balloons are now encircled, joined but not connected. Now keep going and repeat this figure-of-eight drawing until you have drawn six of them, including the first one. Next, reverse the action and draw six the other way.

Safely sealed

When you have completed all these figures-of-eight, contemplate the finished picture. Reflect on how these slow but deliberate movements have erected a sealed barrier between the two air balloons. They appear to be floating freely in the atmosphere, but they are not able to touch. Anything unpleasant escaping from one cannot impact on the other. The person who has hurt you is now prevented from penetrating the protective wall you have drawn around yourself.

Setting yourself free

When you are satisfied you have weakened their power over you sufficiently, using your MindPower once more, visualize the constant crossing and recrossing of the line you drew between the two balloons and notice how, as each new figure-of-eight was drawn, the point where the lines crossed has become frail. Snap it off and feel your balloon shoot up higher into the atmosphere, unfettered by damaging emotions, free as a bird to carry you away into the distance. Look back and send love to the person in that other balloon. Remind yourself that people only have power over you if you let them.

EMOTIONAL EMBROIDERY

Exaggerating is one of the commonest defenses against uncertainty. Often people enlarge on a situation because they are not convinced the reality will carry enough impact, or they feel they do not have enough credibility to be taken seriously. Their poor sense of themselves undermines their own confidence, and they believe other people have picked up the same message.

This also happens in reverse. Hiding hurt feelings and pretending to be unaffected is to exaggerate in the opposite direction. Many people pretend they are not in pain or not disappointed or upset because they do not want to worry anyone or be seen to show weakness.

Exaggeration is another word for distortion. Whether we are reducing our real emotions or enlarging events out of all proportion to their true size, the mind accepts as fact what our emotions endorse. So if that oversized event becomes real in the mind, you will have oversized emotional reactions to it. If you tell everyone else nothing is the matter, you are denying your real emotions.

Seeing the real picture

Try this short exercise. Close your eyes and visualize a situation in which you have elaborated on events to create more interest. Now imagine you are the person to whom you have told this story. See yourself sitting opposite, listening to the person that is you. What do you see and hear? Try to be as objective as you can, and listen as if for the first time. Notice your body language and the expression in your eyes. Do you look like a rabbit caught in a car's headlights? Or, do you look calm and speak in a straightforward manner? Now ask yourself, which person would you believe?

Now imagine a second scene. You are deeply upset, and as your eyes well up with tears, you

RIGHT **Visualizing how you look as you talk to other people will show you how others see you, and help you to understand the way they respond.**

reach for a handkerchief and begin to weep openly. Again, witness this scene as though you are standing on the sidelines and notice what is happening to the other people around you. Are they uncomfortable? Are they embarrassed? How are they reacting to this overt display of emotion? Has anyone become angry?

Now watch one or two come over and put an arm around your shoulders and ask what they can do for you. Instead of feeling helpless, they feel useful. Instead of feeling frustrated at your pretence, they feel admiration for your openness.

Pretending it does not matter is to be over-conscious of the way others see you. If it matters to you, then it matters.

What these scenes reveal is the extent to which we all, to a lesser or greater degree, take other people's feelings on board, trying to guess what these feelings are without necessarily knowing what they are. Exaggerating your own feelings transmits an inaccurate message. No one knows any more about you than you know about him or her. But if you want to get the real picture, give others the unadorned truth.

Mixed emotions

We all experience positive, passionate emotions which motivate, inspire, and enhance our lives. There are also bleak, negative emotions that are just as strongly felt but which produce the opposite effect and which disturb, depress, and paralyse our progress.

But just as life is never either entirely black or white, so it is with our emotions. There are many shades of gray in our attitudes and feelings, and because they are so uncomfortably close to one another, it only takes the slightest movement to upset the balance.

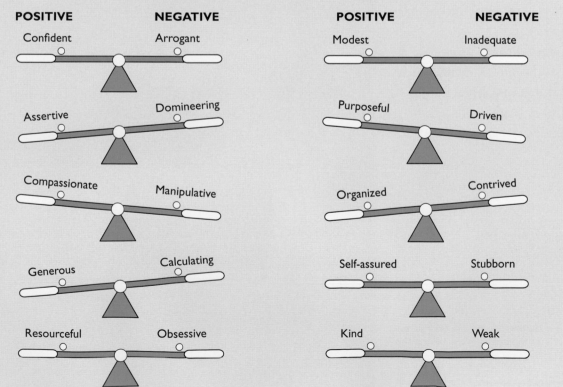

THINKING WITH OUR HORMONES

If you ever wanted an excellent example of mind–body connections, you need look no farther than the different hormones that affect all our thoughts and actions. The wider understanding of our brain chemistry and endocrine system has shown how the secretions of hormones through our blood stream maintains our system's delicate balance. About 50 have already been identified and science is still discovering more.

Hormones are extremely complex soluble chemical substances secreted by the endocrine glands, which act as messengers. Each one carries its own specific code that can only be interpreted by its "target" organ, and between them form a sophisticated communication system, regulating the rates at which various processes take place. They are the guardians of the body's internal environment.

There are growth hormones and reproductive hormones, pain-relieving hormones and energy-producing hormones, as well as hormones that control the amount of calcium in bones, glucose in blood, and cortisone, which defends against disease.

Out of balance

When there is an imbalance, the subsequent detrimental effect on the body can lead to serious problems such as heart and kidney disease, high blood pressure, and many more related conditions. The effect on the mind can lead to violent mood swings and depression, elation, and euphoria.

Louis Pasteur introduced the idea that disease always has a specific cause. For instance, tuberculosis comes from the bacillus *Mycobacterium tuberculosis*, and rabies from the rabies virus. However, his theory fails in the light of the fact that hormones are often activated and affected by emotion. In other words, a physical reaction to a mental stimulus – a mind-body reaction.

RIGHT **Athletes focus their minds before a race to build up optimum energy. The combination of pushing the body to the maximum and winning against the competition releases endorphins, which produce a feeling of euphoria.**

Emotional responses

Our emotional wiring depends on these messenger molecules because their receptors are found throughout the immune defense system as well as other organs in the body, and serve as mediators to our thoughts and feelings. This means that they also hold the key to our emotional response to illness.

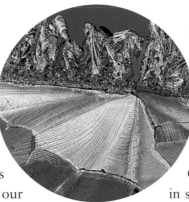

ABOVE **Crystals of beta-endorphin, a brain protein, alleviate pain and control our body's response to stress.**

The activity of every organ in the body can be traced back through the nervous system, which highlights how important their balance is to our state of mind. These nerves, that ultimately connect to the brain, can trigger physical reactions to heat and cold, pain and fear, anger, anxiety, and excitement as we have already seen, such as fear or tension flooding the body with adrenalin.

Performers will deliberately cling to the "edge" produced by an adrenalin rush before going on stage, convinced this state of mind adds to their performance and claiming complacency would do the opposite. School examinations or driving tests produce a similar flow of adrenalin, sharpening concentration and focusing energy.

The feel-good factor

Watching an inspiring film or play, meeting someone whose conversation is fun and entertaining, spending time with good friends in a pleasant atmosphere induce emotional responses of warmth and pleasure. These are the feel-good factors – naturally produced endorphins that can also be set off by exercise, known as "athlete's high," and similar activities or achievements. These same endorphins are also the body's natural painkillers.

You only have to look at a couple in love to realize what an incredible effect their emotional state has had on their physical bodies. They seem to walk suspended off the ground, they have no time or appetite to eat, and the excitement of being with one another makes their adrenalin flow and extends their energy way beyond its normal level.

Restoring equilibrium

Quite how long anyone can survive in such a state of suspended animation is debatable, and the reality is that everything in their system that has speeded up eventually calms down once the initial euphoria has run its course. It does not mean that once this happens the couple no longer love one another. It is simply the body's natural mechanism exercising its option and bringing peace and tranquillity to restore equilibrium.

RIGHT **Louis Pasteur discovered that micro-organisms cause disease, but "dis-ease" is also caused by signals sent from the mind to the physical body.**

MIND–BODY HORMONES

The thyroid gland produces a hormone known as thyroxine and is a typical example of an imbalanced hormone directly affecting both mind and body. When an individual has too much thyroxine, all their body processes speed up. They begin to ignore the cold and perspire a great deal, their heart races and palpitates, and the intestinal muscles work faster, causing diarrhea. This increased metabolic rate burns energy much faster than usual, which leads to weight loss and muscle wastage. The emotional impact of too much thyroxine is distressing because sufferers become extremely agitated and tense, unable to sit still or relax.

Conversely, too little thyroxine can produce the opposite effect and the body slows down. This person feels cold, eats little but gains weight, has a slow heart rate, and a swollen, puffy appearance. The emotional impact of this deficiency leaves people feeling jaded, lethargic, and depressed.

Hormones in decline

Hormone-replacement therapy aims to bring deficient hormones up to what would be a normal level for each individual. Insulin controls the body's blood sugar levels and is given to combat diabetes. When a diabetic has a low level of glucose in their blood, they become dizzy and weak. Emotionally, they are difficult and uncooperative, often aggressive, although largely unaware of the change in themselves.

Replacement hormones are often given after the menopause to balance declining levels of estrogen, which is another typical example of a hormone impacting on both mind and body. Too little can lead to physical problems, such as thinning bones and hot flushes, and the emotional effect of low levels can produce anxiety and irritability, loss of concentration and memory, insomnia, and depression.

RIGHT **Hormonal treatments can now intervene in the body's biochemical processes to preserve vitality. The question of whether these treatments are "natural" or "unnatural" provokes a great deal of debate.**

Similar mood swings emerge when a woman is premenstrual and after giving birth, usually when her hormones have not yet returned to their normal balanced levels. The emotional impact can be severe depression, aggression, and irritability.

The popularity of replacement therapy during and after menopause has been hailed as a mixed blessing. Some doctors are cautious about side effects and warn this is not an elixir of youth. Others believe that it is unnatural for women to be without estrogen, saying nature never intended it to be this way. Two hundred years ago, when life expectancy averaged around 35 years, a woman's child-bearing years would end as she neared 30. Her remaining years would be so short that she was unlikely to experience life with lower estrogen levels.

Boosting natural hormones

Today, administering naturally occurring hormones to boost existing levels is a fashionable episode in medicine. As well as female hormones, people are now taking growth hormone, which is credited with reversing the aging process, and melatonin, which is said to combat jet lag and insomnia. I use the word "fashionable" very deliberately because these hormones reflect trends and their popularity varies from one year to the next. But the use of any substance to check the natural aging process prompts a great many philosophical questions.

Biochemical emotions

Whether our emotions make us laugh or cry, both trigger biochemical reactions that lead to physical results.

CALMING TEARS

We are the only species with the ability to weep. We do it when we are deeply saddened, deliriously happy, or when we are recovering from a shock and we literally cry with relief.

The part of our brains that registers these emotions sends a signal that prompts the physical reaction of tears. These droplets are natural tranquillizers, and once a bout of weeping is over, we tend to feel much more relaxed and free from tension.

HEALING LAUGHTER

Laughter also gives us a healing boost. Smiling exercises our facial muscles, and whenever we shake with laughter, the muscles in our chest, shoulders, and diaphragm relax, which dissipates any tension that has built up. This has a calming effect on the entire nervous system and releases "feel-good" endorphins, helping the lungs generate more oxygen which tunes up our cardiovascular system.

Laughter also cuts down the levels of a stress hormone called cortisol, produced by the adrenal glands, and increases the levels of lymphocytes into the blood stream, which fight infections. It also lowers blood pressure by raising the levels of immunoglobulin A, an antibody that defends the body from viruses and bacteria.

SELF-HEALING
Meditation for Inner Balance

These questions are your contemplations to take into your meditation. Remember to have a pen and paper beside you so you can write down your thoughts immediately afterward.

Contemplations

→ When a close friend says something hurtful, do you find it difficult to shrug it off?

→ Have you been so wound up before an important meeting that you have found yourself unable to eat or even think about food?

→ Would you be embarrassed if someone saw you crying?

→ Have there been times when you have been rushing around so much that you suddenly feel shaky inside, your hands tremble, and you reach for some sugar?

→ Do you wish you had the time to exercise because you never seem to have much energy and would like to be fitter?

Meditation

Nature's natural balance makes sure that our physical bodies tick over very nicely. But when that balance is upset, such as when our emotional and mental energy bodies are in disharmony, this throws the system into confusion. Emotions in turmoil cause turbulent thoughts that impact on our body's complex mechanisms. The result is that the body pumps out too many hormones here, holds back on a few there, stockpiles another, just in case – of what? With no clear directions, it has no idea what it should be doing so it does a bit of everything. We need to restore this precious balance.

Relax, breathe deeply, and meditate

Look at the back of your eyelids and create a scene in which you are walking across a wide stretch of desert under a cloudless blue sky. You are well-protected from the full force of the sun, but you can still feel the ripples of warmth that radiate from it as you make your way slowly across this huge wilderness of sand dunes. This is a vast desert, and although you are completely alone, you feel perfectly safe and begin to enjoy this solitude.

The heat is pleasantly dry, and as you become aware of the sand shifting beneath your feet with each footstep, you realize the soft fall of sand beneath you as you walk is the only sound in what would otherwise be absolute silence.

There is a marvelous peace in this silence, undisturbed by the sounds of birds or insects, just an absolute quietness hanging in the atmosphere, washing over you, bathing you with its calming presence as waves of warmth from the sun cover your body.

You look around and realize there is not another person in sight. This fills you with a sense of elation, because you know how privileged you are right now

to have such an incredible stretch of wild desert entirely to yourself. The dunes undulate ahead of you as far as your eyes can see, and you just want to enjoy walking at your own pace, absorbing this new experience, reveling in the quiet and marveling at the way this desert makes you feel so safe.

The miles of sand lay expansively ahead, behind, and all around you, and yet you know exactly where you are going even though no signposts exist and you have no idea of your destination.

You are beginning to savor the freedom of relying on your inner knowledge. The soothing vibrations fill you with such a sense of certainty about yourself, and you feel absolutely free of any concerns or problems. You are now able to be utterly relaxed. There is no need for vigilance or caution – there are no uncertainties ahead and no unsolved problems behind you. You can live in this moment without a thought for the past or the future. Feeling so sure is an exhilarating sensation, sweeping away the last remnants of doubt and anxiety as though they had never been a part of your life. Imagine all this concern and worry as a dense cloud of color that you can simply gather up into a large bundle. Tie the bundle tightly so that nothing can fall out.

Now watch the bundle being lifted up and quickly carried away, caught up in the spiral of a whirlwind of sand that rushes past you. A few seconds later, it is miles away in the far distance, and a few more seconds later, it vanishes altogether, taking that bundle of worries with it. Now everything that ever gave you an anxious moment has disappeared. Your mind and body are entirely free and clear and you sense a new, wonderfully healthy feeling as if every part of you has been restored.

SELF-HEALING
Meditation for Inner Balance

Suddenly your eyes see everything around you in a different way. The scene is the same but somehow much more vivid and exciting. The blue sky now appears impossibly blue, as though there was never a blue as exquisite before. The sand dunes rolling away into the distance now have tiny golden grains of light twinkling as they catch the sun. Undisturbed and unspoiled, they are pristine and perfect.

The sand beneath your feet is so clean that you stop to kneel down and look at the grains more intently. You notice they are actually all different colors, from granite to palest gold. You pick up a handful of sand and watch it trickle through your fingers, noticing that as well as those tiny golden grains, other grains are transparent and filter the sun's light as they fall, glistening and glittering. You are filled with wonder at this because now you are looking at them so closely you can see that they are more like stars. This is the first time you have ever been able to pause and take the time to examine a grain of sand, and yet you feel absolutely convinced that this is an important use of your time.

You look up and allow your eyes to wander along the sand dunes and imagine these grains multiplied billions of times over. You picture yourself walking over their soft mass, hardly feeling them beneath your feet as they spread out like a silken carpet as far as infinity.

You feel as though time has stopped for a while and you are existing in a unique space where everything matters and nothing is important. You just want to keep walking in this wild place, because each step makes you feel stronger and more comfortable about yourself, more certain and sure of yourself. It seems as if the act of walking is working in reverse and instead of using up energy seems to actually generate more. Your muscles feel toned and powerful and you experience a sensation of excellence – an extraordinary state of mind and body where the harmony within you is perfect.

You can stay in this place as long as you want to, but when you decide to return, bring as many of these feelings back with you into your everyday life.

LEFT **Imagine you are walking over these dunes of silken sand, and with every step you feel stronger and more at peace with yourself, until you achieve a state of perfect harmony.**

Record your first thoughts

Remember to try and capture as much as you can remember by writing down your immediate thoughts and feelings.

What your responses reveal

Mostly "yes" answers

If your answers are mostly "yes," you are clearly fearful of moving away emotionally from the lifestyle you know and the people who influence you, whether or not it makes you happy. It seems not to have occurred to you that you are a free spirit and can choose to reject whatever you want to, particularly if it is not satisfying. You are absorbing the impact of others' opinions and not giving vent to your own, so all this emotional energy is charging around without a clear direction. Your body will reflect this and compensate by becoming impossibly demanding without giving anything back. Own some of your healthy emotions – only when you let them emerge can you build a healthier body.

Consider this: Your spirit is precious and needs nourishing every bit as much as your mind and body need a healthy balance.

Mostly "no" answers

You have obviously discarded the trivial and identified the things you consider important. You have learned from your early life experiences and this is all part of a healthy process in which you evolve and develop. You already know that you may change your outlook a hundred times more before finding out what you really believe in. You are not apprehensive about this because you have learned to rely on your surest guide, your inner wisdom and intuition.

Consider this: Giving yourself permission to be who you are is a rare luxury and health excellence a privilege. Anything is possible if you want it enough.

Half "yes," half "no" answers

You have found yourself an emotional niche in which you can tuck yourself away when you want to hide and which reinforces whatever you need to hear to be encouraged. You have moved out of the slow lane but the fast lane still seems scary. Even though the excitement and stimulation continually attracts you, deep down you suspect that exhilarating things only happen to other people.

Consider this: Dipping a toe in the water is relatively safe, but you need to find the courage to plunge in. That is exhilarating.

Affirmation

I will open up my mind and trust my own judgment. I will challenge the unacceptable, and if one door closes, I will find another.

There will always be circumstances that are beyond your control which can cause stress. We all worry about money, our careers, our relationships, and our families. We also worry about our health, and the pollutants that infect our environment only add to our anxiety. The crucial factor that makes the difference is how much you allow external situations to affect you internally. Absorbing all the stresses and strains of everyday life will leave you stressed and strained. MindPower protects you emotionally, mentally, spiritually, and physically. It means you distinguish between the really important things in your life and the ones that matter very little. So, what is everyone worrying about?

7 | WHAT ARE WE ALL WORRYING ABOUT?

WHAT IS STRESS?

Stress is like a large umbrella with all kinds of negative emotions and destructive-behavior patterns sheltering underneath it. I imagine it as a molten liquid flowing into all the vulnerable parts of the mind and body where its corrosive effect burns little ulcerlike craters. Inside these craters, the liquid sits in little pools, sending out shafts of piercing pain that leave small areas pitted and damaged. Eventually, if the process continues uninterrupted, those small scars join up, and the ensuing havoc creates a scale of destruction that resembles a war zone.

A trigger for illness

This scenario may sound melodramatic, but I assure you it is not an exaggeration. Stress gets blamed for an awful lot of problems, sometimes quite unfairly. But if it is ignored for too long, it manifests itself through a variety of conditions that have come to be called stress-related illnesses. These are usually conditions to which people are susceptible anyway and have probably shown a predisposition toward at some time in their lives.

When negative stress levels are allowed to build up in your body, they can tip the balance and trigger an illness that in other circumstances might not have developed. Equally, stress can have such a destructive effect on the entire immune defense system that the patient's natural powers of recovery are overwhelmed. The mind has created a body that can no longer defend itself.

Like the problems we all face, the details may be different but the essential nature of them and the way we allow them to affect us is what determines our negative stress levels. We have two ways of dealing with stress that we may not even be consciously aware of but are sophisticated processes evolved over thousands of years.

Going with the flow

Life today is run at a fast pace. We communicate in minutes through telephones and in seconds through fax machines and e-mail. As a result, responses are expected almost immediately.

Our minds and bodies perform at different levels of efficiency all through the day as we cope with the demands of our modern lives. The most common down-time is after lunch, when we are more likely to experience drowsiness and our work deteriorates accordingly. Staying at your desk will not help. Get up and stretch your arms and legs or get some fresh air.

Do not go on working too long or you will drop into your energy down-time again. If you carry on working, whatever you then produce will not be up to your normal standard. If you have to stop in the middle of a job, leave a note to yourself where to pick up from the next day, which will send your mental energy a switch-off signal, clearing your mind so that you can forget about work altogether.

DEALING WITH NEGATIVE STRESS

Imagine you are crossing a desert on a camel, and having set out at dawn, the temperature has been tolerable. But as the hours pass and the sun gets hotter, you are relieved to find a tree that offers you welcome shade. Now imagine you are in a Turkish bath or steam room, and as the heat builds up, your veins begin to stand out, the surface of your skin is covered in beads of sweat, and your color becomes a deep pink.

In the first instance, your common sense steers you toward taking extrinsic, or external, action to control your body temperature. In the second instance in the Turkish bath, your body is taking intrinsic, or internal, action to do the same. Both mind and body are involved in relieving your discomfort in the two different situations.

When the desert sun began to burn, your mind received a signal from your body to say it was feeling too hot. When the temperature in the steam room soared, the brain registered discomfort and sent a signal to your body, which then set up a chain of actions that led to cooling down the skin surface with sweat.

ABOVE **In desert heat, your mind registers your body's discomfort and prompts remedial action, but stress can distort perceptions and responses.**

Distorted vision

If that person in the steam room is in a confused state of mind, his thoughts would register discomfort but might not connect it to the obvious cause, because his perception is distorted by his stress. Stressed people often fail to separate themselves emotionally from a problem, and because they are on such a negative course, immediately identify and home in on the parts that have the most meaning for them. They might well ignore other parts that are more upbeat because they simply do not associate themselves with anything optimistic.

These two examples show different reactions to a potentially stressful situation, but there are no clear lines drawn as to the center of control because the mind and body are so closely interlinked. It also demonstrates that the health and condition of one has a crucial effect on the health and condition of the other.

A balanced view

When a problem needs to be addressed, not necessarily solved but just looked at objectively before any decisions are reached, it makes it much easier to assess when someone is in a balanced state of mind. Being under stress inevitably means a person is less of themselves and their judgment will be equally diminished.

Ideally, building up your mental and physical stamina is one way to minimize the effect of a problem. Instead of absorbing its full weight, you can learn to direct your mind to take on board only what you need to and no more. This does not mean you should just get half a story to protect yourself from the more unpleasant elements. It means that when you look at the whole picture, you are able to see it in its proper perspective and eliminate the elements that are unnecessary. In this way, your powers of judgment will be at their most acute, uncluttered by negative emotions that might otherwise have clouded the issue.

OUR CHANGING ROLES

When people feel they cannot cope, they usually describe this as feeling "lost." It frequently happens when all the different roles that we take on in our daily lives overlap. We play a number of diverse roles from the moment we are born through to our adult lives, such as son, mother, employee, client. But these are progressive roles and tend not to cause us problems. The trouble usually begins when our various roles produce conflicting demands.

Young mothers who work become employees, employers even. Fathers may become house-husbands and take on the responsibility of the children while the wife becomes the breadwinner. More often, we all do a bit of everything and this can be confusing. Each generation has always grown up with a slightly different set of values and attitudes to that of their parents, and the changes, though significant, are subtle.

The last 100 years, however, have seen more dramatic changes than ever before, changes that have challenged every area of people's lives and turned traditional customs upside down. The things that had been unthinkable emerged as possibilities as the structures that enclosed communities and governed their lives were first weakened and then, as education enlightened people, eventually crumbled. More and more people questioned what had previously been accepted as inevitable.

Class, sexual, and racial barriers have come down, and legislation makes discrimination an offense, answerable in court. The more rigid rules that restricted previous generations have gradually evolved to meet the new criteria of equality and freedom. They have changed the way we interact with one another and altered traditional roles to such an extent that we have had to adapt our lifestyles accordingly.

> *Class, sexual, and racial barriers have come down, and legislation makes discrimination an offense, answerable in court.*

LEFT **Changes in society broaden our outlook, giving us the opportunity to integrate different cultures and new ideas.**

GREAT EXPECTATIONS

The greatest change lies in our expectations. With all the wonderful modern inventions and the efficiency and swiftness of technology, we expect to be happy – often much happier than we are. Many people find themselves in lives they do not like very much, but have no idea how to change them. Others keep trying to change their lives, moving house continually, switching partners, jobs, or careers, believing that each new beginning will mean a new and better life. When it does not happen, they start to plan their next change.

This frantic searching can take them the length and breadth of the country, but the distance they travel may make no difference because the solution they are seeking lies within themselves. They are projecting all their unhappiness outward, putting it on things they can see and touch, such as their houses and possessions, or blaming other people, making them the scapegoats when their lives have not worked out. This desperate attempt to rationalize their actions is exhausting because they are wasting their precious energies, dispensing them into a meaningless vacuum.

Finding the real thing

Whatever we unconsciously avoid or whatever ploy we adopt to alter things can only have a fleeting success before the reality sets in. Only by looking at our patterns of behavior can we start to make sense of our lives and experience the feeling of relief when the frantic search for everything to be newer, better, and happier calms down. Although these people are creating and expending massive amounts of energy, they are only tapping into a fraction of their real power.

Emotionally they are running around in circles and need to stop, take time out of this whirlwind of activity, and look inside themselves. The potential they have ignored is always there, waiting to be channeled, and discovering their healing power could have an incredible effect on every area of their lives. It can help them make all the things they were searching for actually happen. Or it can enlighten them and help them realize how many of those things have very little value for them any more.

STRESS IN PERSPECTIVE

Did primitive man suffer from stress? Could his cave have made him claustrophobic? Did the continuing demands of providing food for his family keep him awake at night? Was medieval man tense and anxious, depressed about his living conditions and obsessed about his worsening state of health? Well, yes, and why not? It is entirely possible that all through history, humanity has

BELOW **An increase in our expectations of happiness has driven many people into a frantic, never-ending search for something more in their lives to enhance their existence.**

Careful exercise for better health

Doing moderate exercise is an excellent way of helping to relieve the effects of stress and to focus the mind away from life's problems. Daily exercise can significantly lower the risk of heart disease, and it is never too late to start. A study of men in their 50s who had done very little exercise and were already suffering symptoms of heart problems showed that once they began a moderate program of activity, their risk of a fatal attack was five times lower compared to those who were inactive.

Sudden vigorous activity, instead of helping your heart, can strain it, so get proper advice so you are fully aware of your limitations as well as your potential.

been thoroughly miserable, deeply depressed, worried, anxious, tense, and yes, modern though it sounds, stressed.

Literature records men being "out of their minds with worry," people whose fear made them sleepless night after night. Others were racked with pain from their ailments. Our ancestors could be forgiven if they became obsessed with simply trying to survive, which meant finding enough to eat and a warm, dry place to shelter.

Historic events often carried dreadful implications for the people caught up in them, disabling what little power and control they had over their lives. Some generations of our ancestors might have been forced into battle against invading armies. Others faced starvation if the politicians of their time imposed impossible taxes or decided to abolish laws that had previously offered them protection. Many of our ancestors were executed because their religious beliefs did not match those of the ruling monarch of their time.

Age-old worries

Today, many people might be content to know that they could just get through a day that was relatively trouble-free. Compared to our forebears, we are certainly better off. Their lives were focused on their needs, just as we focus on our needs today, but the misery, fear, and anxiety they must have endured would have produced the same damaging effect on their physical bodies as our worries inflict on our physical bodies today.

There is no reason to suppose that because life was so much harder that those people suffered any less emotionally than people do today. The appalling levels of misery and fear surrounding their physical lives must have created emotional turmoil and left them much more vulnerable to the ravages of disease, just as uncertainty and anxiety in our minds destabilize our physical systems in our modern world.

THE REALITIES OF EXISTENCE

We know that in the past, sickness and disease were much more widespread, but we will never really know the extent to which the poor quality of life attracted so much illness and how much the physical vulnerability of those people weakened their capacity to overcome their ill health.

I am not for one moment minimizing the very real worries that go hand in hand with modern life. What I am suggesting, however, is that whether we live in this millennium or whether we lived 200, 400, or 600 years ago, life always comes with a set of problems. The size and extent of them is less significant than the fact of their existence.

Quality of life

It is unrealistic to expect that at some point in our lives we could tick off problems, that everything would one day be perfect. Life consists of highs and lows, light and shade, pain and pleasure, whether we live in the modern or the medieval world. Our expectations become the yardstick we use to measure the quality of our existence. Each generation of our predecessors had a slightly different set of expectations, just as generations in this century have come to expect more than their grandparents and parents experienced.

Spiritual sustenance

What we do know is that the spirituality that sustained so many of our forebears and the enormous emphasis placed on mankind's spiritual life could well have proved the deciding factor when it came to overcoming sickness and disease. The strength of people's faith was tested continually through the ages, and even when they were ordered to change their religious beliefs, thousands chose to die rather than give up their faith.

This stubborn refusal to deny their beliefs shows the remarkable courage men and women displayed to protect many of the ancient wisdoms that were passed from one generation to another. People trusted in the naturally intuitive part of their minds, allowing their own instincts to guide them and their beliefs to elevate them from their physical suffering.

Rising to the challenge

Today, we tend to doubt the existence of our natural knowledge and are cynical about the validity of our own healing potential. As I have said before, life will always be a mixture of

LEFT **Archers take aim at Saint Sebastian, condemned to death by the emperor Diocletian for converting Roman soldiers to Christianity in the third century.**

heartache and happiness. How we deal with those events is what makes the difference. How we react to challenges and potential dangers is a measure of the state of our minds. How much we love life and how exhilarating and enjoyable we make it will be reflected in our emotional and physical health.

Yet, we are more powerful than we think. We no longer need to put poor health down to bad luck. If your life is far from blissful, you may already be aware that luck has little to do with the ways in which things happen to you. You may identify with the suggestion that emotional upheaval and mental turbulence can lead to physical illness and that your poor health comes from your poor state of mind.

COPING WITH LIFE'S CRISES

Our happiness depends on our attitude to life and the way in which we interpret events. Our lives may not go the way we planned them, but you can never compare an ideal with reality. The happiest people are those who recognize life is not perfect and that they are responsible for their own happiness.

The most bitter people are those who target other people and events for their unhappy state, blaming everyone and everything but themselves when their lives have not turned out the way they wanted them to. There are probably a thousand reasons for plans to be overturned and knowing half of them would not change the outcome. But accepting that other forces may intervene and understanding that we often attract what we send out goes half-way to explaining what otherwise seems a random process.

Illness seems to strike without warning and to pick its victims without any cohesive plan. One person's serious illness can send shock waves right through an entire family and often brings people's emotions very close to the surface.

If you look back at a crisis once it is over, you will see that it is possible to extract some positive benefits, although they might not have appeared

that way at the time. Tears and laughter can bring people together. But you do have to look in the right places. If your head is turned around so that just the negative elements are visible, you will only hold onto the worst of your experience. The crises that come out of the blue may devastate us for a time but that does not mean they will unhinge us. We can lean on MindPower at such times because the inner strength it creates provides our strongest support system.

> 'The happiest people are those who recognize life is not perfect and that they are responsible for their own happiness.'

ABOVE **Our attitude to life determines our ability to overcome obstacles and achieve success, self-esteem, and happiness.**

AN IMPOVERISHED SPIRIT

Living in a decaying environment has an enormous impact on our emotional lives. Look at any run-down housing estate where the buildings are dilapidated, the stairwells dirty, and the overall effect is one of neglect. The signal being sent out is one of hopelessness and despair.

Anyone who has ever walked through one of these places I am describing will recognize the aura that pervades these homes and the people who live in them. It is almost tangible in its despondency as though you could reach out a hand and grasp it, because it hangs in the air, as dense and thick as a fog. It feels so heavy that it weighs everyone down.

I grew up in such an environment and it was very hard to care about that place. When people spend their lives in such a depressing environment, it is no surprise that they absorb the effects and become depressed, too. When that happens, no one has the will to make anything happen any more. No one is motivated to change things, stir things up, and start putting them right. With this infectious lethargy comes a defensive indignation. People ask themselves why they should care more than anyone else.

Of course there are hundreds of reasons for not doing anything. If cash is stopping people from making improvements, it might be a case of whose money, who pays, who is responsible? If it is down to the local government and they need reminding that there is work to be done, who is going to remind them?

Perhaps those impoverished souls who smear graffiti on the concrete walls of their environment are acting on impulses they are not fully aware of, but which compel them to destroy and deface the hideous landscapes in which they live? Perhaps the graffiti represents a signature? Are those messages much more articulate than we give them credit for?

Changing things is more than a question of money, and often a question of will. Improvements

> *Enhancing the environment in which we live is an enormous morale booster.*

might be wrecked straight away because when such a black, depressing cloud penetrates people's systems, it can produce mindless acts of vandalism from people who do not even know why they feel the need to destroy.

Natural inspiration

There are many ways of improving the situation. A coat or two of paint, a few repairs here and there, the addition of some window boxes or hanging baskets to lift the drabness with splashes of color, even planting a tree or two would make an enormous difference. If everyone made just one change, the place would be unrecognizable.

Anyone who has been brought up in the countryside or has moved there now will identify with the uplifting effect of the sight of green spaces and the sweet smell of clean air. The greenery and colors of the natural world nourish the spirit. Town-dwellers compensate with colorful displays of flowers on their windowsills, and more and more city streets are planted with trees. Enhancing the environment in which we live is no frivolous, cosmetic exercise, but an enormous morale booster in the midst of a gray vista.

I always feel my spirit lift at the sight of lush green foliage, rolling fields, and hills stretching as far as the eye can see. When I have to visit a town or city, I try to find a route that takes me past those town-dwellers' homes in which they have cultivated whatever outdoor spaces they have, whether it is a balcony, a windowsill, or a tiny patio. The whole process has beneficial effects – the pride people take in their plants and the pleasure they get from the sight of them is tied to a sense of achievement, as well as satisfying their need for creativity.

For the passerby, this life and color gives more than pleasure. It also inspires the uninspired.

OUR DANGEROUS ENVIRONMENT

We would not have to travel very far back in time to see the enormous contrast between life today and the way people used to live. The journeys that took days and weeks are now completed in a matter of hours and minutes. We can cross the world in less than 24 hours, while our ancestors would have to set aside months, sometimes years.

We can modify the natural climate to meet our individual ideas of comfort and pretend it is high summer inside our homes in the middle of winter. We have soft bedding, thick carpets, and clothes that never crease. We can eat out-of-season fruit and vegetables thanks to the freezer, and thanks to the microwave oven we can produce a meal in minutes where once it took hours. We live in a world where time has been telescoped. The chores that once occupied days of people's lives can now be completed in minutes.

But the lifestyle we enjoy today comes at a price, and that price is the high level of pollution which exists inside our homes, in offices and workplaces, in our cars, and out on the streets. We have mountains of waste materials we cannot dispose of safely; the rivers and oceans have become dumping grounds for the world's garbage, and the discarded chemicals we no longer need have not, inconveniently, automatically dispersed. This is the environment that fish and mammals depend upon for their survival and which are now forced to ingest the substances that have the potential to harm them.

BREATHING CAN DAMAGE YOUR HEALTH

Who would believe that something as natural as breathing could be dangerous, that the air we take into our lungs can endanger our physical health to such an extent that it damages our immune systems? In some cases, the substances we inhale weaken our systems to the point where they can no longer be relied upon for support, because their resistance is so reduced. Who would believe that the air we breathe could kill us?

From the moment you step outside your front door in the morning, you risk breathing in a cocktail of chemicals that has been pumped into the atmosphere from hundreds of different sources, from light industry to gas and diesel fumes produced by cars, buses, and trucks.

If you are a car driver, you may think you are better off once you are safely inside your vehicle, but you are wrong. It may look as though the pedestrians outside on the street are worse off than you, relatively safe inside your own vehicle. They have no choice and are forced to inhale the emissions coming from all the car exhausts on the road.

But statistics show that car drivers and their passengers suffer the greatest damage from these exhaust emissions.

INDOOR POLLUTION

The level of comfort we enjoy in our homes is one of the main reasons for the pollution inside them. Our houses are warmed with heating systems and the windows are either double-glazed or have some sort of insulation to prevent drafts. We effectively seal ourselves inside airtight cocoons, and it makes no difference to our lives whether it is snowing outside or sweltering in the middle of a heat wave, because we can control and modify the temperature inside our living spaces.

We can make our indoor environments into whatever we want them to be. If the atmosphere is too dry, we can turn on a humidifier; too damp, and we turn up the heating. We can go from tropical rain forest to arid desert without moving off the couch. We can walk around our homes in lightweight summer clothes in the middle of winter if that is our preference, because the natural climate cannot come in.

Not-so-green machines

The five key pollutants pumped out by diesel and gasoline engines are nitrogen oxides, sulfur dioxide, carbon monoxide, benzene, and minute particles that are byproducts of the combustion process.

The introduction of catalytic converters has proved to be a mixed blessing. Their effectiveness is minimized by the fact that the converter needs time and distance to warm up, and only begins to work after a journey of, say, 2 miles, which is the average length of most car journeys.

LEFT **We can choose whether we want our comfortable, centrally-heated homes to be like tropical rainforests or arid deserts, but we have less control over the parasites that lurk in our beds or languish in the wall-to-wall carpets.**

Omnipresent allergen

The downside of all this has been to turn our homes into wonderful breeding grounds for the things that affect us so detrimentally. Dust is the main culprit and has been around for centuries, when people probably left it laying in even thicker layers in their homes than it is allowed to remain today. In fact, disturbing it is part of the problem.

If you release what looks like a cloud of dust from your mattress, what you are really seeing is a collection of microscopic mites' excrement and flakes of human skin. A lot of this "dust" can be found on our beds and soft furnishings, such as chairs and couches, and is also lying on the floors and carpets. This is household dust and almost impossible to eliminate from everyday life, which is why it is one of the commonest allergens. Providing it stays where it is, and however distasteful that may seem, this dust does not actually cause much trouble.

The main problems begin once we start cleaning our homes and attempt to remove all traces of dust. Using a duster inevitably leads to spreading some of the dust around the room, and some of the particles are bound to escape when trying to suck it all up into a vacuum cleaner. A few manufacturers fit filters to their vacuum cleaners to trap stray bacteria and viruses, but this heightens the problem because they only succeed in spreading the very things they want to extinguish since the particles can leech through these filters and are then blown out into the air.

Some cleaners, such as the *Dyson* range, are now specially equipped to kill bacteria and viruses, and in tests have been found to be capable of killing the AIDS virus. If that sounds melodramatic, it is worth noting that meningitis is caused by forms of bacteria that are not only capable of living in air-conditioning systems but can also be dispersed through a vacuum cleaner.

There is even a suggestion that the disturbance we create when we clean our homes also means we often breathe in radon particles. This naturally occurring substance is suspected of causing certain kinds of cancer.

THE EFFECTS OF AIR POLLUTION

The very high levels of air pollution directly disturb our breathing function, restricting our lung capacity and limiting the amount of oxygen we take in. Anyone trying to function on 25 percent less oxygen than their body normally needs will become breathless and tired very quickly. If you see your doctor about this, you will be asked to blow into a tube and this will assess the state of your lung capacity.

Assisted breathing

Salbutamol, which is the drug used in some inhalers and a derivative of ephedrine, is designed to bring rapid relief to the sufferer by jolting the lungs and bronchi out of their spasm and forcing air through more easily. You might be prescribed a preventative drug in an inhaler to preempt this breathlessness.

Our natural resistance to ill health is gradually reduced because of the levels of pollution in our systems. The increased numbers of 40 and 50 year olds who now suffer from asthma can be largely blamed on the high pollution levels they have had to become accustomed to, and which have built up to the point where their immune systems just cannot cope.

I am constantly amazed at how many people have their own inhaler to help them deal with their asthma, and astonished at the casual way they take a couple of puffs when their breathing becomes restricted. Remember, breathing is the most natural, life-giving, life-sustaining process, which continues on a 24-hour basis automatically, and when it stops, it usually signals that we are no

Children are the most vulnerable group to suffer the destructive effects of modern pollution.

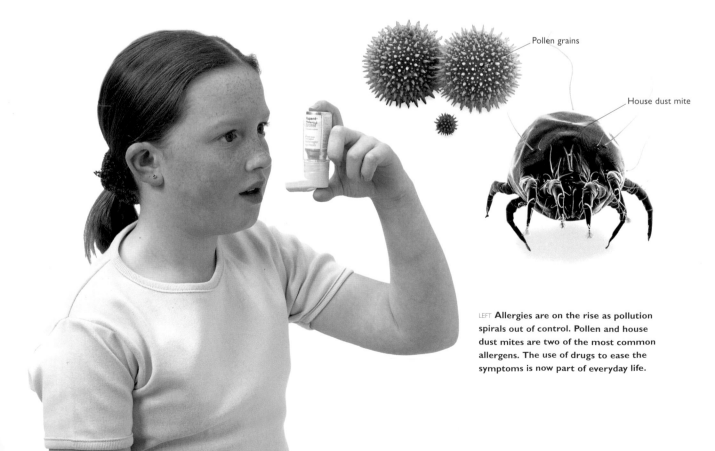

Pollen grains

House dust mite

LEFT **Allergies are on the rise as pollution spirals out of control. Pollen and house dust mites are two of the most common allergens. The use of drugs to ease the symptoms is now part of everyday life.**

longer alive. Yet, these inhalers have become so commonplace now, they are almost regarded as an everyday accessory to remember to include when you leave the house alongside your watch, credit cards, and wallet.

My son Daniel, who used an inhaler occasionally, became scared to leave home without it and I had to persuade him to treat it with more discrimination. I have even seen someone take a few puffs on their inhaler before lighting a cigarette, which, although an extreme example, is nevertheless significant. It indicated a profound apathy in their attitude to their own health, an abdication of their own responsibility in safeguarding their health, and confidence that this drug would rectify the self-inflicted damage. What I did not see was any awareness of the potency of this drug, or any attempt to treat it with the respect it warranted.

Who is affected?

Children are the most vulnerable group to suffer the destructive effects of modern pollution because they have been consistently exposed to these damaging effects for their entire lives. Anyone who grew up in a home which was not heated or double-glazed and lived in an area where there were few cars is probably far less affected because their immune system will have built up a certain amount of resistance and they will be able to withstand the worst ravages of poor air quality.

The increasing trend toward younger and younger asthma sufferers is testimony to the higher levels of pollution that their systems have to contend with, and the younger they are, the more vulnerable it makes them. They are exposed to a double dose of pollution, both in their homes as well as outside in the streets, long before they have had a chance to build up any resistance. This means their immune systems have never really been able to get going. Immunologists now believe that if a child could be insulated against atmos-

pheric pollution, indoors and out, until around the age of four, they would have a better chance of developing a stronger immune system and might even escape any allergies.

HYGIENE RISKS

When our forebears began installing plumbing and drainage systems, the effect revolutionized people's lives. Sanitation led to cleaner water, and the dirt and infections that threatened everyone's health disappeared and were replaced with antiseptic and hygienic conditions. Over the years, a combination of preservatives and refrigeration stopped butter from turning rancid and kept food fresher for longer.

Ironically, the figures for cases of food poisoning today are on the increase compared to ten years ago, with outbreaks of potentially lethal bugs such as salmonella and E coli bacteria. It seems that the generations who grew up in this safer, cleaner world with no memory of the horrors that previous generations had to contend with have gradually become apathetic about cleanliness.

The invisible enemy

If microscopic bacteria were visible to the human eye, we would see how millions of them lurk in our kitchens, crowding onto dishcloths and counters, mixing with the knives on chopping boards and the silverware in sinks, and silently contaminating the cooked meats hastily shoveled into a refrigerator while still warm and stacked alongside uncooked meat.

Sometimes the danger comes from the preparation or lack of it, such as frozen poultry that has not thawed out properly or is only partly cooked, or fresh fish landed and unloaded in full sunlight for just a little too long. At best, a bout of food poisoning is unpleasant, but for elderly people and small babies, such cases can kill. The danger from these invisible but microscopic bacteria is always present, just as continued vigilance is essential.

LIVING WITH ELECTRICITY

Living around electricity can be dangerous, but just how dangerous is still being debated. Electricity supply wires tend to be low frequency, but are still linked to clinical depression and childhood leukemia, and electrical sensitivity causes headaches, dizziness, and nausea. As the levels rise, higher than normal fields of electricity become linked to more and more illnesses. This is thought to be because they affect our immune systems, which are then unable to reject the damaged cells that can lead to cancers.

There are two types of field produced by electricity. The electric field depends on the voltage, and you can reduce the levels in your home fairly easily. The magnetic field is caused by electric current flowing when people are using electrical power, and it is difficult to block because it will travel through brick walls. Your electricity company will be able to locate the proximity of underground cables that carry electricity to your home and measure the electric and magnetic fields.

Pole-mounted transformers, overhead cables, many home appliances, and electrical outlets in the home have been implicated in risks to health. The magnetic fields from substations come mainly from the underground cables feeding the supply of electricity. Pylons, depending upon their voltage, need to be situated within the prescribed safe distances from your home. The electric fields come from the cables running between the pylons, not the pylons themselves.

Safety precautions

Minimize the risks by making sure that frequently used furniture is placed at least 2 yards away from electric meters, fuse boxes, and electrical outlets. Avoid children playing in areas where there are high-voltage overhead lines, and stand at least 3 feet away from a working microwave oven. Where you sleep is probably the most important place to minimize fields. If you live next to an electricity sub-station, move your children's bedroom so that they sleep as far away from it as possible.

DAMAGING RAYS

The thinning of the ozone layer means that many more potentially damaging ultraviolet rays can now penetrate what was once a protective layer, rays with the capacity to burn plants, crops, and people. The cosmetic damage from sunbathing is very high – the sun dehydrates and prematurely ages the skin, accounting for some 80 percent of the wrinkles that emerge. Much more worrying is the risk of a life-threatening skin cancer, such as melanoma, following prolonged exposure. This increased risk is due to a combination of factors, of which depletion of the ozone layer is just one.

Out of those people that continue to worship

Cosmic radiation

There is growing concern that frequent flying exposes jet-setters and airline cabin crews to larger doses of radiation than is believed to be safe. Those of us who are more earthbound receive doses equivalent to 13 x-rays a year, compared to those who take two long-haul flights each month and probably absorb the equivalent radiation levels of more than 100 x-rays a year. This puts those who travel by air on a frequent basis in the most dangerous category for radiation exposure, even above people who work in nuclear power stations. The main health risk from radiation is cancer, and that risk varies according to geographical location, as well as to the particular altitude of the aircraft.

the sun, the people most at risk are those whose skin is exposed to very little sunshine all year and who then take a short vacation and subject their bodies to a sudden concentration of fierce sunshine. The most vulnerable complexions are pale skin with blue eyes and red hair and freckles, compared to olive skin with brown eyes, which carry only a medium risk.

High-risk groups

Children are in the highest category risk group of all. Sunburn in childhood is one of the major causes of melanoma in later life. This is probably the most dangerous of the skin cancers, but just as the sun's cosmetic damage may not show for 20 years, the young children destined to suffer the worst effects of the sun may not be revealed until they are adults. Any evidence of sunburn before the age of 16 heightens the risk of melanoma.

The growing incidences of skin cancers over the last 10 years has led to a very different type of sun product being developed, which either limits the sun's effects or totally blocks the skin's absorption of its damaging rays. It is the burning stage that is believed to be the starting point for skin cancers. Remember, if you choose to toast yourself in the sun, you will certainly get lines and wrinkles. Toast your children and they could get cancer.

RIGHT **Sun-kissed skin was once seen as a sign of health, but we now know this signals a danger to health – particularly in children.**

Sunshine safety

- Use a reliable sun protection product. Always apply additional sun protection if you plan to visit a place at a high altitude or where the humidity is high and you are likely to perspire heavily.

- All sun protection products should be applied continually throughout the day at regular intervals.

- Children should be protected with a total sun block, which is also waterproof, and should wear a floppy hat to cover the back of the neck and a thick t-shirt, especially for swimming. Even safer, t-shirts and swimsuits in a sun-protective fabric give maximum protection of SPF100+ wet or dry.

HAZARDS IN THE WORKPLACE

If you work in an office, you will be subjected to the damaging effects of computers and printers, photocopiers, scanners, and fax machines. Even the lighting can cause you problems. All this equipment drains every drop of moisture from the atmosphere, and leaves people with dry, itchy skin and aggravates eczema and other skin conditions. The same effect is produced when you travel on airplanes.

People who spend hours hunched over a computer can develop postural problems. The muscles in the neck and across the shoulders begin to ache or lock in a spasm, and tiny nodules of tension form clusters of uncomfortable knots. Fluorescent lighting overradiates, pumping out unnecessary light, and causes headaches and migraines. The unnatural brightness can set off eye strain, affect people's vision, and lead to conjunctivitis. Air-conditioning systems recycle many sore throats and infections. Again, the air inside an airplane, which passengers inhale for hours at a time, is frequently responsible for circulating viruses and infections.

Constant keyboard use leads to joint complaints from tendonitis to carpal tunnel syndrome, and is associated with repetitive strain injury. Sometimes, these everyday ailments manifest themselves in a different form, as low-level, insidious depression. People working in such an unhealthy environment often complain they have no energy.

RIGHT **A cell phone is convenient, but clamping one to your ear is likely to endanger your health.**

Cell phone microwaves

Cell phone users may be endangering their health. There is widespread concern that the microwaves emitted by cell phones can lead to a variety of health problems, from skin and eye problems to headaches, anxiety attacks, poor short-term memory, and increasing fatigue.

The major concern is that these microwaves can cause brain tumors, as well as other cancers, because digital cellular phones emit pulses of microwave radiation that can be recorded heating tissues in the head. Research has implicated long-term genetic problems, eye damage, and chronic leukemias, as well as Alzheimer's and Parkinson's Disease.

A shield can be fixed to the phone to cut down the amount of radiation absorbed, and some companies have produced leather protection cases with built-in protective shields and advise their customers always to extend the aerial fully and position their phones away from their bodies. Research continues to determine if analog-type cordless phones are potentially hazardous. I use a hands-free cellular phone with a microphone and an earphone. It has a long wire connection that allows me to hold the phone at arm's length, away from my body.

Lifestyle issues in today's world

DR. WENDY DENNING, one of five partners in an integrated medical practice in London, England, which offers alternative therapies alongside modern medicine.

❝Many people believe they have allergies, but they are often feeling the effects of increased pollution levels in their homes and on the streets. We eat out a lot more than we ever did compared to 10 or 20 years ago and subject ourselves to other people's standards of hygiene, and you cannot eliminate the possibility of human error. Hygiene rules are often disregarded, and the number of food-poisoning incidents is reported to be rising.

There are natural mechanisms in the body to eliminate toxins through the kidneys, but I also recommend drinking at least 2 quarts of water a day, because this flushes out the system. I would say that it is one of the most important things you can do for your health because it rehydrates the body generally.

Many people are dehydrated from drinking tea and coffee, and this shows in the tightness of their skin and more pronounced lines, so you could say drinking water is also crucial to maintaining your looks because it keeps everything flowing, literally.

Walking is good exercise and it gets people out into the natural world. Wherever you live in a city, you can usually find a park where you can reconnect with nature, while the walking gets your endorphins going. I always recommend that patients find an exercise method that

ABOVE **Drink plenty of water every day to keep your body working efficiently.**

ABOVE **Walking is an excellent, relaxing form of exercise and an enjoyable way of keeping in** touch with the natural world and our surroundings.

they enjoy, because if you push yourself to continue with something you find you hate, you are working against the natural grain of the body.

Your job may not be that enjoyable – you just need not to hate it. This is the single determining factor affecting recovery in people returning to work after illness or an injury. If they hate that job, it will prolong the time it takes them to get better. Many unemployed people miss that sense of being appreciated, and this is often linked to poor health. I encourage people to try volunteer work if they do not have a job, so they feel they are making a contribution.

Not taking yourself too seriously, working out your priorities, and being able to laugh are all vital, as is finding a purpose or deeper meaning to life, because without it, why would we bother to do anything?
I know there are people who do all the things I suggest we should not do and still live a long life. Being purist in your approach to a healthy lifestyle becomes another stress in itself. The key is moderation, so everyone can find their own level. ❞

LEFT **Each of us has a responsibility to protect the environment.**

WHO CARES MORE THAN YOU DO?

Today, most of us are aware that the modern world has led to a physical environment that can adversely affect our health. The progress of industrialization has a downside and every manufacturing process produces dangerous, potentially toxic waste materials that are proving more and more difficult to dispose of safely.

The huge percentage of us who drive cars realize we are inadvertently contributing to the thousands of poisonous particles being pumped into the atmosphere daily. The oceans are becoming polluted and the world's tropical rain forests are being cut down, leaving barren dust bowls where nothing will grow and inevitably changing the world's climate for ever.

Yet, the environment is not exclusively the preserve of those who care about conserving it. The word has been hijacked and turned into a cause, but in reality our environment describes the surroundings in which each one of us lives. We all have our own space on this planet and this becomes our habitat. The condition it is in dramatically affects the health of all those who live out their lives in it.

Daunting tasks

Environmental problems seem enormously difficult to solve. They make people feel uncomfortable because the solutions could cost money and cause inconvenience. Some are too complicated to solve with money because what they really need is a drastic change of attitude before they will go away.

Most of us pride ourselves on our awareness, which has to be better than ignorance, and perhaps salve our consciences by writing a cheque to an appropriate charity. Most parents help and encourage their children to produce projects for school covering conservation issues, and appreciate the concept of protecting our natural environment.

An awful lot of people prefer to distance themselves – recycling is something other people do. They vaguely assume that those who claim to be looking after things will somehow sort them out. In many ways, we have become a dependent, reliant society in which there is a growing tendency to pass responsibility over to someone else and then put the problem out of our minds as though it had already been solved. If and when things go wrong, there are experts to turn to, other people who can be relied upon to put things right.

The collective will

The places in which we live and work are fundamental to our welfare, just as our bodies need a healthy environment in which to thrive. The responsibility for achieving the best possible conditions for ourselves and our families belongs to everyone.

Individually, we may not be the experts who can devise ways of making our lives better, safer, and healthier, but we can alert these experts to the fact that we are not a compliant society content to settle for less because we cannot be bothered to fight for more.

Caring for the natural world is an extension of the way we care for our loved ones. We want the best for them and for future generations, and we want to nurture and protect them from anything destructive or harmful.

We do have the power to change situations and make them much better than we ever thought possible. One voice may not be heard, but several voices certainly will, and a few thousand can create a huge clamor.

SELF-HEALING
Meditation for Tranquillity

The following questions are contemplations that can be taken into your meditation.

CONTEMPLATIONS

→ If the telephone rings late at night, does your heart turn over and your mouth become dry, because you automatically think something dreadful has happened?

→ Would you doggedly watch a depressing television program right to the end, convinced its pessimistic scenario could actually happen?

→ Do you turn out all the lights at night, then go back downstairs and check again, even though you have never missed one yet?

→ Have any of your friends or colleagues accused you of being overcritical?

→ Do you suffer from a recurring condition that your doctor is unable to explain?

→ Do you find you are always running out of time and always in a hurry?

Meditation

How many times have you worried for nothing? How many times have you played the same worry over and over in your mind so that you experience it over and over again? The courageous man dies a single death; the fearful man dies a thousand times.

Relax, breathe deeply, and meditate

You do not need me to tell you whether or not you are a worrier. Worriers have nowhere to escape to because their worry invades every aspect of their lives, often preventing any laughter or enjoyment, casting its heavy shadow wherever they turn. Worriers are absorbed by a restless fear and benefit from meditation because it calms their frenetic mental activity and offers them respite and peace of mind.

This meditation works well if you can lie down with a comfortable pillow tucked under your head and a blanket or cover over you, so that you do not feel cold.

SELF-HEALING
Meditation for Tranquillity

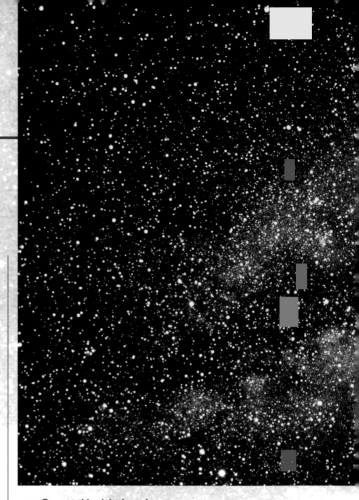

Imagine yourself lying in a field on a warm summer night, looking up at the dark velvet blue of the sky. As you look at the stars, they become brighter as others fade and resemble a series of brilliant diamonds, twinkling and shining in a seemingly endless display.

The more you watch, the more you see of these never-ending stars, as their brightness trails off into infinity. Feel the perfect peace of this picture above you, painted by nature it seems for your pleasure. Imagine this peace as a ray of light and call it down to where you are lying. Now this ray of light becomes brighter, and as it gets nearer, it broadens out so its rays encircle you and you can feel their calm warmth penetrate through to your spirit.

Imagine your spirit as a part of you that has been shattered like brittle glass and this light is healing the sharp edges, piecing them together one by one, very slowly. Notice the sensation as each new fragment connects, mending your broken spirit. Feel each piece send a surge of hopeful energy through your body. Imagine that energy as a color and see the heat it generates as it sends flickers of light here and there, reconnecting, repairing, mending, and fixing.

As you lie looking up at the stars, bathed in this healing light, take the time to savor the sensation as the healing rays penetrate your spirit and it begins to reflect and radiate the brilliance. Now you are like a star, twinkling and reflecting all the other stars, and your brilliance is like a beacon, lighting up your life so that you can see your talents and your accomplishments more clearly than ever before.

ABOVE **Gaze at this nighttime sky, studded with brightly sparkling stars, and feel their powerful healing light beaming down on you and penetrating right through to your spirit.**

This light is so bright that no darkness can survive its astonishing power. Now take all the negativity that is cowering in the shade and scoop it up in a compassionate color before sending it soaring off into the distance, off into a place that is thousands of light years away.

Revived and invigorated, you can now send this healing light back up to the stars where it will twinkle and glitter every night, always ready to shine its brilliance on your spirit so you can absorb and reflect its healing power. Watch the light grow smaller and smaller until it reaches the other stars and takes its place in the diamond display. Notice how dark the blue of the night sky is and how safe and secure you feel under its velvet presence. Stretch your legs and arms and allow yourself a gentle return to earth.

Record your first thoughts

As always, write down the effect that your meditation has had on your mood and your emotions as soon as you possibly can.

What your responses reveal

Mostly "yes" answers

You doggedly pursue each day and refuse to allow your emotional state to stop you from getting through it, taking fleeting comfort in criticizing others. Pulling them down, even for a moment, puts you up, but this is a transient elevation. You need to acknowledge that you are on overload, your mind cluttered with worry, and your body rigid with tension. You need relaxation periods in your life as much as you need food and water. The state of anxiety in which you exist has become your normal state, and it affects the way you think as well as behave and drains your energy levels.

Consider this: Your steely determination to keep going at all costs is undeniable. But would you treat someone else as badly as you are treating yourself?

Half "yes," half "no" answers

You are at least recognizing the mountain of work for what it is, partly self-constructed as a visible alibi to justify being held back, partly a reason to excuse you from moving forward. Let go of the part of you that approaches everything from under a black cloud and cling to the part that wants to be free of this burden.

Consider this: Meditation may have been tailor-made for you – it settles you down, eases the pressure, and clears your mind, giving you space to love yourself more and find a healthier way to live.

Mostly "no" answers

You are dealing with life very well and avoiding the worry trap that pulls so many people down. You have a fine sense of priorities and know the difference between trivial concerns and life-enhancing considerations. In learning not to expend energy unnecessarily, you have found out how to flow with the tide of life.

Consider this: The intense wisdom of your inner voice will be reflected in the health of your mind and body as long as you are able to hear it.

Affirmation

I will trust my intelligence and listen to my inner wisdom, and they will be my protection. My mind will be my shield, not my sword.

Ivan Pavlov was a Russian scientist who believed that all behavior is learned and can also be unlearned. He also believed this learning happened because of simple associations rather than thought processes. He devised an experiment in which he "conditioned" some dogs. First he rang a bell, then he produced some food and the dogs began to salivate. He repeated this over and over again and they reacted by salivating each time. They had learned to associate the sequence of the bell ringing with food arriving. Then Pavlov rang the bell and did not produce the food, but because he had reinforced the link through repetition, the dogs still salivated.

8 | THE RHYTHM OF LIFE

FAMILIAR RETREATS

All through our lives, we repeat the same patterns of behavior whether we realize it or not. In day-to-day situations, we fall back on the same emotional responses, and when we are angry, sad, irritated, or pleased, our reactions rarely vary. The details may be different, but the messages we receive and send to all our brains are the same.

Most of the time we are unaware or unable to alter these patterns because they are so deeply embedded in our psyche. Often the only protective technique we use is avoidance. The more we do things, the more they become part of our psyche, and often we define ourselves by our lifestyle. When we meet new people, we rarely judge them on appearance or their name, but when we know what their occupation is and find out if someone is a brain surgeon or a refuse collector, we then form an opinion and slot them into a category.

Predictable behavior

Many people find they have had a series of unsuccessful relationships in which their partners were similar in character and looks, and which all ended for the same reasons. How many people remarry only to have their friends remark on the similarities between this spouse and their previous one? We develop habits that often threaten to take over our lives but which we feel unable to give up. We have opinions that have been unchanged since we were young, just as we uphold the same moral codes of behavior and beliefs.

Some people hate to stay in other people's homes because they "like their own things around them." They may return to the same place for their vacation year after year, confident that they will not be disappointed because they know exactly what to expect.

Conditioning from the cradle

A baby smiles and its parents smile back. A baby cries and is comforted with a cuddle. It learns very quickly which actions produce the best response, and once registered, repeats them again and again. It is believed that the way parents react to their baby forms the foundation of their child's emotional base, laying down a pattern that will last a lifetime. If parents prove reliable and constant, the baby connects this to security and safety in the same way that a baby who becomes accustomed to being ignored can grow up feeling neglected and lacking in confidence.

LEFT **Our emotional stability as an adult is profoundly influenced by our early relationship with our parents. A loving environment is the best start in life.**

COMFORT IN BELONGING

You have probably noticed how people in offices tend to bring in their own plants and photographs, and make their desks their own. When a bus full of passengers sets off on the return journey, the passengers usually sit in the same seats they occupied when they departed. No one needs to put up a notice because this is tacitly understood, and it would be a brave person who ignored these unwritten rules and actually sat in a different seat.

The ensuing surprise and indignation over this transgression would not be because someone was sitting in a different seat, rather that they were sitting in what was generally perceived to be someone else's seat. Making things our own is a very widespread human trait, and however illogical, none of the other passengers would be likely to support the rebel because of this unwritten rule that governs our behavior.

Tiny babies warm to routine because their world is still small and there are only a handful of faces they recognize with pleasure. Leaving a small child with someone they hardly know can be terrifying. Starting school where they will have to take on board all kinds of new faces, situations, and rules can be overwhelming.

ABOVE **Belonging to a group makes us feel safe because we are sharing experiences with other people. Being with a** group of like-minded people can reassure individuals that their values are sound, that they have a place in their world.

> *If life is making you unhappy, constantly worried, or even ill when it could be doing the opposite of all those things, this is a clear signal that something needs to change.*

Reassurance in social structures

Familiarity is comfortable. If we have a sense of where we belong, then being in places we belong to reinforces that. It also applies to people we spend time with, such as friends. These familiar faces know us as well as we know them, and we build up shared memories together, perhaps shared troubles. With friends, neighbors, and relatives, we evolve the social structures of our lives and often have certain days of the week when we regularly meet.

Throughout history, just as birth and death have been attended by ceremonies, courting rituals have been set out, social rules drawn up, and manners and customs laid down. They may have varied over the centuries, but the essence of their purpose has been constant. Society finds it reassuring. Life has its rhythm that is constructed from the patterns we choose, and when those are disrupted, how we react is a measure of our dependency on these rules.

STRUCTURED OR STIFLED?

It may be, however, that your routine or way of living was constructed so long ago that it no longer fits in with your way of life as it is today. Without change, maybe all you can see ahead are years of boredom. Your problem may be how to tell your partner that the way you live is no longer the way you want to continue. Simply facing up to that fact is rather frightening.

It is a little like pulling the rug out from under your feet, because this has been the program that has sustained you for a long time. This dilemma affects many people – staying with what you know fills you with fatigue, but moving on is filled with uncertainty. What you know feels safe, and without it you might feel unsupported, unstructured, and unprotected. Identifying the things that are dissatisfying is the first hurdle; deciding what you want to do instead comes next.

Taking time out will allow you the space and peace of mind to indulge in self-exploration. It gives you a chance to look at all the areas of your life and work out whether they synchronize or whether they leave you overburdened. In this way, you may come to a realization that the undisturbed rhythm of your lifestyle needs to be interrupted. What you once enjoyed and regarded as a smooth-flowing, ordered existence might now have disintegrated into a mundane, empty way to spend your days.

Painful changes

Much as we fear change, we ourselves change, and the things that pleased us once may cease to satisfy, while the problems that once bothered us most might now make us laugh. Facing up to the facts means being very honest with yourself, and not

necessarily liking what you find. But if life is making you unhappy, constantly worried, or even ill when it could be doing the opposite of all those things, this is a clear signal that something needs to change.

Readjusting your life patterns can be painful but vital. The only way out of a process is through it because you need to complete it in order to understand what it means. All the good advice in the world will not be as effective as personal experience. Well-meaning friends may tell you not to continue on with this difficult process of upheaval, but giving up halfway through will only leave you feeling dissatisfied, just as any other unfinished business leaves nagging doubts.

RIGHT **Many people prefer to hide their misery behind a mask of happiness, fearful of looking too deeply at their problems.**

SELF-HEALING
Reconditioning

Make a note of 12 different everyday activities, such as reading the morning newspaper, cleaning your teeth, making breakfast, walking the dog, sorting the laundry, or planning meals. Choose the kind of mundane tasks you could probably do with your eyes shut.

Take two of them and deliberately do them in a different way. If you usually sort the laundry in the morning, do it in the evening. If you habitually drive with the radio on tuned to a talk station, put on some music instead, a type of music you do not often listen to. If everyone at work goes to a nearby café at lunchtime, go somewhere totally new. Eat a different kind of lunch than you usually choose. Wear a different style or color combination of clothes for work. Take a different route home. Read a magazine from back to front.

A plan of change

For one week, try to find two activities that you can do in an entirely different way from the norm for the whole seven days. The next week, add two more, then the following week, two more after that until all 12 have been tackled using a different approach. It does not matter how small the change seems, whether it is switching your toothpaste, changing your hairstyle, or rearranging your living room.

Breaking free

If you feel disorientated, stay with it because this feeling will pass. Stick to your plan and you will begin to notice how liberated these changes make you feel. Even if you only try writing your name with your other hand, do this every day for a week and the effect will be significant.

The shape and form our lives take can become deadly dull and the need to conform, meet deadlines, stick to routines, and pay the bills can be stultifying. The free flow of creative thought gets trapped in the back of our minds, and this exercise helps to push different buttons and provoke new responses.

BELOW **Changing your appearance can alter the way you feel about yourself and encourage a fresh perspective on life.**

ABOVE **If you have always longed to do something different, such as mountain climbing or sailing, you can make that dream a reality.**

Four-step changes

The interlinking parts of the mind and body influence each other. Your state of health may depend on whether you can make changes to your state of mind, or if you can interrupt destructive behavior patterns and generally bring about major lifestyle alterations. It may be a matter of giving something up, beginning a program of exercise, or following a specific therapy.

Across the top of a page, make four columns and on the left-hand side list the changes you need to make. Head the first column "beliefs," the second "thoughts," the third "emotions," and the fourth "behavior." If you are trying to stop smoking, for example, put smoking in the left-hand list. In the following columns list why you believe you should stop, what you think about stopping, what you feel about stopping, and how your behavior is affected if you stop smoking. Keep returning to this page and rereading what you have written from time to time. It will be a visible reminder that will support you if you lose sight of your goal or your motivation runs down or if your lifestyle makes it all seem too hard.

ACHIEVABLE ASPIRATIONS

Suppose your occupation means you spend your working life confined to an office environment five days a week, barely able to deal with your heavy workload, let alone contemplate pursuing hobbies outside work time. Suppose you nurture a dream of climbing Mount Kilimanjaro in Kenya, or you had a secret longing to sail across the South China Sea, or a desire to run in a marathon? These are all achievements that are entirely possible if you have the determination to do them.

Self-evaluation

The very nature of self-evaluation generally means that those people who look back and examine their lives have already notched up quite a lot of experience. This accounts for the fact that the most unlikely adventures are frequently begun in mid-life by people who have come through an illness or a trauma of some description. Suddenly the office job, the financial responsibilities, and the future can be sorted into equal parts of a very full life that has many facets to it. The whole becomes greater than the sum of the parts, the whole being the person and the parts the minutiae of that individual's life. This brings us back to the holistic approach of health management.

A balancing act

If the parts of your life are not apportioned out in equal balance, but concentrated in one area, you are vulnerable and exposed should that area of your life change. But dividing the different parts of your life into equal, harmonious sections is not just to cover yourself in case something goes wrong and provide you with a fall-back position. Equilibrium is about using all your different body energies in equal quantities so you never neglect, sublimate, or mask one with another, avoiding things you would rather not face by over-indulging in another area.

PATTERNS FROM THE PAST

That we are all creatures of habit to some extent or another is not important if those habits are doing us good, but when they are causing us harm – perhaps even ruining our lives – they take on a greater significance.

Many of our habits are retained through our memory. The parent who tells their child that he or she is fat is instilling an idea that will lodge in their memory. This child could grow into an adult after having nurtured this vision of themselves as a fat person even if they are really thin.

Children learn by copying others, beginning with their first role models, their parents, then close family such as aunts, uncles, and cousins, followed by their teachers and school friends when they go to school.

They watch and listen, and whatever they observe tends to be what they will also learn to do. When a person is "conditioned," they have been fed a set of thoughts and a pattern of behavior as if there were no other choice. Their thinking then follows the same rigid lines that have been set out for them and their behavior is dictated by the same conditioned behavior they have been taught to emulate.

When someone continually repeats a habit, this reinforces that habit a little bit more each time. If a child is frightened of, say, mice, this fear will be repeated each time they see a mouse, and each time the fear will become more entrenched. By the time they have grown into an adult, the fear might have become too severe to tolerate and they will probably have to avoid totally any situations in which they might meet a mouse, thus avoiding their terrible fear.

Sometimes an opinion formed during childhood will remain in the memory throughout that person's life, whether it is relevant or not. The toddler who turns down a particular food will continue to avoid that food and possibly never consider whether his or her more mature taste buds might now like it. It is likely that the child whose parents dictate what he or she may like or dislike will carry those opinions through life without questioning their origin or validity because they are so deeply embedded in that individual's mind.

BELOW **Encouraging children to believe in their abilities will boost their confidence and help them to fulfill their potential.**

Evolving self-perception

Children begin to develop a sense of themselves quite early in childhood and this is usually based on the quality of their relationships with others – their mothers, fathers, relations, and friends. This is their environment, and they begin to see themselves and their place within this relatively small circle. By the time they become adults, this will have widened considerably, but this same self-concept continues, reinforced by interaction with all the people they meet in their everyday lives, from college students and work colleagues to personal relationships.

RIGHT **It is important for a child to develop a sense of their own identity, rather than living out a plan laid down by their parents. Their hopes and dreams can be a source of great motivation.**

How do we become addicted?

DR BRIAN WELLS, *a consultant psychiatrist and specialist in addictions:*

❝ Many people today suffer from addictions. Whether they are addicted to drugs, alcohol, sex, food, shopping, or exercise, the common thread that links most addicts is a state of low self-esteem. Generally speaking, doing something to excess is an addiction, and the core of such behavior is being addicted to sources of instant gratification.

In the case of alcoholism, there is a known genetic link, and we also see addicts who have grown up in families where there is an addiction in one of the parents. We see addicts emerging from a childhood in which the father was perhaps a workaholic and the child felt ignored, or where there was some other kind of emotional or physical childhood abuse. The effects of this can present later in some form of addiction.

Many addicts are people who have failed for whatever reason to develop a sense of their own identity, and have grown up with very little idea of what they want to be and what occupation they would like to follow. ❞

But if those early experiences were miserable and unhappy, their perception of themselves will be a negative one. If they have received very little love or been heavily criticized as a child, they will feel unloved and unacceptable in adult life. If teachers and other significant adults in the child's life offer very little support, this only compounds the situation and that child grows up with little self-esteem. As such, they will be poorly equipped to tackle their lives, unable to trust their own judgment or plan their own future.

Maybe the patterns you are sticking to so rigidly in your life are making you ill because you have not recognized how damaging it is for you.

WHEN ILLNESS INTERRUPTS

When a person becomes ill, depending upon the seriousness or duration of the illness, they can become reflective. Perhaps they find themselves with time to dwell on where they are in their life and whether they even like their lifestyle.

Illness can prompt a spontaneous desire to reassess values and think about priorities, separating the nonessential items from the important ones. This can have a cleansing effect, which is also a form of healing. You can describe it as a mental and emotional spring-clean, and sometimes it is the precursor to a much deeper exploration. Such a reassessment can become the starting point for living a different kind of life, because the news of an illness can sometimes make someone feel like a different kind of person.

Illness can be inconvenient because it interrupts your life's normal rhythm, but it can also have an impact on your emotional life. People frequently discover areas of their emotional makeup that may have been hidden when they were well but that now come to the surface. Being incapacitated can highlight a variety of needs that have not been met, and trigger a desire to make enormous changes once that person has recovered. Illness makes people aware of the passage of time, many of whom become determined to make the most of their lives in future.

Turning your world upside down

Illness certainly does not fit into the ordered routine of life and brings with it all kinds of uncertainty. Its impact can be far-reaching, affecting all the people in your life as well, or it can be something very personal that leaves you feeling very isolated.

Within the family, younger children can feel threatened when a parent is ill, as though a rock they have always found firm and dependable has suddenly turned to jelly. Partners, however loving and well-intentioned, may still show resentment over the other's illness. An adult child nursing an elderly patient may feel as though they have swapped roles and become the parent of the child.

Illness strikes different chords in people and can turn values upside down. It can bring out aspects of people you were unaware of. The most unlikely people can prove stalwart in their support, while rock-solid friends may show a selfish side of themselves you would never have believed possible. Illness can surprise you, revealing the generosity of spirit shown by others, which is of course just another form of healing. It can also act as a mirror and intensify your real-life situation, perhaps activating thoughts you had tried not to dwell upon.

There are lots questions you can ask yourself about the causes of your illness. Maybe the patterns you are sticking to so rigidly in your life are making you ill because you have not recognized how damaging it is for you? Maybe you can see that changes are about to be forced upon you and this fact is making you sick with fear? Some illnesses emerge from frustration. When you are reluctant to acknowledge your emotions, they can turn inward and ignored for too long can eventually make you ill.

Sleep hygiene

DR. WENDY DENNING, *one of five partners in an integrated medical practice in London, England, which offers alternative therapies alongside modern medicine*

❛Most people do not have enough sleep, and I see more and more people who are chronically tired in our society. This is usually because they do not go to bed early enough. After 10 p.m. there are critical signals of tiredness, and when these are ignored, the body kicks into an activity phase as though it was daytime, and this can continue until 2 a.m. Those people who then go to bed at midnight find it difficult to shut down their mental activity.

I believe in sleep hygiene, which is actually a routine where you have a regular bedtime and prepare yourself for bed so your body winds down in readiness for sleep. It involves avoiding coffee, cigarettes, and alcohol late at night because they all disrupt sleep. Half an hour's walk after dinner helps digestion as well as the winding-down process. You can listen to relaxing music and have a milky drink or a hot bath with a soothing essential oil added – anything to make sure your body registers bedtime. The main point is to avoid starting anything that activates the mental processes. ❜

RIGHT **Establishing a regular routine before bedtime helps to wind down your mental processes. A hot bath, perhaps with a soothing essential oil added to the water, or a scented candle placed in the room, is a highly pleasurable and effective preparation for sleep.**

WHEN CHANGE IS THREATENING

When change is forced upon us and everything we know and love is under threat, we react with understandable anxiety. That is a normal moderate reaction. Taken to its most extreme, the prospect of change can be so frightening that it escalates into anxiety and then panic. Panic, of course, paralyses. We do nothing, we are helpless. Yet, if we stopped to list all the things that could go wrong, we might not even step outside the front door. The best laid plans can be overturned by circumstances impossible to predict – losing a job or being rejected in a relationship to illness or tragic accidents.

Huge life changes can be very difficult to come to terms with. Many families are geographically separated, such as grandparents in one country with their grandchildren growing up on the other side of the world. The older generation might be filled with trepidation at the idea of a new country and a new life, but a younger couple see their family growing up in an excitingly different environment.

ABOVE **In many countries the traditional family unit no longer exists, as younger generations develop different priorities to their parents and grandparents. Bridging the gulf between hereditary values and modern thinking can be a difficult process.**

When someone loses their job after working in the same position for several years, the loss is often much greater than mere employment. Apart from the financial insecurity, alongside the loss of the job goes the loss of identity with an organization that they might well have been linked to for so long and the loss of camaraderie with work colleagues with whom they shared a common bond, being employees in the same firm. There is also the loss of purpose or routine, because they no longer have a structured day and a place to be at a given time.

Fresh challenges

While enforced change can be threatening and devastating, it can also be stimulating and exciting. Sometimes it can be all those things at once. New parents are thrilled by the arrival of their first baby, but when it arrives they find themselves emotionally unprepared for such a total disruption of their lives. Their usual routines may not have been particularly structured, but they still formed the pattern of their

LEFT **The arrival of a baby can be an emotional rollercoaster. The parents' excitement is tempered by the new and overwhelming demands made on their time and energy, and having to come to terms with fundamental changes to the pattern of their lives.**

Testament, Job says: "For the thing which I greatly feared is come upon me, and that which I was afraid of is come unto me." In our modern language, we would describe this as a self-fulfilling prophecy and say that giving a dire scenario so much energy is to give it validity.

That helpless feeling

When something is left up in the air, many of us do just this, "worrying" at the unresolved problem, often through a long night of disturbed sleep. Logic may dictate that since we cannot resolve the problem immediately, we should put it out of our minds until we are in a position to sort it out.

Worry makes people less sure of themselves because the criteria they normally use to define themselves are suddenly no longer there. The metaphorical goalposts have been moved, and there is a yawning gap where everything familiar used to be. We have no way of sorting things out because we do not have the normal criteria to help us reach for an answer, so this new, unfinished business leaves us feeling helpless.

Hitting out

The prospect of profound personal change sometimes leads to the rejection of people we have been close to for most of our lives. When we look inside ourselves for a deeper meaning, we also look for places to put our anger, guilt, and blame. The very people who have provided our crucial emotional attachments, such as parents and family, are sometimes targeted and turned into scapegoats. They become the recipients of our emotional debris.

MindPower gives you the power to heal, not cause pain and hurt, and is also about taking personal responsibility for yourself, trusting yourself, respecting your own judgment, and owning your own thoughts and actions. The fundamental essence of self-healing is just that – healing yourself.

lifestyle. Not only do they have to become accustomed to being parents and the awesome responsibility of a tiny infant making enormous demands on them, but they have to become used to their lives changing quite drastically.

WHY UNCERTAINTY UNSETTLES

Routines and patterns form the boundaries of our world. When they change, when we do not know what to expect or we have to do something we have never done before, uncertainty sets in.

Not knowing what will happen can be worse than having several scenarios spelled out in graphic detail, because however dreadful, at least they would be your scenarios. Maybe solving this problem is not as cut and dried as we would want. We might have to wait for someone else's decision first, or there might be a time factor involved or other facts have still to come to light. We often describe a dog as "worrying" at a bone because it will keep gnawing away long after all the meat has been devoured. Some people have become so accustomed to worry that they visualize the worst possible outcome even though it has not even happened. As their imagination magnifies these negative events, their anxiety increases. In the Old

SELF-HEALING
Meditation for Certainty

Here are a few questions to take into your meditation and contemplate.

Contemplations

→ Do you think people who embrace every new idea as if it is a life-changing discovery are unrealistic and naive?

→ Do you have a problem convincing your doctor that your symptoms are real because his dismissive attitude makes you feel like a malingerer?

→ Do you feel very nostalgic when you look back at your childhood?

→ Have you felt disappointed when someone you admired for their professional expertise turned out to have a petulant, childlike attitude in other areas of their life?

→ Do you daydream about winning a fortune and fantasize about what it would buy for you?

→ Do your suffer from anxiety before an important meeting to the extent that you cannot eat?

Meditation

Rhythm in our lives can be reassuring and consistent, as well as predictable and stultifying. The more we keep to that rhythm, the more stable its influence seems. We often pick up the rhythms devised by others and continue them throughout our life because familiarity is so comfortable, and we may never stop to ask if they suit us. It may not occur to us that someone else's patterns are the wrong design and we need to develop our own. We may not realize how automatically we respond to situations just because that is the way we have always responded.

Relax, breathe deeply, and meditate

Imagine you are sitting on a rock at the top of a high mountain looking out at the view spread before you. Your mountain is the highest in this range and gives you an unparalleled view of all the other mountain peaks from where you are positioned.

This rock is very safe and you feel very comfortable. Above you the sky is cloudless and a very vivid blue. The rocks beneath your feet have a fine dusting of light snow. The air is crisp and cold because you are very high up and the sun is very hot. The combination of the chill freshness of the air and the heat of the sun's rays is very invigorating. It makes you think of other similar situations that would produce such a blend of sensations, such as plunging into a cool river on a hot day or walking in snow-covered countryside at midday under a winter sun.

As you breathe deeply, you can feel the sharp freshness of this air going down deep into your lungs, filling you with its cleansing, restorative energy. Each time you breathe out, you have a sense of your physical energy becoming stronger and stronger. Your body feels light and powerful, as though every muscle and fiber has been instilled with a dynamic new force that has injected so much vitality into your system that you believe you could climb this mountain effortlessly, hardly pausing for breath.

You look across again at the vista spread out before you like a feast, snow-capped peak after snow-capped peak, a range of mountains, ancient and immovable through hundreds of centuries. As your eyes wander down the mountains' sides, you see the lush deep green of forests give way to the magnificent colors of the different species of wildflowers that grow there undisturbed in a wild profusion of scents and shades.

This is a timeless scene, recreated routinely year in and year out. The wildlife on these mountains depends on its consistency. Every bird and insect, every wild animal large or small instinctively heads for the plant it depends on at the time of year it knows it will be flourishing, whether to sample its nectar or feed off its fruit.

As you watch, your eyes are able to pick out tiny squirrels harvesting nuts, and you catch the glitter of a fish darting through one of the mountain streams. A family of deer are nibbling at some branches and a fox moves delicately through some trees. You recognize its unmistakable gait with its back slightly arched as it looks furtively to left and right, alert to danger at all times.

This scene is majestic and calm and you now remind yourself of how it must look to others. The danger that hovers over the head of the tiniest field mouse when an eagle's eye spots it from high above; that eagle is beautiful and that field mouse is exquisitely formed. The predators rely on the appearance of their prey to remain unchanged, which allows the routine of hunter and hunted to continue as it always has.

Look again at that fox. Reflect on how its hunger compels its continued search for recognizable food, and if nature should suddenly change its rules and the fox's prey take on a different appearance, remind yourself that the fox would not starve.

SELF-HEALING
Meditation for Certainty

Life moves onward and evolves all the time. Moving routine references simply means relocating those references. When a road no longer goes where the signpost is pointing, it does not necessarily follow that everyone gets lost. The signpost has to be turned to face a new direction so it points where people need to go.

Look across at the view again and notice how this combination of warm sunshine and cool air produces an atmosphere of extraordinary power. Your thoughts are clear and uncluttered, your perceptions intensified and sharpened. Every sensation, from the cool of the air on your skin to the warmth of the sun on the back of your neck, is heightened. You become aware that being on this high mountain perch has made you invincible. You are unstoppable and untouchable. The accuracy of your instincts is razor-sharp, and you know with absolute certainty that by following them you will always go where you were always meant to.

As you sit on this mountain rock, it feels as though you are on top of the whole world, with choices spread out beneath your feet. Just as your thoughts and senses have increased in intensity, this high altitude and pristine environment have added a special quality to your inner voice and given it incredible clarity.

Take one last glance at those mountains and remind yourself of the continuing rhythms on those slopes that represent survival for the wildlife that live on them. If and when the patterns change, those who cling to the old routines suffer the consequences. Then remind yourself of the miraculous process that enables us all to evolve and adapt when the patterns of our lives no longer suit our needs.

Record your first thoughts

Collect your thoughts from this meditation and put them down on paper as quickly as you can. You will notice over the next few days how clear your thinking has become. When you return to these notes after some time, you may be surprised at how free and uncomplicated your life has since become.

What your responses reveal
Mostly "yes" answers

Your emotional health is affecting your physical state. Clinging to the memories of your childhood so tightly has distorted them, so that only the best elements have been saved and the real memories discarded. An imaginary version of events has been dragged into your adult life like a comfort blanket, and your dilemma is now that real life does not match up, so you have to pretend. But you can only fool yourself for so long, and this realization makes you bitter and resentful. These two negatives eat away at you, sapping your confidence and your energy. It is not that your goals are impossibly high, but that they impossibly unrealistic. Go back to your childhood and look at it with different eyes and savor the good along with the bad, take something from both elements and see them for what they are. Then look at how you can adapt them to meet your present needs, and if they will not fit, get something new instead.

Consider this: Finding out that a truth is not a truth and accepting the emotions around that discovery means you have accepted and understood yourself.

Mostly "no" answers

You have taken stock of your life's early experiences and calculated how best they fit into your present and future world, making the most of the good ones and learning lessons from the others. You like routine because it gives your everyday life a shape and makes it work efficiently, but you love new and exciting challenges, too. The state of your health is also dynamic and you probably keep very up-to-date on ways of maintaining your health.

 Consider this: You attract into your life whatever you give most thought to, believe in most strongly, and imagine most vividly.

Half "yes," half "no" answers

If your answers are half and half, you are getting where you want to be, but just when you need your confidence and energy most, you cannot summon it up. The little darts of fear that penetrate your system override your best intentions and doubts creep back. Have a look at your rhythms. You may find that your periodic lapses of confidence follow regular patterns without you necessarily realizing it, and your confidence could be fluctuating because that is the only program it knows.

 Consider this: Real change is not a superficial process, so do not let superficial problems block a real transformation.

Affirmation

I will not put off a decision and will look around each problem through fresh eyes. I will always take action even if that action is a considered decision to do nothing.

OUR BELIEF SYSTEMS

Individual perceptions describe the different ways each one of us sees things. These are unique perceptions, formed from our own lives and shaped by our personal experiences, and their perspective can be clouded or heightened by our emotions. They emerge from our belief system which probably began in childhood, when the rules we were taught to live by were first set out by parents, and were usually based on what their parents taught them. Schoolteachers and your minister or rabbi probably adapted other rules to fit the then-current social and religious climate.

Laying down the ground rules

These were the first beliefs most of us knew, and they formed the framework of our lives, governing the social codes we adhered to. They showed us what was right and what was wrong, and when we grew up, we would be socially aware, civilized beings. Those who broke the social codes were punished, judged unable to fit into society or even dangerous to other members of society.

Beliefs allow us to make sense of our world. We believe what our parents tell us until we grow up and start asking questions. Tilting at authority is a classic student phase, as idealism flourishes on a wave of newly found freedom, when the old rule books can be dismissed, their restricting views reflecting the last generation's old-fashioned belief systems.

Life experiences

As we have already seen, our perception of ourselves grows from childhood, and if we feel pain or pleasure when we recall memories of events or the way people treated us or the way we faced new experiences, that is likely to be the way we continue to feel into our adult lives. When, for example, a baby duck is abandoned and rescued by a human family, the first person to care for it "imprints" on its young mind and the duck believes that this person is its mother – it does not see another species, only a creature who sees to its needs. How we see ourselves can be clouded by emotional memories and the imprints can be indelibly stamped on our adult minds.

Emotions vary in intensity. Different cultures display them in different ways. By the time we are adults, we have played out many different roles – sister, brother, son, daughter, pupil, student, best friend, employee, citizen, patient, client, passenger, member. At times, those roles produce conflicting demands and cause tension and anxiety.

Individual beliefs

As I said earlier, we exist in a society that shares a common human bond – the need to belong. Most of us at some time in our lives have identified ourselves with a specific group, whether it is our family, our class, a student organization, or our social club. When someone does not fit in, our society regards them as the aberration, the loner.

The loner may have rejected the normal boundaries we have come to accept which restrict how we behave and think. The loner may have come up

with a different set of values to those most of us live by, but this does not make such a person either good or bad. It simply means they are different.

Being different requires courage, confidence, and conviction. Through the centuries, such people were outcasts, literally cast out of society, and to be exiled was to be punished. Other loners may have been avoided because of their eccentricity and hailed as heroes once they died. There are loners who have become high achievers, unable and unwilling to identify with the herd, recognizing their innate leadership qualities and believing absolutely in their own judgment.

So what are beliefs? Some of us take them for granted and never stop to question them, happily existing within the structures that have been designed for us. Others grow up to challenge them with such a fervent idealism that the older generations dismiss their earnestness as youthful exuberance. Those that continue to question the established rules tend to stand out.

BELOW AND RIGHT **From student riots in Paris to punk rock in Britain, rebellion has always asserted individuality and provoked change.**

Self-belief

A lack of self-belief can dominate people's lives and prevent them from being happy. Without a sense of their own value, they never move forward because they simply do not believe it will happen. They program themselves to fail. If anything good does happen to them, there is still doubt and disbelief, as if their prize will be taken away at any moment.

Such people become adept at erecting a confident facade which they present to the world, even though they may feel like jelly inside themselves. They use up a great deal of emotional energy because they constantly fear being "found out."

Christianity Islam Hinduism Baha'i Confuscianism

Sikhism Judaism Shintoism Jainism Taoism

Zoroastrianism Buddhism

ABOVE **Some cultures have simply no understanding of the things admired or held sacred by others, which erects insurmountable barriers between them.**

BELIEFS THAT SEPARATE CULTURES

Beliefs are the rules that separate cultures. Humanity takes pride in its differences and clings to them defiantly. Most wars begin because one group of people with a set of beliefs does not want to live next to another whose belief system is different. This is the cause of tribal wars all across the African continent, and the religious wars between Christian and Muslim in Eastern Europe and between Arab and Jew in the Middle East.

People in different countries often begin their thinking from a different place, and the things valued or abhorred in one community will be disregarded or revered in another. Some cultures have no understanding of sentiment; others place civility and politeness high and are appalled if one person openly criticizes another, preferring a dignified silence to speak volumes instead. Others interpret the roles of men and women in ways that many of us would consider intolerable. Certain cultures devise punishments that others might find unthinkable.

In some countries, great emphasis is placed on producing large families, in spite of the increasing world population and the burden it places on natural resources. Certain cultures believe in the importance of keeping their cultural philosophies intact from one generation to the next, disregarding the changes that the modern world has introduced.

Strict regimes

Often these philosophies are a combination of social and spiritual beliefs which are so closely interwoven that the two cannot be separated. Belonging to such a community or culture means accepting the religious beliefs as well as the social rules and leaves much less room for maneuver, let alone modernization. Some belief systems are so controlling that breaking out is virtually

*‘Even the most assertive,
opinionated people can become submissive
and docile when they are ill, and see
nothing unusual in handing over their
welfare to someone else.’*

impossible. For many people raised in the freedom of a 20th-century liberal atmosphere, many of the very extreme belief systems other people live by are far removed from anything they have known. With no childhood references to share and no rules with which other cultures can identify, many extremist communities could be living on a different planet because they stretch people's understanding. They defy belief.

BLIND BELIEF

Even the most assertive, opinionated people can become submissive and docile when they are ill, and see nothing unusual in handing over their welfare to someone else. Of course, this someone else is usually an accredited health expert, so this attitude is not entirely without a rationale. But there is also an element of not wanting to usurp authority or appear to be "stepping on toes," particularly if that person is very knowledgeable.

Even today, the old-fashioned perception of a doctor's authority, which has become known as "the aura of the white coat," can still induce unquestioning compliance in patients. Few doctors or therapists regard such a situation as therapeutic.

Relinquishing responsibility

Sometimes people are not consciously aware that they might be preventing their own recovery. The mind can become conditioned to react in certain ways, and such conditioning is reinforced each time the process is repeated. If we learn in child

hood that at the first sign of illness we automatically hand ourselves over to a healthcare expert, then that is exactly what we do for the rest of our lives unless something happens to change that program of behavior.

The international pharmaceutical industry pours billions of dollars a year into the promotion of its products, targeting both the general public and the medical world. Pharmaceutical remedies have made us fairly passive about actively participating in our own healing and they do seem, initially, to work like magic. Often the science that devised them is quite brilliant. As a result, patients' expectations can exceed the reality of their situation. Sometimes a drug can be overused to the point where it ceases to be effective and that person's system becomes immune to its action. There are many cases in which antibiotics have been prescribed so liberally that patients fail to respond, often at times when they are most needed.

There are also instances where patients' expectations have become so embedded in their unconscious mind that if a situation arises in which the doctor has no "magic" cure to offer, the patient is often very shocked because they have never allowed themselves to consciously consider such an event.

The mind is powerful enough to heal as well as destroy, and if the will to get better is not present, it does not matter how many doctors or therapists are consulted if the patient is unwilling to contribute to the healing process as well.

TAKING BACK RESPONSIBILITY

What does a dependent patient do when the remedy fails or a cure does not exist? How does such a person cope when all the doctors and therapists shake their heads sadly and say they have nothing to offer? Having handed responsibility over to others and abdicated their role in their own welfare, such people have lost touch with their own abilities.

I have emphasized that healing can take many forms, but nowhere is its effectiveness more dramatic than when it comes from within. Self-healing means being receptive to your own body's needs and providing the kind of nourishing environment in which you will thrive.

There is no need to relinquish responsibility for your illness. Your doctor or therapist will not be offended and you are not intruding on anyone else's territory. There is a mutual recognition today shared by a growing number of health experts that a two-way healing process is more likely to produce recovery. Who knows you and your body better than you do yourself? You may not consciously realize this yet, but whatever you need to know can be found within while your doctor or therapist can treat the outer you. Surely the two best people to cooperate in solving a health problem are the patient and healer, when one is an expert on health and the other has the potential to be an expert on themselves.

❛Self-healing means being receptive to your own body's needs and providing the kind of nourishing environment in which you will thrive.❜

RIGHT **Being true to yourself in your dealings with others and not hiding behind a façade in order to fit in or deferring to those in a position of authority ensures that your inner and outer selves are in tune, and that you are in an ideal state to be receptive to your body's needs.**

SELF-HEALING
Meditation for Renewal

When you have read the following list of questions, take the awareness of them into your meditation for contemplation. After the meditation, I would like you to write down your thoughts as spontaneously as you possibly can.

Contemplations

→ Do you find yourself accepting invitations or spending time with people you do not particularly like because you do not want to appear rude?

→ Do you get confused when all the things you have been brought up to believe in are a source of amusement to people at work or friends you admire?

→ Do you avoid confrontations because tension makes you blush or stammer, or experience a sense of panic?

→ Have you ever been provoked into a loud argument with someone in public?

→ Supposing you complained to the waiter about the poor service in a restaurant and then discovered your companion was embarrassed. Would you feel guilty over your action?

→ Do you have butterflies in your stomach or feel sudden pressure on your bladder whenever you are anxious?

Meditation

Sometimes people live their lives by other people's rules almost without realizing it. Even if they do not agree, they make allowances, change their opinions, defer, and apologize. It is like sitting on the edge of your seat all the time in case leaning back tips the chair over. The permanent tension this causes is almost unbearable.

Relax, breathe deeply, and meditate

Imagine you are in a favorite place. It can be a gorgeous tropical beach with white sands and waving palms, or in a beautiful garden where all the flowers you love most are growing in abundance. You may prefer the countryside in which there is no sign of another human being, and all you can see for miles around are green hills stretching into the distance under a vivid blue sky.

Take yourself to this place which is known only to you and see yourself in it, either walking through the shallows, feeling the sand beneath your feet, smelling the scent of the flowers in your garden, or wandering through the hills. Make it as real as you can. Pause and savor all the sensations, feel the sun on the back of your head, smell the flowers, hear the birds in the hills.

This place is your sanctuary – a place you can return to whenever you feel hurt, angry, or unhappy. It is a healing place where all the natural energies you have suppressed can emerge freely. It is a place where you can form whatever opinions you want to, change your mind, and challenge your doubts, and you can do all these things without considering anyone else.

As you enjoy being in this place, call upon some healing colors and see them as soft, billowing fabric encircling you so softly and gently that you can hardly feel their touch, yet their presence is also firm. Feel the effect of these colors on your mind and body as the folds of silky fabric carefully gather all the pieces that have become disconnected and lay them smoothly side by side, layer upon layer, folding and smoothing, until it seems as though they had never been disturbed.

SELF-HEALING
Meditation for Renewal

Notice how good it feels when everything is back where it belongs and there is nothing to disturb the smooth flow of your system. Notice how your energy bodies interlink so effortlessly that the movements are almost undetectable.

Now go to the parts of your physical body that have suffered as a result of the enormous burden of tension you have been carrying around, and pause. Focus on them for a few minutes and remind yourself how healthy these parts of your body were when they were tension-free and imagine them to be relaxed and healthful again.

Visualize them healed and restored. Start with your face. Smooth the frown lines that dug deeply into your forehead as though your tension was etched across your face and gently lift away the tightness around your mouth where life's problems caused you to clench your teeth. Feel your lips fill out with softness as you stretch out the thin, taut line that formed when you clamped your lips together so tightly in order to avoid letting your words and feelings out.

Continue down through your body, soothing your neck and shoulders, softening the hunched muscles that held so much of your constant anxiety. Keep going on your passage down through your body until you reach your toes, pausing at every place where you sense there is healing needed, and watch yourself flourish under the effect of this powerful healing energy as each part of you is restored to its original state. Spend as long as you want, as long as you believe you need to complete the process of renewal.

When you are ready, pause again and notice how good you feel, how nice it is to be whole, to be balanced again. Notice how strong this perfect harmony makes you feel, as though your mind has been flooded with certainty and your body with strength.

Remind yourself very briefly of how you were when all your energies were fragmented as your worries sent you spinning in endless chaotic circles, and rejoice in the way you are now back to who you are and where you were, completely restored and renewed. Before you leave this place of ultimate sanctuary, allow yourself a moment or two to enjoy a sense of achievement in creating this renewal for yourself and send yourself the love you deserve.

Record your first thoughts

Remember to write down your thoughts and feelings as soon as you are able to after the meditation. Come back to read through your notes when some time has passed, and you may find that they will take you by surprise. The image you have of yourself can change quite dramatically.

What your responses reveal

Mostly "yes" answers

You may already have suffered a lot of ill health from tension and anxiety. Have you asked yourself why you take responsibility for other people's behavior? People-pleasing is hard work and drains your energy. Every time you sublimate your true self, you suppress something of value which escapes and sends off warning signals, such as a stammer or a blush, or generates enough fear for a panic attack.

Consider this: Courage and hope are two precious commodities – the first starts you up and the second keeps you going. Experiences, however devastating, can eventually be enlightening.

Mostly "no" answers

You have a very clear and confident self-image and manage to assert yourself gently, show compassion without condescension, and enjoy the harmony that hovers over your inner and outer world. Your decisiveness is to be admired, as is your quest for quality, and your refusal to settle for less when more is entirely possible will carry you onward and upward in excellent health.

Consider this: Your inner voice is guiding you brilliantly, so always resist the temptation to test its power.

If life seems too good to be true, do not be suspicious. Accept it and be joyful, because the mind really does have the power to turn the unthinkable into reality.

Half "yes," half "no" answers

You still have work to do but you have already done a great deal. The most imminent scientist whose brilliant mind has thought up a miraculous invention may be impossible to live with and a disaster socially, but that does not detract from the value of the invention. Are you a weekend migraine sufferer, someone who denies your anxiety while you cope with a problem, but when it is over and you relax the headache floods in?

Consider this: The migraine may have begun as a slight headache, but because you ignored the signals it sent, you had to feel even more uncomfortable before you would take any notice. Try a migraine relief pill for an instant remedy, but listen to what your body is telling you so it does not have to repeat the message again and again.

Affirmation

I have no more room in my life for things that hold me back – only space for the things I cherish.

In our conscious minds, we do things we long to stop. Giving up things that damage our health and taking up things that improve it would be wonderful. So what holds us back?

Everything you think or do is logged in the vast computer that is the unconscious mind, and the thoughts you access and the thoughts you repress are determined by your private logic. This personal reasoning, as opposed to common sense, has no rational basis, and is formed from all the people and experiences that have influenced you. If your own actions occasionally frustrate and bewilder you, it is probably because the motivation behind such puzzling behavior comes from the hidden agenda lodged in your unconscious mind.

9 | PRIVATE LOGIC – COMMON SENSE

WHO NEEDS ILLNESS?

Some people really do need to be ill from time to time. These episodes usually coincide with certain events happening in their lives. Illness protects people from all the things they do not want near them. Illness can provide the perfect alibi, the supreme excuse to duck and dive.

Being ill can change the way others think about you and evoke sympathy, compassion, solicitude, and attention. Being ill can enliven a humdrum existence and conjure up an air of melodrama and mystery. It can make you more interesting.

Manipulating illness

Hypochondriasis is a very real illness and sometimes it can be so severe it masks any other symptoms of physical illness from which the patient might also be suffering. In fact, a great many people who are hypochondriacs have already experienced serious illness and often this happened in their childhood. While it may have been boring at times, even uncomfortable and painful, it commanded constant attention.

A patient is a pampered being and might get used to being washed and fed, amused and comforted. Visitors bring gifts, parents produce treats, and no one expects a sick child to do very much for themselves.

When the child patient grows up to become an adult, difficult periods in their life make them long for the times when they felt cosseted and comforted. If they suffered long periods of illness and missed a lot of their school years, they might suffer from feelings of inadequacy because of the gaps in their general knowledge. They might feel they have nothing to offer that will capture anyone's attention, and the only way to present themselves in a more interesting light is to create a drama. Literature and history are full of tragic heroines and melodramatic heroes, and whatever other attributes they had, nothing compared to the distinctive status that came with their sickness.

Just as we are reluctant to "speak ill of the dead," so sickness gives people power. It is not a healthy, useful power because it is fueled by a form of emotional blackmail as though being ill places the sick beyond criticism. Serious illness can make them free to say or do whatever they like because the normal social rules have been waived on compassionate grounds.

Man and his Symbols

Carl Jung

❝A man likes to believe that he is master of his soul. But as long as he is unable to control his moods and emotions, or to be conscious of the myriad secret ways in which unconscious factors insinuate themselves into his arrangements and decisions, he is certainly not his own master.❞

Hiding behind illness

When illness becomes an alibi and provides a place to hide when life becomes too difficult to deal with, the underlying fear of facing up to problems may have a very unlikely source. What seems small and unimportant might be disregarded, whereas an obviously large problem would not.

Yet, many of the fears that cause such disruption in people's lives can be much larger and far more worrying than the problem itself. But when they are distorted out of all proportion to reality, these fears can be too frightening to face. Developing an illness is some sort of solution because it buys time for reflection, but it hardly ever makes the problem go away. This is one of the hardest facts a hypochondriac has to face.

DETERMINED TO BE ILL

The degree to which a hypochondriac will feign illness depends on the state of their lives because their circumstances will have affected the state of their mind. At one extreme is the occasional pretence at illness, when something or someone has been upset by events and cannot face going into work for a day or for some reason needs to avoid their friends. At the other end of the spectrum is the serious hypochondriac whose desperation is so acute that they are prepared to cause themselves actual physical harm if that is what it takes to make anyone believe that they are sick and in need of help.

ABOVE **Jobs in which others depend upon you for their safety can place immense strain on body and mind. Developing an illness can provide a temporary escape route.**

Needing to be ill indicates needs that are unmet. It can be a sign of unhappiness and loneliness. In some cases, life can be so dull that illness is an improvement on boredom. Some people think illness is a way of making people like them more, seeing it as the solution to their unpopularity. How can anyone dislike you if you are sick? Surely they have no choice but to view you with compassion and sympathy.

The mind gets locked into a program, and if there is no will to move out of that program or take in anything new or different, the mind will go on acting and reacting as it always has. If this keeps up for long enough, the patient stops worrying about whether or not the pretence of illness will be exposed because they have now convinced themselves that they are actually ill.

When illness becomes such a familiar presence in someone's life, they may not know any other way of behaving or where to begin to develop an alternative strategy. To break this destructive pattern, it is important to evaluate exactly what benefits are derived from being ill and then try and find other ways of getting to the same place without the need for subterfuge. Compassion is a precious currency and squandering it can lead to a deficit.

The physician with such a patient may gradually become more and more irritated at being continually presented with this variety of imagined symptoms, and may begin to refuse the hospital referrals that once would have been automatic. It makes life very uncomfortable and unhappy for the hypochondriac whose view of life may be distorted but who also has some awareness of the pointlessness of their behavior. Many have a great deal of insight into their own condition and the way it leads them to behave.

This is another example of mental and emotional energy working at full strength but being used for a negative effect. If a person is able to draw upon such enormous reserves of mental energy and invest it in such a single-minded determination to be ill, it is entirely possible that they could reinvest it toward making themselves better. They probably realize the supreme irony of their

> *If a person is able to draw upon such enormous reserves of mental energy and invest it in such a single-minded determination to be ill, it is entirely possible that they could reinvest it toward making themselves better.*

situation. They know that the only way to build up their emotional strength and regain their health is to stop being ill.

DENYING ILLNESS

Some people need to be ill more than they realize. They are reluctant patients who firmly believe that succumbing to illness is giving in to a weakness and taking to their bed is something of a disgrace. They deny their physical symptoms and soldier on in the hope that this will make their symptoms disappear, just as a workaholic will ignore the signs of stress they are putting themselves under.

Exerting the power of their mental and emotional energy, they stubbornly refuse to acknowledge anything that will interfere with the pattern of their lives. Fear of the smallest disruption drives them on. The workaholic may be worried about losing a job. He has convinced himself that if he puts in longer and longer hours,

RIGHT **Those who, out of fear, refuse even to admit the possibility of illness drive themselves into becoming martyrs to their work and responsibilities, like modern-day St. Catherines.**

this will be to his credit. It is as though as long as his physical presence is there, the job will be, too.

The reluctant patient who never allows him or herself to be ill may nurture a dreadful fear of stopping. With depleted energy levels and increasing fatigue denied, they know that if they stop for an instant, they might never start up again. They are locked into a program that motivates them into a state of extreme martyrdom. Their self-esteem is low and they have persuaded themselves that sublimating all their personal needs is the only way to behave.

Strange though it may sound, illness can sometimes actually improve your health.

WHEN NATURE TAKES A HAND

If someone is stretched to breaking point, nature sometimes takes matters in hand and kicks in with a survival strategy. Sometimes people really do need to be ill because it is in fact the only way they will be able to survive in the end. Getting sick means having to stay at home and probably resting in bed.

Whatever denials are lodged in that person's mind have been countered by their unconscious mind, which has summarized the situation and forced the issue. A stressed-out mind will create enough physical symptoms to place that person effectively in the situation they need most. An individual in this predicament needs to get ill in order to get better.

When blood drains from the head and rushes downward, it precedes a faint, which is nature's way of putting people into horizontal mode when they need to be taken out of themselves for a few seconds. When people faint at extreme pain or shock, it is because their mind finds the situation intolerable and so therefore organizes this brief respite.

Unconscious caring

The power our minds exert over our bodies may not necessarily register consciously at the time, but when you look back at what has happened, you may well picture things differently. With the wisdom of hindsight comes a greater awareness, and what seemed pointless then suddenly becomes very clear now.

We look after ourselves on different levels, whether overtly or whether prompted by the deepest of our natural instincts, often buried so far down in our unconscious mind that we hardly even know of their existence. If we send out any instructions at all, we may not realize it fully, but that does not necessarily mean that our inner voice is not communicating with the outside world. Just because we are not listening and cannot or simply choose not to hear, it does not automatically make it ineffective.

Survival is a very ancient and primitive instinct, and however socialized and civilized we regard ourselves as being today, when the health of our body is jeopardized for whatever reason and desperately needs a period of rest to recuperate, or the mind is so overworked that it also needs some respite, very often an illness is the only way of making these things happen. Strange though it may sound, illness can sometimes actually improve your health.

ALIENATED BY ILLNESS

In some communities, healing involves everyone. When we lived near our extended families with grandparents, aunts, and uncles just down the street, if anyone was ill everyone rallied around. Today, young people grow up and leave home then move away, often to a different town or city, even a different country and continent. In these circumstances, when sickness strikes, the automatic assumption that friends will help out the way families used to is often misplaced, prevented by geographical distance.

Many people have no idea what to do or say when someone becomes ill and are overcome with awkwardness and embarrassment in the face of sickness. Illness still has the capacity to inspire fear in others, just as it did in the Middle Ages. Given the number of contagious and potentially fatal diseases, there was some justification for such trepidation. However, there are a great many people today whose fear of close contact with sick people is based on superstition rather than fact, and they refuse to even visit a hospital in case they are somehow tempting fate and might also become ill themselves. Those people who avoid the sick are generally not callous but often just terrified by illness – their perception of it is colored by their own fear. Many of us think of ourselves when others are ill. What will we say? Will we feel uncomfortable? How do you comfort someone when their illness is really serious?

Helping to heal others

Touching and hugging can be healing. People find sanctuary in silence, and sometimes saying nothing is important. Many people who have become ill find they cannot share their thoughts because they are too painful, muddled, incomprehensible, or just too personal. Silence leaves a space for these thoughts to be sorted out and dealt with whenever that person is ready. Allowing them that space of silent companionship is a valuable healing gift.

Illness can be isolating. Just as thoughts inside one's head can become distorted, so the thoughts of a sick person, left alone to dwell on their condition, can run away with them, taking on a perspective they do not merit. Being there acts as a valuable and gentle reminder of reality. Compassion for another person is healing, and someone sick will always respond to this soothing energy. By concentrating your own power, you can become a channel through which your own vibrant, healthy energy can be transmitted to another. This is sharing your power.

RIGHT **Silence is often more soothing in situations where words are inadequate, and the power of touch can be the most effective healer.**

INVESTING IN ILLNESS

People who failed to learn the art of self-reliance when they were children may well have had parents who deliberately created this dependency, possibly because they were adults who used this device to satisfy their own needs.

The love that parents extend to their children is unconditional and takes no account of faults or failings, because that kind of love surpasses such things. Nothing in later life compares to such generosity. Many adults whose childhood was devoid of this affection emerge emotionally bruised, never feeling particularly wanted or needed by anyone.

Hunger for love

When such people are starved of their fundamental emotional needs, the arrival of an infant who depends on them for everything is greeted with an enormous emotional hunger. The parent whose self-esteem is low and longs to be loved unconditionally has a vested interest in keeping his or her child in an emotionally needy

> *The love that parents extend to their children is unconditional and takes no account of faults or failings, because that kind of love surpasses such things.*

state. The moment the child prefers school friends to family is a precursor to another day this parent dreads, the time when the child becomes a young adult and decides to leave home.

Instead of encouraging the child to grow into an independent being equipped to face the world, this parent will encourage illness instead, because then she will always have a role in her child's life. Having a sick child fulfils her need to be needed.

In extreme cases, parents have actually injured their children or given them food or drinks that make them sick, and generally create an impression of illness before seeking out a doctor. Their love for their child has been swamped by their desperation and they are even prepared to hurt that child if that is what it takes to keep the child needy and dependent on them.

LEFT **A secure child, aware of being much loved, will develop into an independent adult. Wise parents encourage independence, realizing that they will not always be on hand to deal with life's ups and downs.**

Stunting the emotions

Spoiling a child can stunt their emotional growth. Every time they scream or cry, the parents rush to soothe them, giving them whatever they demand, desperate to placate this angry child. The angry child then grows into an angry adult, who bullies their way through school and goes on to become a demanding husband or wife and bullying parent. The only way they have of measuring their own success is through the defeat of others. The only way they know how to win is through the process of intimidation.

The pampered child also suffers from stunted emotions. Unlike the spoiled child, they have no need to even scream or cry because the dedicated parents rush to do everything for them before they even have a chance. Every need is met long before the child has time to even think about what they want or what will suit their needs best. This child grows up with no sense of discrimination and without courage. Life has never had to be tested, and, therefore, they have never had to learn through failure.

But they have also been denied the triumph of a success. They have no visions or dreams of their future because they have never had to stretch their imagination to think beyond the here and now. Because everything they could need or want was provided when they were young, it comes as a shock to discover that the adult world does not behave this way. These are adults with childlike minds, innocent and unaware of their own abilities.

Faking illness

Naturally, life is difficult for such people and from time to time, usually when those difficulties overwhelm them, they seek comfort and solace in the sort of situations where it was always provided. They revert to the behavior that most children try at some point in their schooldays, in which they attempt to persuade their parents that they were too ill to go to school that day. But where most mothers and fathers are far too astute to allow their children to get away with fake illness, adults rarely have to face such a confrontation.

If anyone suspects the condition is convenient rather than genuine, there is generally an embarrassment surrounding such a deception and an understandable reluctance to challenge such a person. It is this hesitant attitude that such people rely on. How dreadful it would be to accuse someone of faking an illness only to find out that their suffering was real.

LEFT **The spoiled child cries and its parents immediately give in to its demands. This can establish a pattern of bullying that carries on in adult life.**

SELF-HEALING
Meditation for Reconnection

Here are some questions to contemplate during your meditation. Please make sure you have a pen and paper to write down your thoughts as quickly as you can after meditating.

CONTEMPLATIONS

➜ Could you name, without hesitating, the most important person or event in your life?

➜ Would you make up an excuse to cancel a meeting with someone if you heard they had a bad cold?

➜ Do you welcome other people turning to you for emotional support and find it flattering?

➜ Do you wish you were stronger physically so you could try and excel at different and more energetic sports?

➜ Do you find it difficult to visit people in hospital because illness makes you depressed?

Meditation

When we try to escape from ourselves, all we usually do is end up in a different kind of prison. Whatever devices we use to adorn the truth only makes it emerge in a different guise. Games of hide-and-seek lead to revelations and discovery. Self-discovery frees you from the shackles of self-deception.

When your eyes are closed, I want you to think about the four seasons of the year. Begin with summer and imagine you are sitting in a garden as the season is drawing to a close. The heat of the noonday sun has lost its intensity and the long, light evenings are beginning to feel slightly cooler. Walk around this garden and look at the flowers, stopping to enjoy their scent or their blooms.

Notice how some flowers are still in a state of glorious splendor, seemingly oblivious to the impending changes that will come with the fall season, changes that will alter their appearance dramatically as their petals droop and fall.

Now imagine you have a very old oak tree in this garden. It was planted hundreds of years ago, and as you look up at its branches, think about the different generations to whom it has offered refreshing shade on the hottest days of summer. Think about the children who played beneath it, then grew up beside it and enjoyed the quiet respite it offered them as they sat beneath it in the later years. See it as a living legacy of days gone by.

Many dramatic events may have taken place, wars won or lost, presidents and monarchs come and gone, children born, married, and passed on, and through it all this magnificent tree stood firm and solid, a living witness to history.

Notice how this tree is always the last to open its leaf buds in the spring and the last to lose its leaves in the fall, as though its sheer height and breadth is so vast that the changes of season take longer to permeate its wide trunk and filter out to its many branches.

Now walk across the lawn toward a vegetable garden. As you do this, notice the buzz of insects and the sounds of the birds, the rustle of leaves in the slight breeze. These are the sounds of nature at this particular time of the year, and if you walk across this same patch of lawn in two months' time, those sounds will have changed as nature reflects the new season.

Look down at the vegetables still growing and imagine how this piece of land will look in a few months' time, perhaps with a covering of light snow, hardly recognizable as the fertile soil in front of your eyes now. The ground will be hard from frost and difficult to turn over, and without the warming rays of the sun will feel cold to the touch.

Look back now to the other part of the garden you have just left behind you and visualize it in the spring. See the first spring flowers appear, and watch the birds flitting to and fro, building their nests under the eaves. The old oak will look very majestic with its bare branches spanning an ever greater expanse, and notice the tiny buds on other trees racing to open and soak up the sunshine after the long winter.

Reflect on the way the seasons change so smoothly, passing from one season into the next as they have done since the beginning of time in an unchanging pattern. Reflect on the way the energy of each season changes as one makes room for another. The frenzied growing energy of spring as the first pale rays of sun appear gives way to the strong energy that comes in with the splendour of summer, bringing long days and warm nights.

Fall introduces a calming energy as the leaves turn from green to yellow and gold, and the nights begin to close in. As the last leaves drop from the trees and the frosts appear in the early mornings, the ground hardens and prepares for the long winter sleep. Winter's energy is about sleep and change, rest and restoration, conserving its strength for the period of renewal ahead.

Reflect on how many changing seasons you have seen and how many more lie ahead of you, and no matter what happens in your world, these changes are inevitable and have been taking place since the dawn of time. They can become your personal boundaries, offering a secure and reassuring structure on which you can build up and renew your own energies, using their absolute reliability as your yardstick for measuring your judgment.

SELF-HEALING
Meditation for Reconnection

Reflect on how little subterfuge occurs in nature – what happens is what you see happen. The invisible growth energy that is busy during the long winter sleep makes its presence felt in the spring. The strong energy of summer flaunts itself with pride and the calm fall energy gently soothes all this activity, so that when it is time to sleep, the restorative energy can do its work.

Reflect on how this relates to your own energies. Compare your energy vibrations with those of the seasons and see how the pattern emerges with perfect precision as long as you trust its ability and believe in its constancy.

Notice how the seasons provide a backdrop for every kind of activity, emotion, thought, or sensation, and whatever happens in your life, however important, sad, or happy, barely touches the seasons whose only concern is to maintain their ancient patterns. Notice the oak tree again and consider how many people have lived out their life span while it steadily spread its branches and reached even higher.

Imagine all the happiness and sadness, delight and despair, brilliance and absurdity, joy and hopelessness it would have outlived, steadily and consistently offering its sturdy presence as a reflection of how much tiny details can be exaggerated and how little the very important things matter.

Before you end this meditation, keep this oak tree and the changing seasons in your thoughts and use them as a metaphor for the health of your mind and body, giving you insight as to ways of conserving your energies so that they can coexist constructively.

Record your first thoughts

As soon as you can, write down the first thoughts that occur to you after this meditation.

What your responses reveal

Mostly "yes" answers

Illness, yours and other people's, has a starring role in your life. It fascinates you and also fills you with fear because it means so many other things. You use illness. You hide behind it, turn it into an alibi, or manipulate it for emotional leverage, either to attract sympathy or as a bolster for your self-esteem. Your beliefs may well go right back to your childhood, but they are not healthy, merely a habit. You have no sense of where you belong in the world or the value of your place in it, so you return to the only structures that you believe define you. Use your precious energies to discover more about life instead of wasting them clinging to the past. You are like the male spider whose compulsion to mate with a female is stronger than his fear that she will kill him. You both suspend belief but the inevitable nearly always happens. The spider will die and you will attract all the illness you fear.

 Answer this: Only you can know how deep your discontentment goes, just as only you can decide to shake it off. Have you considered that letting go of the past means you are on the brink of discovering how much bigger and better life can be?

LEFT **Contemplate this magnificent old oak tree and consider its ability to outlive generations of human beings. Use its example of strength and endurance to find ways of conserving your own energies.**

Mostly "no" answers

Your outlook reflects your healthy mind and body because you do not allow illness to impact on your life or prevent you from enjoying it to the full.

 Reflect on this: Making your life healthy does not have to be a struggle. It can be a joyful experience.

Half "yes," half "no" answers

You are in state of limbo. Your lack of self-worth means you are quite surprised you have come as far as you have, and this same lack of confidence is keeping you from going any farther. The symptoms of ill health are signals and if ignored for too long become warning signals. If you can examine some of your fears and find other meanings, you will discover how much you can learn and acknowledge the tremendous progress you have already made. There is no league table to compare achievements and accomplishments because we all define them differently.

 Consider this: You decide what matters to you and make it happen that way just as only you can fully understand the pleasure and satisfaction it gives you.

Affirmation

I will see things as they really are, but not worse than they are. Then I will see them the way I want them and make them the way I want them.

ASSESSING TREATMENTS
FOR ILL HEALTH

When illness strikes, you need to play your part fully in securing the most effective and appropriate treatment. As I have stressed before, no one else knows as much about you as you do yourself, so it makes sense to find out as much as you can about your condition and see what treatments suit you best, whether modern medications, complementary therapies, or a combination of both. Apply common sense, follow your instincts, and above all listen to what your mind and body are telling you.

How modern medications work

The medicines most of us are familiar with today can be divided into major groups aimed at specific points in the body, designed to minimize or alleviate symptoms rather than cure a condition (see pages 209–15 for a guide). In fact, it is doubtful whether any drug exists today that can do this. However, if you remove all the symptoms of an illness, you could argue that this is, in fact, the same as curing it. Without symptoms, after all, how can such a condition exist? What drugs can do is knock out the symptoms while the body's natural defenses promote the process of recovery.

While some of today's medications can save lives, there are other drug groups that specifically target the various discomforts people experience. There are drugs to anesthetize patients for surgery, relax tension, lift depression, curb appetite, bring down blood pressure, slow heart rate, accelerate kidney function, and replace depleted hormones. There are antihistamines to combat allergies, antiseptics to fight infection, antibiotics to kill bacteria, and antifungals to deal with fungal outbreaks, plus a whole range of betablockers that "block" mechanisms when there is damage to be repaired.

Newer drugs that will supersede the existing ones are being developed all the time, some improved versions of the originals, others working in a totally different way. Naturally, some drugs are stronger than others – the range of painkillers

RIGHT **Pharmaceutical drugs offer relief from symptoms rather than tackling the underlying cause of an ailment, and their increasing sophistication means that they are being aimed more and more specifically at precise target areas of the body.**

available today can deal with the gentlest of headaches to the much more severe pain of, for instance, renal colic or gallstones.

The right dose

No one can guess how a drug will react on a particular patient. Doctors can estimate the dosage through a set of reliable, established statistics and generally such measures prove correct, but no one can eliminate the chance of individuals reacting differently. The dosage that works with one patient may have no effect on another.

Some adults may only need a child's dose and find a larger, adult-sized dose is too much for their system. What may be recommended as a therapeutic dose for one patient may hardly impact on another. Often a drug such as a synthesized hormone stimulates the body into producing more of its own natural version, which immediately throws the levels out of balance. This can happen when women are prescribed hormone-replacement therapy and their medication comes in prepared packs, one dose for all.

Some women experience such severe side effects that they stop taking their drugs, in spite of the benefits they might bring. But each individual metabolizes substances at different rates, and it could be that a reduced dose would reduce the undesirable side effects and still be sufficiently therapeutic. It could be that these women are not actually having a bad reaction to their medication, but are perhaps just suffering from the effects of an overdose that could easily be adjusted. Sometimes the smallest observation is enough to change the entire outcome, and your instincts are able to guide you very accurately on such issues.

Weighing benefits against risks

Drugs often produce side effects, which means the patient experiences various symptoms that have nothing to do with the beneficial, intended effects for which the drug is prescribed. These can be minor, harmless symptoms that are easily tolerated. An adverse reaction, however, can be more serious, such as an allergic reaction. Among the commonest allergies to medications are penicillin and aspirin. Reactions are preventable in both cases as long as the patient informs their doctor, because there are adequate alternatives to both.

However, an anaphylactic reaction is much more serious and can be life-threatening. People who risk the allergic symptoms of anaphylaxis are normally aware of the substances that trigger it and avoid them for the sake of their own welfare. The commonest ones come from either eating nuts or being stung by a wasp or bee, and people with these allergies carry a syringe containing adrenalin for use in the event of emergencies because this reaction can very rapidly lead to unconsciousness and cardiac arrest.

ABOVE AND LEFT **An anaphylactic reaction, to such things as wasp and bee stings or nuts, can be fatal. It can happen within seconds or can be delayed by 30 minutes or more. If adrenalin is not administered immediately, the individual may lose consciousness and stop breathing.**

177

Harming not healing

Drugs can be toxic. This means they can actually poison you if you have too much or if they clash with your system and produce an adverse reaction. Taking too high a dose of any drug can change it from a beneficial medicine into a poisonous substance with the potential to kill. That said, what is a high dose for one person may not be for another, and in an ideal world, the dosage of every medication would be measured individually to suit each person's needs.

This accounts for the different levels of tolerance when drinking alcohol, because there are many variations in the rate of absorption and one person may become intoxicated far more quickly than another, even though they have both drunk the same quantity.

Many drugs are abused today, which means they are obtained illegally. Some of the most potentially dangerous drugs that can lead to both psychological and physical addiction come under the category of "controlled drugs," or they are "dangerous drugs" and issued under very specific conditions only. However, many of the drugs available from drug stores without a prescription can be lethal if an overdose is taken, including aspirin, leading to substantial damage and often death.

Many of the drugs available from drug stores without a prescription can be lethal if an overdose is taken.

YOUR RESPONSIBILITY

Learn about your drugs. Many side effects can be countered by avoiding certain foods or alcohol, or by selecting a suitable complementary therapy. Read the directions carefully. Check the label and store in a cool, dry place well away from moisture or sunshine. If the directions call for the drug to be kept in a refrigerator, do not freeze it.

Always make sure your doctor has your full medical history so that any indications against certain drugs will be on your record. Your medical history can also alert your doctor to any current medication you are on, so that you are not given any drugs that might clash.

For the same reasons, never save leftover medication or offer it to others. What suits you could be disastrous for someone else. Women should always tell their doctor if they suspect they are pregnant, even if it is only by a matter of days, because many of today's drugs could cause damage to a fetus even in the very early stages.

LEFT **Always consult your doctor before giving medication to a child. Children need a much smaller dosage than adults to achieve the same effect.**

20 questions for your doctor

Ask your doctor these questions before taking any new medication he or she prescribes.

1 How should you take the medication – before food, with food, or after food?

2 What time of day should you take it?

3 What should you do if you forget a dose?

4 How does the drug work?

5 How long before it begins to work?

6 Should you avoid any substances when taking it?

7 Does your drug cause photosensitivity, does it react adversely in bright sunlight?

8 Is it safe to drive, operate machinery, or pilot an airplane, when taking the drug?

9 Is it safe to take while you are pregnant?

10 Will it have a damaging affect on your baby if you are breast-feeding?

11 Is the drug likely to combine well or badly with other medications?

12 Will drinking alcohol, tea, or coffee, or smoking while taking the medication limit the drug's absorption and hinder its effectiveness?

13 How much do you need the prescription? Will the condition cure itself without medication?

14 What should be done in the event of an accidental overdose?

15 What are the likely, most frequently experienced side effects?

16 What are the more uncommon side effects?

17 Do the side effects increase with prolonged use compared to a short course of the drug?

18 How should you stop taking the drug – at the end of the course or should it be reduced gradually?

19 Do your drugs have a use-by date?

20 Is the name of your drug its brand name or its generic name?

RIGHT **A visit to your doctor should be relaxed and informative. Do not be afraid to ask questions to make sure you are receiving the right treatment – an enlightened physician will be happy to help.**

HELPING YOU TO HELP YOURSELF

How many times have you heard someone say they are taking pills but have no idea what they are, what they do, or what they are called? It is unlikely these same people would order a dish in a restaurant without knowing its name or what ingredients it contained, so why bask in ignorance when it comes to taking a potentially highly toxic substance? If your doctor fails to give you advice on taking medication or undergoing any other treatments or refuses to answer any of your questions, trust your instincts and change your doctor. There are plenty of enlightened physicians who are only too pleased to give their patients as much information as they want and so help them to help themselves.

Following instructions

Your doctor or practice nurse should be able to give you information concerning the action of the drug, the side effects, the time in which it is likely to work, and when and how you should discontinue it (see page 179). The latter is important, because while you can simply stop taking some drugs, others need to be reduced gradually, and in the case of antibiotics it is essential to complete a full course of treatment.

There may be occasions when the side effects of a drug you have been prescribed are unavoidable. In other words, the reasons for giving you this drug are sufficiently important and the benefits it will bring are enough to warrant its negative side effects. In such a situation, there is a balance of risks. Saving your life might mean taking a drug that has unpleasant side effects, and many patients undergoing chemotherapy for cancer suffer the difficult side effects of their treatment because they realize that it often leads to a cure.

The more information you have about your medications, the greater your chances of experiencing fewer side effects and speeding your recovery. There are many therapies that literally complement mainstream medicine, as opposed to presenting an alternative, and these are often able to counter the worst side effects which, in turn, boosts your sense of well-being and improves your rate of recovery.

THE ROLE OF NATURAL HEALING

Does the new millennium herald a subtle change in our approach to healing? Researchers at Harvard Medical School have reported a 50 percent increase in the number of people visiting practitioners of alternative therapies over a 10-year period. Now that may only reflect a fraction of the population, but the increase represents nearly half as much again as that fraction.

Consumer choice

The fact that this swing to natural healing therapies has been called one of the biggest consumer phenomena of the last 100 years is not without its ironies if it indicates that people are rejecting conventional medicine. One hundred years ago, no antibiotics existed and blood poisoning from a cut finger could prove fatal. Childhood diseases were not preventable, tuberculosis killed thousands, and the high mortality rate of mothers in childbirth and their new-born infants was one of the biggest challenges facing the medical profession.

LEFT **The touch of a complementary therapist corrects subtle imbalances in the body before they cause serious problems.**

The shortcomings of conventional medicine

HAROLD GAIER, a qualified naturopath, homeopath, and osteopath:

❛There has been a great division in medical thought as far back in time as Hippocrates. My father was a professor of medicine at the University of Vienna, my sister is a veterinary surgeon, and my uncle is an orthopedic surgeon in Austria, and I have seen the shortcomings of rationalist medicine. It has always looked to science for explanations, and I found that quite frightening because, other than antibiotics, nothing actually cures.

The constant prescribing of medicines such as cortisone creams and inhalers, steroids for arthritis, sleeping pills, and antidepressants just keeps the cash registers ringing for the pharmaceutical industry. They all work while the patients continue to take them and stop when they stop. People continue to suffer from their problems and need repeat prescriptions, and it becomes a bottomless pit financially.

Also, pharmaceutical drugs have various effects – I believe the description "side effects" is actually misleading because what the patient experiences are all effects, just not all the desired effects. For example, a steroid may reduce the pain in a joint but you may have bleeding internally and mineral loss from your bones.

I use acupuncture and osteopathy, homeopathy, and herbalism to manipulate diets and correct a lifestyle – whatever I think is going to make the patient better. But what the patient wants to know is – does this work?❜

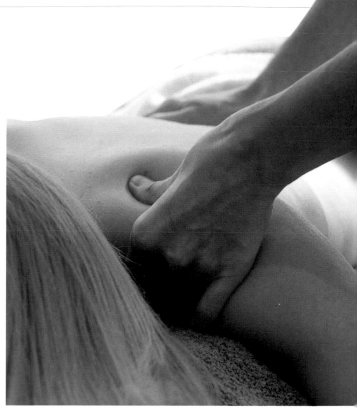

ABOVE **One of the oldest forms of remedial therapy, massage is an excellent way to relax both the mind and the body, and so bring relief from everyday stresses and strains.**

What seems to be happening instead is that an increasing number of people are combining the old wisdoms alongside the new, making so-called alternative therapies literally complementary in the truest sense of the word. We are seeing a growing number of integrated practices springing up in which medical doctors offer a variety of therapies to patients as adjuncts to pharmaceutical remedies.

Differences of opinion

Doctors and therapists involved in healthcare, however, have widely differing views. Some think the multidisciplinary approach offers patients the best of both worlds, while others believe in the pragmatic, evidence-based scientific systems for testing all remedies, whatever their origin. Some health practitioners believe that orthodox medicine and its symptom-based, chemical remedies should be avoided.

LEFT **Much of modern medicine is based upon early herbal practices – most conventional drugs contain synthesized extracts and essences of herbs and plants. The active constituents of many ancient natural remedies are the key ingredients of many of today's proprietary drugs.**

OLD WISDOMS – NEW WISDOMS

As far as ancient wisdoms go, it might be true to say that there is nothing new under the sun. Modern medicine has adapted ancient remedies and synthesized them for a mass market. Aspirin, one of the most widely used drugs today, originates from willow; digitalis for heart conditions comes from the foxglove; the Mexican yam gave us the contraceptive pill, and the rosy periwinkle, which grows in tropical rain forests, has dramatically reversed the outcome of childhood leukemia.

The alternative remedies marketed directly to consumers include St. John's wort for depression, hailed as the natural version of Prozac, echinacea against colds and influenza; gingko biloba to heighten mental alertness; and goldenseal to boost the immune system. Ginseng is sold as an energizer, kava and valerian are recommended for their calming properties, and there are many, many more such remedies, some dating back thousands of years. There are also dozens of mineral and vitamin supplements aimed at a dispirited consumer market whose food is so refined that it often fails to contain the much-needed nutrients it once delivered.

LEFT **Much of modern medicine is based upon early herbal practices – most conventional drugs contain synthesized extracts and essences of herbs and plants. The active constituents of many ancient natural remedies are the key ingredients of many of today's proprietary drugs.**

Substances that were once freely available have now been banned. Certain cough mixtures containing morphine were sold without a doctor's prescription. The Victorians' liberal use of laudanum as a panacea for most conditions led to many people becoming addicted to this narcotic derivative.

The promise of good health

All this tells us how anxious people are about their health and how susceptible we can be when it comes to being offered what purports to be the elixir of life. As we have seen, conventional medicine once nurtured the aura of the white coat, in which the doctors' authority was never challenged. In those days, most patients had no idea what medication they were on, and because the consultations were so brief, they had little time in which to ask. Thankfully, today those attitudes have changed dramatically, but not entirely.

If practitioners who offer herbal medicines and supplements seem to have a greater appeal for people, maybe it is because they spend more time

BELOW **Herbal remedies and supplements can be contaminated during growing** **and processing, so try to buy them from a reputable source.**

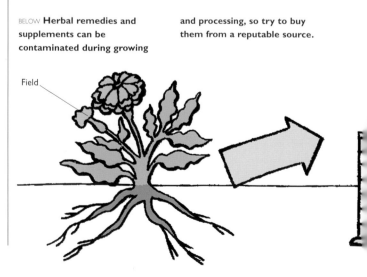

Field

with their patients who appreciate being able to discuss the dynamics of their own health needs. Perhaps it is also because the ethos of alternative therapies hands responsibility for health back to the patient.

"Natural" effects

Perhaps the biggest drawback when a substance is called "natural" is the implication that it is therefore safe. Many of the products sold as food supplements bypass the normal regulations that apply to drugs, and are often mass-produced in factories, while many more are grown in countries where the liberal use of pesticides is common practice and the contents are inconsistent and inaccurately described.

I would certainly recommend that everyone explores the alternatives, and at the same time keeps their medical doctor fully informed, particularly if taking a herbal remedy alongside a pharmaceutical one. Everything medicinal originates in nature and has many different effects as well as the desired one, and any one of them can conflict with other substances. Trust your intuition and be guided by its wisdom. We live in a far too enlightened age to be misled by promises that fail to deliver, just as we can keep fully informed about the modern medicines we are offered.

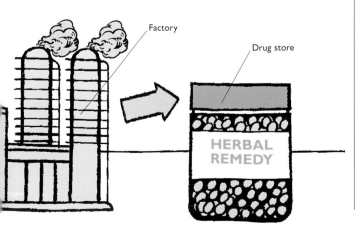

Factory

Drug store

HERBAL REMEDY

Iscador therapy

HAROLD GAIER, qualified naturopath, homeopath, and osteopath

❝With certain types of cancer, Iscador therapy is effective. This substance is an extract of mistletoe, and the philosophy behind its use is based on anthroposophy's "doctrine of signatures," which believes in using nature as an indicator for remedies.

In this case, mistletoe is a parasitical plant, a foreign body that adheres itself to a tree to grow, just as cancer is a parasitical "foreign" body growing in a person. This is the indicator or signature, and on a dynamic level, mistletoe may regard the cancer cell as a competitor that threatens its own survival unless eliminated. This is the basis of its action.

Since published studies show that Iscador therapy alongside conventional treatment can increase the five-year survival period, this means it is better than doing nothing and as good as, if not better than, the best existing treatment results. This includes the three mainstays of orthodox medicine – radiation, chemotherapy, and surgery. An improvement on longevity means just that.❞

Your attitude and lifestyle profoundly affect your state of mind because your immune system is responsive to the subtle messages you send to your brain. Waking up each morning feeling happy sends positive signals. Beginning the day as though a black cloud were hovering over you produces a negative effect. Since the mind has the power to regulate the body's physical responses, we should, therefore, try to be as contented as possible to ward off ill health and fight disease. It also follows that the happier we are, the greater access we have to the sixth sense, the intuitive part of our mind that shapes our lives.

10 | THE SECRET OF LOVE AND HAPPINESS

THE NATURE OF HAPPINESS

In an ideal world, everyone would choose to be happy and enjoy peace of mind, but the reality is much more complicated to achieve. If some people's lives seem destined to thrive while others are disaster-prone, is this a matter of good or bad luck? Why are some born into wealth and influence and others into hardship?

We all know people who seem to lead charmed lives. They have a lightness of spirit that is infectious and affects everyone whose lives they touch. They enjoy each day to the full almost as if they were born with such a gift. Others have a darkness about them, a deepness and intensity that signals a troubled attitude, weighed down with worry in their serious world in which frivolity and laughter are simply out of place.

The energy they send out feels very different. Those for whom life is happy and joyous attract others to them because their vibrations are attractive and appealing. People feel relaxed in their company and pick up their mood, joining in the lightness of the atmosphere, enjoying the laughter.

The other kind of energy is spiky, as though it signals "proceed with caution." It hints at underlying tensions and warns you to choose your words carefully. The vibrations being sent out jangle your senses, and instead of being relaxed, you pick up the tension in the atmosphere and adapt your own behavior accordingly.

It is natural to find happy people much more appealing company than somber people. Happy people attract others because they are easier to deal with and are less likely to react adversely should you put a foot out of place. They would probably find humor in your mistake compared to the other kind who would suspect a motive instantly.

In search of happiness

The importance of happiness in our lives drives us to look in all kinds of places as though it were a commodity that we could find in a store. Or, we look to someone else to provide it, to make us happy. Or, maybe we search for what we think we want only to discover that our needs have changed. Some look in the wrong places, others expect it to come to them automatically as if by divine right.

LEFT **Happiness is infectious. If you send out positive signals to other people, the warmth you experience in return will enrich your life.**

1 85

WHEN HAPPINESS IS UNDERMINED

Some people give up on happiness believing they will never be happy because of what they have already endured in their lives. An unhappy childhood can prevent enjoyment of adult life, just as events and influences can cause emotional damage and block happiness when the child grows up. Being unhappy can be a normal state of mind, and in such situations, if this is what you know best, it is also what you cling to most.

Adverse circumstances

Circumstances can create victims as well as motivate people to move metaphorical mountains. The influences surrounding our lives determine the way we could be but not necessarily the way we will be. How we deal with circumstances is what makes the difference.

If yours have held you back and you believe they have contributed to the way you are today, you can do two things. First of all, identify the parts of yourself that you believe have been affected, the kind of memories that trigger certain thoughts and actions. The second step is to work out positive ways of making these negative elements work for you instead of against you.

Children who suffer insecurity about their own potential can develop a deep fear of failure when they grow up and give up trying before they have really started. These feelings provide an excuse to ignore their other fears – fear of not being good enough, fear of not measuring up in a highly competitive world. These fears can turn inward and become fear of living and lead to anxiety, stress, and depression as well as many physical conditions.

We know the mind is capable of producing such illnesses as well as capable of curing them. But healing from within demands concentration and a crystal clear mind, uncluttered by distracting self-doubts. Love is vital, yet we rarely give love to ourselves, often failing to appreciate the person we have become, neglecting our most attractive qualities, because our perceptions are cloaked in the false modesty of our upbringing.

Preparing for the worst

What happens, then, if everything is taken away? What happens when the unimaginable happens, an unforeseen event? Where do the mental resources for coping come from? How can we live with both pleasure and pain?

No one can be complacent about life, and we should all make allowances for the unpredictable to disrupt our best-laid plans. Naturally, those who enjoy peace of mind and contentment will be

in a better state to deal with the worst that life can throw at them compared to those people already in an unhappy state of mind.

Measuring happiness

Love and happiness are vital ingredients for well-being, but they are defined in many different ways. For some people, the idea of happiness is having 50 pairs of shoes, a set of solid gold tableware, or a fabulous car such as a Ferrari. Some might define it as the kind of financial security that means never having to worry about money ever again. Happiness can come from being in a job you enjoy, from passing an examination, or from a long and rewarding relationship. Others attach a moral value to happiness, claiming money cannot buy it. But there are plenty of rich, happy people who are living testimony to the fact that happiness can come from material things – not from their acquisition as such but from that person's ability to enjoy them.

Happiness is often a state of mind we are not aware of until we look back at our memories, which then remind us how happy we were at such times. Happiness is a continuing, ongoing state of mind in which we live normal lives and do normal things. It comes from relationships, raising children, and pride in achievement, or often just from the pleasure of being among good, close friends. It usually takes a significant problem or a major upheaval to interrupt our lives for us to realize how happy we actually were until it came along.

What makes you happy?

One of the first steps in your search for a happier and more contented life is to identify the things you would love to do but have never thought possible, or never been in a position to achieve. Do not apply the normal life limitations or allow your thoughts to become weighed down by concerns about your responsibilities, your job, friends, or family. Do not even begin to consider whether other people might laugh at your ambitions or be scornful of them.

Happiness is often a state of mind we are not aware of until we look back at our memories, which then remind us how happy we were at such times.

ABOVE **We all have different ways of measuring and defining personal happiness, whether it is owning a luxury yacht or a diamond ring, living in a mansion, or jetting off to a dream destination. But happiness is a state of mind we can all possess through the course of our normal everyday lives.**

RIGHT **Family relationships, a great source of contentment, need sustenance in the form of love and understanding.**

THE MEANING OF SUCCESS

Open your mind and allow yourself to dream, expanding all your normal boundaries as you create a world inside your mind where there are not any barriers and anything is possible. Then ask yourself, however unlikely it might seem, is there anyone who has ever achieved such a thing, or at least something close to it?

If the answer is yes, then look at that person, because you have now identified your personal role model. Take a long, appraising look, because there are questions to be asked here and the first one is – why them and not you? If the response is clear cut and there are several practical reasons, begin looking at those reasons with the same eagle-eyed observation. You may discover that they are not so much reasons as in fact excuses for problems that have to be overcome.

Paying the price

Look at the success that your role model has enjoyed and ask yourself seriously if you both share the same definition of the word success. Sometimes the emotional price that successful people pay can be disastrous, demanding a level of dedication and self-sacrifice that leaves little room for anything else in their lives. This kind of success can mean that loved ones – wives, husbands, and children – have to be slotted into a packed schedule, which calls for an inevitable shifting of priorities.

Then ask yourself – is this really what you want? What prize is worth so much that anything that detracts from your goal gets ignored?

On the other hand, there is another kind of success that does not require such a ruthless disregard of other commitments. People who achieve what they want without abandoning other elements of their lives, such as their family and friends, have merely allocated their time differently to accommodate the things that they hold dear. They have carefully planned their lifestyle to take on board their priorities, instead of accepting that there is only one way and no other.

They do not want a life that eliminates anything except the final goal.

Freedom of choice

What they have effectively achieved is the freedom to make decisions about what happens in their lives instead of allowing life events to become the decisive factors. This in turn reinforces their self-confidence, since it reminds them of the way they have created a life that suits their needs instead of rushing headlong into pursuing goals that fail to make them happy.

People who are focused can visualize a positive ending when they set out to achieve, and they keep this in their mind through all the difficult setbacks. Sometimes their desire for the prize changes and they do not want it as much as they did before, or they see something else they now realize they would much prefer. This is where the ability to be flexible is vital.

Your right to change

Being able to acknowledge a mistake or a change of mind will make you far happier than clinging desperately to whatever you first thought of, as though changing your mind is somehow unstable. Switching your thinking is actually healing. A mistake is only a mistake – holding onto things you no longer want just because you feel you ought to is damaging.

The sheer relief of letting go of whatever is unwanted and giving yourself permission to alter your course should you want brings a refreshing sense of freedom into your life. Most of us have

People who are focused can visualize a positive ending when they set out to achieve, and they keep this in mind through all the difficult setbacks.

probably been adapting at different stages throughout our lives without necessarily realizing it. The things we choose as adults are the result of our more sophisticated selection processes.

As a child you might have chosen a vivid bright color which as an adult you would consider garish, and so you opt to wear something much more subtle. The idealism surrounding a child's perception of life makes way for practicalities in the future. Little boys who wanted to be engine drivers or little girls who thought they might become nurses grow up to see their choices through much more pragmatic eyes.

As a child, being singled out in a classroom would be viewed with trepidation, and you might have agreed with all the others in the class just to safeguard yourself against this. As an adult, your opinions may consider other factors, but ultimately whatever you decide is what you believe in. If you are still conforming in spite of your misgivings, you are denying yourself the privilege of being true to yourself.

LEFT **Allow yourself the opportunity to make your own choices about what you want to achieve in the future, rather than letting events determine the outcome. But also give yourself the freedom to change your mind about what you want to achieve.**

THE APPEARANCE OF HAPPINESS

We are all born with what seems to be varying degrees of good fortune, and life can seem like a lottery in selecting winners and losers. Physical beauty is a matter of inheritance, although it seems like luck because our genes dictate our physical makeup. Whether you are tall or short, blonde or brunette, slim or rounded is decided at the moment of conception in a split second of time, based on your parents' genetic patterns.

When a baby is born, we peer endlessly into the cradle, scrutinizing its features to see whether it most resembles its mother or father. This ability to reproduce in our own image fascinates us all, and although it happens all the time, we still marvel at such similarities.

The lottery of looks

Looks can change the way your life goes – some young girls will have inherited exactly the right genetic ingredients to forge a career as a top model, and will probably earn large sums of money and enjoy celebrity as a result. What has happened to them is a matter of pure chance – their face and figure matches the contemporary ideal and they are in a position to embark on a career based on assets they were born with rather than achieved.

Living up to an ideal

The majority of people have less glamorous options because if we all looked like models there would be no aspirational prototypes, no quest for perfection. But would that be such a terrible thing? I am sure if a league table of happiness were ever invented, we would see that the construction of this ideal female form has led to far fewer happy people than you would expect compared to the unhappiness that has resulted.

Scores of young women, and increasingly young men, suffer from a wide range of eating disorders and compulsive behaviors in different degrees of severity, and I was once one of them. Many of these disorders originate from a desperation to conform to the role models that society has placed on impossibly high pedestals.

Living in fear

These conditions are becoming commonplace even among the ranks of those models whose so-called gifts have brought them fame and fortune. They suffer their own set of fears, in case they gain weight or lose their looks, and often fear the inevitable, such as growing older.

Curiously, this fear tends not to be based on a reasonably normal concern that a lucrative career could come to an end. Most of us would find such a worry completely understandable and in such a position make plans accordingly. But when someone is feted far beyond their own perception of their worth, it creates uneasiness. The perfect model girl exists in the eyes of others, but rarely in the eyes of the model herself. Since her world is built on her appearance, those looks take on an importance and value way beyond their real price. In some cases, each new day carries the increasing risk of being "found out," perhaps exposed as being less beautiful than people believe, or being revealed in the image they have of themselves.

Real values

Surviving in such a world demands survival tactics. The excitement when all the adulation began has to be tempered with both confidence and realism – confidence in themselves instead of just in their looks; realism in their attitude to the world in which they have found themselves. There are plenty of clichéd warnings on offer when someone is in such a celebrated position as well as plenty of advice.

But the survival tactic that works best is the one that applies in all such situations where the pressure of other peoples' opinions can persuade or confuse issues. Trust yourself, trust your own

judgment, trust your intelligence. The genetic patterns you inherit come with more than physical traits such as height or hair color. They pass on some of the ancient wisdoms that sustained so many previous generations and which are applicable in our modern world, too. Your thoughts may be affected by your emotions, but it is your spirit that is essentially untouched and essentially you.

You can enjoy happiness and still take advantage of all the wonderful gifts you have had bestowed on you without life turning sour and making you ill. We all have gifts, no matter what shape or form they manifest in us, and it is those gifts you have to bring out in yourself. A gift is a blessing, not a curse. Gifts bring pleasure, and they only turn into burdens if they are prized way beyond their true value, because this exaggerates the fear of their loss.

SAFETY IN MISERY

As I have explored in many ways in this book, there is a two-way communication between mind and body, and we send messages from one to the other continually. But are they always healthy messages?

Some of life's saddest situations attract the saddest people. We all know at least one commiserating friend at a funeral who consoles and sympathizes with barely concealed excitement, having found themselves cast in a real-life drama into which they can pour all the emotions they live with every day. They do not need to learn their script because they are already word perfect.

Knowing that others are going through the same bad experience as they are brings like-minded people together. Having felt isolated in their unhappiness, they can be tremendously relieved by the support of others who they believe will really understand their situation.

Feeding off unhappiness

If that compassion, however, just echoes all their worst fears, it only duplicates and enlarges the problem, and the only bonding that takes place is the kind that reinforces all the most negative aspects. Every time they relive what happened and go over the details again, they mentally take themselves back into the situation and suffer the same emotions all over again. This confirms that they are all powerless victims together. It is not a club I would recommend anyone should join.

Instead of looking at the broader picture of what happened to them, these people have concentrated all their thoughts into this one area, which has become magnified out of proportion. They have lost sight of all the other aspects of themselves as their problem has loomed larger and larger, swamping everything else until it becomes the main activity in their lives. What can begin by

RIGHT **It is easy to catch the mood of people around you, as those who have experienced the mass hysteria at a rock concert will testify. But if these infectious emotions are negative and connect with your own negative feelings, they will combine and multiply to form a mass of negativity.**

identifying another person's unhappiness as a brief justification for their own sadness moves on to bolster misplaced confidence.

The person who relishes a funeral has been feeding their negative thoughts for such a long time that they have become this negative person, whose pleasure and self-esteem is now so warped that it comes from other people's anguish. Their identity is now the same as the starring role, and to be part of this real-life scenario is a high point, something to look forward to, much as others might look forward to going to a party.

The grievance group who feed one another's gloom and doom are not unlike the young teenage girls who weep at pop concerts. Moods and behavior can be infectious, and when people find something in their own experience to tap into, they are only too willing to catch whatever is going around.

Handing it all back

When other people's words have the power to hurt you or their actions upset you, one of the surest ways of protecting yourself from these unpleasant emotions and causing you unhappiness is to use the power of your mind to hand it all back gently. If you can unload the weight of your burden, the negative energy it carried will flow out of you and you will feel your spirit lighten.

Imagine the contents of a letter you have received have caused you enormous distress and misery. You reread the letter, as though you cannot believe the power it has to cause you such immense emotional pain. I would recommend you put it into an envelope and send it back where it came from without a note to explain. The fact that you have done this will be sufficient, and the letter writer will know exactly what is going on. Having used their pen to dispel such poison, they will see their words all over again and realize their venomous power has been diminished.

Using the power of your mind, you can send those people who would seek to cause you harm far away from you. Any ill-feeling and anger they have directed toward you will be diluted. Imagine yourself bundling up all the hurt and damage, and using your MindPower, send this unpleasant package back to the place and people it originated from, but always make sure you send it back with positive feelings toward the recipient.

The hurt and misery pulled you down, undermined, and threatened to overwhelm you. By sending it back, you will be able to see your enemy through more compassionate eyes and consequently feel pity, understanding, and perhaps even love toward them.

MAGNIFYING PROBLEMS

What all this behavior reflects is that people give away their own power. They can become so undermined by their troubles that they lose sight of who they once were, allowing their new identity to subdue whatever they once were. The people in the group whose mutual experiences have brought them together also hand over their power to others, because having magnified their problems by constantly revisiting them, they have come to believe they really are much bigger than they are.

The very act of relinquishing power could mean they have given up. Alternatively, this gesture could be interpreted as a cry for help. Maybe they realize, deep down, that the sympathy and help they have turned to is not the kind they need. Maybe, in that same part of the mind that reveals such insights, they know that the only help that will sustain them has to come from within, and to capture a fraction of it will require a stronger emotional foundation.

On the positive side, a group that comes together through mutual experience and compassion can prove to be both inspiring and supportive for the members. Support groups for specific illnesses and for specific problems typify the positive way that mutual understanding can be employed to uplift sufferers instead of merely confirming the enormity of shared troubles.

WE ALL NEED LOVE

Whatever family we are born into and wherever we originate in whatever country in the world, the power of love is universal, permeating every day of our lives from the time we are born until death. Babies deprived of love suffer a dreadful and irreparable loss, missing the vital bonding that connects them to their mothers, never developing the invisible communication that exists between mother and child.

When love is denied

All over the world, the desperate plight of the young babies abandoned in orphanages never fails to shock and sadden. We have all seen them in news reports as their bleak, emotionless eyes stare out at the television cameras, seeing everything and registering nothing while their undernourished bodies reflect the degree of neuroses they are enduring, either rocking to and fro or just sitting motionless with a terrible stillness about them.

They are there either because their parents cannot afford to keep them, or they come from a culture in which female babies are not valued, or simply because they have been orphaned and their parents really are dead. Whatever the cause, they have been born into circumstances that deny them the natural and unconditional love of a mother and father, and the emotional damage they suffer is often incalculable.

Denying love

There are people for whom circumstances have been so horrendous that their thoughts and memories have become intolerable, and they have found the only way to survive emotionally is to block out everything from their minds. Often such emotional damage can be enormous, and only with the help of others can they overcome what has happened to them, or find ways to replace the emotions they have denied. Typically, child refugees who have been forced to leave their homes with or without their parents suffer dreadfully, separated either from their mothers or from all the things they have known in their short lives.

> *Out of such circumstances,
> love generates love. Out of such
> love comes healing.*

BELOW **Many people who have had loving childhoods feel a desperate need to help those children deprived of the precious commodity that they themselves enjoyed in abundance.**

Love generates love

When mother love is available in abundance, the natural telepathy between mother and baby continues to grow throughout life, connecting them and binding them together. This love provides the security and support for the young child to go out into their small world and test themselves and try new things, gradually going on to meet bigger challenges as they grow up. They face their future with confidence because the foundation of love that anchored them initially has always been in place.

Many such babies have grown into the men and women who have seen the television news images of these orphanages or child refugees around the world and who, moved beyond compassion into action, have overcome all kinds of obstacles to adopt or actively support some of these unfortunate children. The contrast between their own origins and those of the tiny inmates of the orphanages or lost and abandoned children stands out in stark relief. These men and women who grew up showered in love are horrified at the thought of a fellow human being never knowing such an emotion. Out of such circumstances, love generates love. Out of such love comes healing.

OUR EMOTIONAL BIRTHRIGHT

Society attempts to understand the people whose implacable cruelty and terrible crimes put them beyond the bounds of reasonable comprehension, and there have been many links established that show that criminals who torture and murder were often deprived of normal loving relationships throughout their childhood. What these links confirm is the enormous value of love and affection, but they do not imply that every deprived child has to grow up to become a criminal.

There are many inspirational examples of the human spirit triumphing in the most unlikely circumstances. Numerous young children, deprived of a great many of their normal emotional and physical needs, often overcompensate to such an extent that they actually achieve a great deal. They go way beyond others who have never had to face such hardships. A person who has been born into the worst of all possible worlds can grow up with the most astonishing mental strength and a single-minded determination to make sure that what happened to them will not be allowed to affect their lives any more. They are defying anyone's right to destroy their spirit or devalue their destiny.

We can choose our friends but not our family. There will always be relatives, sisters, and brothers who squabble, and parents that argue or are too strict or too lenient, or whose offspring find them embarrassing or are proud of them, having never let them down. Our birthright is as varied as humanity itself.

HEALING FRIENDSHIP

First choose a color for love. Using your MindPower, travel to a favorite and familiar place where there is plenty of room for others to join you. Imagine you are holding a perfect heart in the palm of your hand which is the symbol of love. Hold out your hand and offer this heart to the image of yourself. You are now giving yourself the gift of love. Feel the pleasure that receiving such a gift brings.

An affectionate embrace

Using the power of your mind, put your arms around this image as though you were a child being hugged by your mother. Hold this image close to you in an affectionate embrace. Using the color of love, surround yourself with this color and bask in its warmth.

Now choose someone you are close to, such as a good friend or member of your family, and invite them to join you. Create their image beside yours. Hold out your hands to them and offer them a perfect heart as a symbol of your love. Now watch them hand a heart to you. As you both hug in the same warm embrace that you gave yourself, sense the pleasure of giving as well as receiving. Using the color of love, imagine it as a soft mist encircling you and creating a warm glow.

Extending your love

Now invite a person with whom you have had difficulties to join you – someone you dislike or who has upset you and evoked strong negative emotions. When you have visualized their presence beside you and your close friend, extend your love to this person by holding out your hand and offering them a heart as a symbol of love. As they

LEFT **Using your MindPower, visualize hugging a loved one and revel in the pleasure of giving love just as much as receiving it.**

accept this gift of love from you, notice how they change and soften, as the love they have received from you extinguishes all the bad feelings that have existed between you both. Hold out your hands to them again and see them return this gesture. Using the color of love, wrap it around you both, then call your friend to join an embrace, so the powerful energy of your love can form a circle around you all.

Consider how it was as easy to hand love to a close friend as it was to hand love to

BELOW **Help to heal a relationship in difficulty by visualizing the individual concerned and extending a hand of love to that person.**

someone who had caused you pain. Reflect on the simplicity of those gestures and rejoice in the warmth and love it brought you in return.

After completing this visualization, you will discover how much easier it is to face the person toward whom you felt animosity. It will dull your recollection and you may not even be able to remember what it was that caused you both problems.

'*Liking and loving yourself is the result of self-approval.*'

LOVING YOURSELF

Happiness cannot be ignored or neglected – it requires constant attention to maintain the delicate balance it needs for survival. Just as happiness is essential to our lives, love sustains and nourishes us.

We extend love to others but we also need to love ourselves. Truly happy people do not dislike themselves. Liking and loving yourself is the result of self-approval. Self-approval is self-respect, and you need to earn this for yourself, setting up your own standards for living and writing your own rules.

If you never do anything that goes against this code of ethics, you grow to respect yourself and those standards.

We all know someone who does something, then promptly asks everyone else either to forgive them or for their approval. Such people want forgiveness because they have acted against their own instincts, and instead of looking inside themselves for clemency, they seek it outside from others with the implication that their own judgment is insufficient.

Seeking approval from other people stems from the same source, and, of course, it is great to have others applaud you and celebrate successes with you. But if whatever you have done is such an uncertain achievement in your own mind that it needs validation from others, perhaps you should be listening to those instincts after all. Perhaps your first thoughts were spot on and the achievement is not that special? Or, perhaps your self-image is so poor that you are simply unable to evaluate what you have achieved?

Kindness and understanding

Forgiving yourself is healing; "owning" an action is another step towards recognizing the parts of yourself that lead you to behave or think in various ways. Admitting to yourself that your own behavior makes you feel uncomfortable is much more cleansing and infinitely healthier than hearing this from other people. It moves you onward because it means that you are no longer being so harshly judgmental toward yourself, and you can begin to face up to your own behavior.

In much the same way as you would be gentler with others and show more compassion for their failings, you can be gentler and more understanding with yourself. You are treating yourself with respect and loving yourself enough to be honest.

RIGHT **Find time to be alone with yourself. Periods of quiet contemplation will give your mind a chance to sift through the jumble of thoughts that sometimes seem to obscure your view. Remind yourself that you are allowed to be less than perfect.**

Healing emotions

Healing emotions are powerful and can change lives. They can reverse situations and transform them from misery into happiness. They can bring out love and warmth where there was none, and generate compassion and friendship.

People who exude vitality and appear balanced physically and emotionally have discovered how positive emotions can make them healthier, and they are able to block negative emotions and heighten positive ones. These people usually display a continued interest in others, and are always keen to learn something new and stretch themselves mentally and physically, whatever their age. Their curiosity is healthy, not intrusive, arising from their love of life itself, and is fueled by their desire to embrace as much of life's experiences as they can.

Gratitude and appreciation coupled with eagerness and excitement, determination and an ability to be flexible, cheerfulness and humor all contribute to inner tranquillity and self-knowledge. People who have developed their inner wisdom also realize the value of self-respect and self-appreciation.

Treating yourself to time and space is not selfish, nor indulgent, but an important recognition of your own needs. Dividing your time so this can happen is being kind to yourself. Keeping life balanced means enjoying greater levels of energy, propelled by interest and stimulation, as well as renewed vitality.

Self-sustenance

Loving yourself automatically protects you from the normal stresses and strains of everyday life. You will discover the enormous resources of energy within your mind that sustain you in the worst of times and inspire and uplift you when times are good.

Our society tends to disapprove when someone applauds their own achievements and calls it showing-off. Pride is labeled vanity and self-love becomes conceit. We learn instead to become self-deprecating, and grow up unsure of ourselves with little respect for the person we have become. Lack of confidence is one of the biggest causes of unhappiness.

RIGHT **Learning to love yourself is a vital part of happiness and well-being. This means approving of and respecting yourself for living up to your own standards, and giving yourself credit for your achievements.**

Finding the key to your psyche means you can unlock the door you have hidden many of your problems behind.

THE KEY TO SELF-KNOWLEDGE

Understanding yourself means recognizing how your mind works and why you behave as you do. Finding the key to your psyche means you can unlock the door you have hidden many of your problems behind. The point is, others can show you where the key is and perhaps even help you open that door, but this will only take you so far. Only you can go through that door and discover your own secrets. No one else can do this for you.

Learning to trust yourself

As with all decisions in your life, allowing yourself to be guided by your intuition is always the wisest counsel you can follow. The future has endless possibilities, and if you trust your own intelligence, you can climb out from under this blanket of comforting, soothing words. Tempting though it may be, no one can ever help you in quite the same way as you can help yourself.

We all possess wisdom and power, so why allow others, however well-meaning, to dilute it and cloud the issues, wrapping you in their pity and smothering the motivation you need to draw upon to move forward?

We all have free will, and becoming a slave to circumstances is to give in and wallow in misfortune. There are people for whom this "emotional baggage" provides an excuse for failure and they drag their childhood into their adult lives, never blaming themselves when things do not work out, preferring to shift responsibility onto other people's failings.

Loving yourself means being completely comfortable within your own skin – living your life according to your own set of standards, being able to mix in different circles without having to adjust your behavior or your appearance, and never having to erect a facade to meet the outside world. What you feel and believe deep down at the core of your being is what you need to present to others.

LEFT **Find the key and unlock the door to your mind and explore its vast depths. Only in this way can you unearth the problems that you have hidden away.**

Happy mirror

You may be familiar with the technique I call "mirrorizing" (see Lasting Impressions on page 84), and now you can use it in a slightly different way. This involves standing or sitting in front of a mirror and really taking note of everything about yourself. Instead of looking at the "inner you," you can now study the "outer you." The important point is to make sure you do not look in the mirror and see what you expect to see. Instead, remind yourself that you are observing your reflection through other people's eyes.

Changes for the better

I want you to study yourself very carefully. There may well be physical features you dislike and would love to change, but first ask yourself some questions. If you could change three things, which would you choose? Now imagine yourself once those changes have taken place. Really see yourself as you believe you would now look and study the image you have just created. Then go back to how you normally look before you made those changes and examine the things you wanted to change about yourself.

Feeling the effects

Now ask yourself some more questions. Did you feel happier and

RIGHT **This exercise will help you to accept and feel comfortable with yourself just the way you are, as other people do.**

more confident? Are the things you altered so bad that you had to change them? Perhaps you only made subtle changes, changes that few people would notice, but which make a difference to you? Did changing them change you? Would you have more fun? Would people like you more? Would you get a better job, make more money?

Accepting yourself as you are is part of loving yourself. If you dislike yourself, you believe you are equally unacceptable to others. Now look back in the mirror and give yourself a huge smile, and if that seems funny to you, then laugh. When we look in the mirror it is usually either to shave, put on makeup, or check our clothes – we hardly ever catch ourselves really laughing out loud. See yourself laughing and notice the transformation that takes place. Your laughter has made this mirror your Happy Mirror.

SELF-HEALING
Meditation for Love

Read through the following questions and bring them with you into your meditation.

CONTEMPLATIONS

→ Do you tend to defer to the stronger personalities in your relationships?

→ Would you ignore a ringing telephone if you suspected it was someone you were avoiding because they wanted your help?

→ Are you unhappy at work because you do not seem to fit in with your colleagues?

→ Are you very concerned about the prospect of getting a serious illness one day?

→ If a friend lets you down, will you be angry for a long period of time?

→ When you meet people for the first time, such as at a party, do you find it difficult to know what to talk about?

→ Do you feel so close to any of your friends that you could talk to them about anything?

Meditation

We tend to look for love outside ourselves and invest our energy in this search as though we only have a value if another person loves us. Break the links that undermine you and begin to enjoy and rejoice in who you really are. Love is a healing energy. If you give love to others freely, expecting nothing in return, it will come back to you. If you give love to yourself, you will be healing yourself.

Relax, breathe deeply, and meditate

Imagine you are standing on a wide veranda fronting a house overlooking a beach. The veranda runs the whole breadth of the house and there is a view of the ocean from every window. The floor is wooden decking and your hands rest on the wooden rail as you look out to sea. This is a very peaceful place and even the raucous cries of the seagulls seem softer than usual as they mix with the gentle sound of the waves lapping the shore. The sea is very calm and the tide is out. The waves are tiny little ripples, no more than a few inches high, and you know if you were standing at the water's edge, they would only break around your ankles. They are so safe that a small child could play in these shallows.

Feel the cleansing, healthy effect of the salt air as you breathe deeply, taking it down into your lungs. Become aware of the slight salt-sting of the sea breeze as it brushes your skin and brings a glow of color to your cheeks and flicks through your hair. Feel the energy of this wind, fresh off the ocean's surface, sharp and cold and powerful. The elements are making themselves noticed, bringing their presence to your attention, touching you physically as if to remind you that they share the same universe.

You have been alone on this veranda and now you look to your right and notice that other people are also standing at the rail, looking across the beach and out to the sea beyond. You are all complete strangers but you sense that you are all sharing the same thoughts and feelings as you look beyond the terrace.

You walk over to the group and take the hand of the nearest person and smile at them. Then you take another person's hand. You look up at the house. You now notice that there are people at the windows looking out at the ocean and you wave to them to come down and join you. As they appear, you encourage the others to join hands with the newcomers until you are all standing in a circle of friendship. This circle is as old as time itself, a circle that brings you all together, uniting your spirits and forming a universal chain of love.

Now imagine how it feels to stand in such a circle, as you savor the love traveling from one spirit to another, like electric current flashing through a cable. The more love you send to the others, the more comes back in an everlasting exchange. Concentrate on experiencing this sensation as deeply as you can, and find the pleasure and enjoyment that sharing so much love brings. Each person's spirit is touched by love, which then touches the spirit of the next person and the next, until you can all feel this love pouring over you as it spreads around that circle. The energy it generates flows through everyone, passing from hand to hand in the chain, penetrating all the energy bodies and heightening the vibrations they give out.

SELF-HEALING
Meditation for Love

Make this energy into a color and then imagine it as a cloud, soft and filmy, semitransparent, semiopaque, drifting in the air and encircling everyone. You feel as if you can catch this cloud of love in your hand and pass it around the people with whom you are sharing love. Watch it dipping and rising, twisting and turning, in and out, through and beyond, creating more healing energy with every varying movement.

Stay with this circle and look again out to sea. Notice how the elements have made you so aware of your physical body, sending the wind to whip your hair and flush your cheeks; the gulls to call, the waves to lap, and the fresh smell of salt to breathe into your lungs.

Notice how all the people in this circle are equally aware of their physical bodies, as though they have been invigorated by the elements in just the same way as you have been.

Notice now how this awareness of your physical bodies has infiltrated the circle of friendship. You all realize that this emphasis is designed to increase your sensitivity to your spiritual energy and how the love you are sharing has heightened this awareness. All the senses are now so acute that you can all feel, hear, taste, and smell everything around you, because the love you are sharing has brought all your senses together. Touching the spirit of so many people with so much love has had an extraordinary effect. It feels like taking a shower in which the spirit of this universal love has been poured over you and bathed you in its power.

Remain within this circle as long as you want to, enjoying the intensified sensations it has brought you, because the longer you are touching your spirit, the greater your healing power. Giving so much love has brought even more love back to you. Savor the experience and keep it safely within your mind.

Record your first thoughts

Please write down your immediate thoughts and feelings as spontaneously as you can.

What your responses reveal
Mostly "yes" answers

You seem to have lost sight of yourself and have no idea what effect you have on others. You are center-stage in your own world and so wrapped up in your own concerns that you have no energy left to absorb what is happening around you.

You probably feel chronically tired a great deal of the time because you hand out your positive energy in such meagre portions, believing it will deplete you and leave you with nothing when the reality is exactly the opposite. Your fatigue makes you feel very angry and you hide it behind a mask of irritability. When you feel like shouting, you merely snap.

This is a dangerous spiral and it would take very little to tip the balance right over. Stop and take stock of your life. There has to be a healthier way to live than this. Your health will suffer from your constant state of agitation unless you give yourself some love and reward yourself with some healing care.

 Consider this: The state of mind you are in is the state of mind you have chosen. Only you can decide if you need never feel like you do today.

Mostly "no" answers

You have found a way to prioritize without losing your compassion, to give out love without feeling a sense of loss. Trusting your intuition has shown you where your strengths and weaknesses are, and you have not allowed your ego to jeopardize your spiritual growth.

 Consider this: Giving without expecting anything in return is a truly generous spirit. It means that if something unexpectedly does come back to you, it will have double the value.

Half "yes," half "no" answers

You are balancing your negative emotions with very positive ones and not allowing yourself to dwell on what you cannot do and concentrating instead on what is potentially possible. Listen to your instincts and trust them a little more.

 Consider this: Refuse to allow a lack of knowledge to hold you back or an expert to intimidate you. Information is power – arm yourself adequately and then use it wisely.

Affirmation

Giving is a pleasure, but the art of receiving is someone else's pleasure, and learning how to do this matters just as much.

LET YOUR SPIRIT DANCE

All through this book, I have explored ancient and modern wisdoms, delved into the worlds of science and the human spirit, and gradually discovered the links between what we feel and think and believe and the state of our health. I have also revealed to you another aspect of MindPower, in the form of an inner healing therapy.

Mind Medicine is an important book for me and I do not want to disconnect myself from you, the reader, just because you have reached the last page. Whether you have been giving or receiving healing or healing yourself, I would love to hear whether anything unusual has happened to you. Have any incidents that you might once have called strange, taken place while you have been reading *Mind Medicine*? More importantly, would you call them strange now or have you come to a deeper understanding of why and how they happened?

Since reaching the end of the book, have you found yourself looking at your life in different ways, perhaps seeing the people close to you from a different perspective? Have you changed your plans, created new dreams for your future, identified new ambitions and challenges? Have you discovered that many of the things you felt or thought in the past which were once inexplicable have become recognizable now? Are the messages in your dreams very clear to you now?

Perhaps you have tested your own powers of telepathy: The phone that rings with a call from the very person you are thinking about, the so-called accidental meeting with a long-lost friend, or a sequence of events that looked disastrous but turned out to be wonderful? Maybe you have listened to your deepest instincts and been able to sense another person's thoughts? Or, you may have traveled on incredible journeys through your meditations and reached places that have enriched and enhanced your understanding of life.

I want to hear your story: I want to know if the variety of choices *Mind Medicine* offered you really did show you how to find what you needed. Write and tell me whether it made you want to stretch and expand your horizons. Did you discover aspects of yourself that had been buried, such as courage and confidence, just lying there waiting for you to tap into them? Do you now really believe you can be as healthy in mind and body as you want to be? Did you take comfort from the knowledge that all the power you ever needed was yours already?

You can reach me by letter or e-mail at the address on page 220. We have shared a connection through the pages of this book, and I do not want to dismantle those links. I would love to learn of your personal experiences and know that *Mind Medicine* has helped in some way to make your life healthier.

Ancient Oriental wisdom describes the perfect harmony between mind and body as energies dancing together while they strive for cosmic balance. I like to think of health excellence in the same way, as a perfect and harmonious balance between mind and body. I believe that with MindPower we can all make our spirits dance.

Let me leave you with these reflections from two great men of science.

> ❝The most beautiful thing we can experience is the mysterious. It is the source of all true art and science.❞
> **Albert Einstein**

> ❝Your vision will become clear only when you look into your heart. Who looks outside, dreams. Who looks inside, awakens.❞
> **Carl Jung**

The last word

Dr. Peter Fenwick
Consultant neuropsychiatrist

❝A book like this is important because it helps you to heal yourself. We know the mind-brain interface is rich and complex and that what goes on in the mind affects the body. Any techniques which can help us understand this link are fundamental to my work as a scientist.

The nature and structure of consciousness at present remain an enigma for science, which is why I believe we need a new science, a Science of Consciousness. Meditation is important as it takes us deep into ourselves and helps us to examine and make use of the depths of our own subjective experience. We are now gathering scientific evidence that meditation works. A recent study at Harvard University has shown that meditation is a powerful way of releasing the natural healing power within us all and that people who meditate nourish their spirituality. This book shows that we all have this healing power, it teaches us how to find it, and then use it in a constructive way upon yourself.

The world you experience depends to some extent on the way you perceive it – on your own attitude. Therefore, how you relate to yourself is important, and you must be careful that you don't diminish yourself by your own preconceptions. Through meditation, you become more gentle and loving, learn to take time and to set goals, and make them your own. If you don't reach those goals, don't be too hard on yourself, but remake them so that they are achievable.

Meditation produces a profound state of relaxation, and so is a great way of changing the body's physiology, leading to an improvement in stress hormone levels and a reduction in blood pressure. What is often called the Mother Teresa Effect shows that holding loving thoughts improves immune system functioning. So, too, do feelings of happiness and a positive outlook; people who are happy and positive tend to recover more quickly from illness. On the other hand, unhappy people are more likely to become ill and to visit their GP more often, because unhappiness reduces the number of killer T-cells, the cells which mediate immunity.

The philosophy that sums up this book for me is that you can discover a profound and deeply significant part of yourself through meditation. Meditation can change your level of consciousness and this can change the way you see the world. But nothing comes without some effort – the only magic wand is the one you wave yourself.❞

POPULAR COMPLEMENTARY THERAPIES

ACUPRESSURE

A form of acupuncture (see Acupuncture) where fingertip or nail pressure is applied to acupuncture points on the body to remove blockages or pain and enhance the flow of energy within the body's meridians, thereby aiding the healthy function of the internal organs and preventing or curing disease.

ACUPUNCTURE

The Chinese practise of inserting fine needles into specific areas of the body – the acupoints on the meridians – in order to improve the flow of *chi* or *qi* in the meridians and to restore balance and healthy functioning to the internal organs.

ABOVE **Essential oil is a pure, concentrated essence taken from a plant.**

AROMATHERAPY

The use of essential oils from plants to enhance general health and appearance. Each oil has its own characteristic aroma and therapeutic properties, with the ability to soothe and relax or stimulate and invigorate. Since many essential oils are antibacterial, antiseptic, or anti-inflammatory, they can be useful in treating a variety of minor ailments.

COLOR THERAPY

Colors are used to rebalance the body on both the physical and "psychic" levels. On the physical level, therapists believe that as light is received and absorbed through the skin, it works on the nervous system to change the body's chemical balance. Therefore, by adjusting the amount of specific color input,

they can affect physical well-being as well as mood. On the psychic level, therapists work to influence the seven energy centers, or *chakras*, each of which correspond to one of the seven colors of the light spectrum.

CRYSTAL AND GEM THERAPY

Gems and crystals are placed on and around the patient to focus and enhance healing energy. Different stones are believed to possess varying vibrational energy levels which can influence the individual's own healing power. Crystals are also placed around the home in the belief that they improve the atmosphere by absorbing negativity.

FENG SHUI

The ancient art of balancing energies by integrating people, buildings, and landscape to create a harmonious environment. Only when balance and harmony are achieved can the *chi*, the energy or life force of the universe, flow freely, resulting in good health, happiness, and prosperity.

FLOWER ESSENCES

These are used to treat many common ailments, alleviate symptoms, and aid in the healing process. They help to balance the negative emotions that lead to and are the symptoms of disease.

RIGHT **In crystal therapy, crystals are placed around the client to soak up negative energy or to replenish low levels of positive energy.**

HERBALISM

A system of medicine offering treatment for a wide variety of illnesses, but instead of treating symptoms in isolation, it aims to restore the body's own ability to protect and heal itself. Herbalists use plant parts in their entirety in their remedies, rather than trying to isolate the plants' chemically active constituents, in the belief that it is the combination of a plant's various elements that form its healing properties, and this also works to prevent any harmful side effects.

ABOVE **Hepar. Sulph., a homeopathic remedy used to treat some infections.**

HOMEOPATHY

An holistic form of medicine that aims to help the body heal itself. The word "homeopathy" means treating like with like. In practice this involves administering a minute dose of the agent that is the cause of symptoms, which in turn is believed to stimulate the body's own defense capacity.

BELOW **Oil – often scented with essential oils – is used in massage to help the hands glide over the skin.**

HYPNOTHERAPY

The use of hypnosis – the induction of a trance state – to encourage healing and well-being by drawing on the resources of the unconscious mind. This technique is useful in the treatment of addictions, anxiety, and stress-related problems.

MASSAGE

The art of relaxing the body and encouraging healing and well-being through touch. A regular body massage can enhance general health and vitality, while specialized methods of massage help release tension from muscles, ease stiff joints, promote healthy circulation of the blood, and stimulate lymphatic drainage to encourage the elimination of wastes from the body.

MEDITATION

A method of contacting the inner energy that powers the natural processes of healing and self-realization. Meditation has been shown to decrease blood pressure and breathing and heart rates, thereby helping to reduce stress. Besides promoting a state of deep relaxation, meditation also encourages mental alertness and openness.

RIGHT **Some systems of meditation require you to adopt a certain posture, such as the classic half-lotus position.**

NATUROPATHY

This system of philosophy incorporates a number of therapies which are all based on the belief that illness can be healed by the natural processes of the body. Naturopaths believe that four basic components make for good health: clean air, clean water, clean food from good earth, exercise, and "right living." All naturopathic treatments concentrate on various of these elements, and often all of them combined, to restore health and vitality.

NUTRITIONAL THERAPY

Nutrients: are prescribed to rebalance the body and restore well-being, as well as to prevent ill health.

Nutritional therapists: administer dietary or food supplements in the form of pills, capsules, powders, or fluids.

Nutritional therapy: focuses on tailoring diet to the person, examining the individual condition and treating accordingly.

OSTEOPATHY

A manipulative therapy that works on the body's structure (the skeleton, muscles, ligaments, and connective tissue) to relieve pain, improve mobility, and restore all-round health.

REFLEXOLOGY

This is a specialized form of massage of the feet and – less commonly – the hands, to detect and correct imbalances in the body that may be the cause of ill health. Reflexologists believe the body is divided into 10 equal zones that extend the length of the body, from head to toe, and that stimulation of an area of the foot in one zone affects other parts of the body in the same zone. Reflexology is a good all-round therapy for people of any age.

REIKI

The word *reiki* means "universal life energy," and gives its name to a system of healing which uses this energy that surrounds us everywhere for self-healing as well as for healing others. Initiation from a reiki master involves a simple laying on of hands to activate the individual's ability to harness the life energy. Besides being used to help treat many specific health problems, reiki promotes spiritual, emotional, and mental well-being.

SHIATSU

Based on the same principles as acupuncture (see Acupuncture), shiatsu aims to restore a balanced flow of energy within the body's meridians, and to enhance vitality and well-being. However, shiatsu does not rely solely on acupressure or massage techniques, but also incorporates elements from physiotherapy, osteopathy, and from other forms of healing tradition.

T'AI CHI CHUAN

Also known as *t'ai chi*, this is an ancient Chinese system designed to develop *chi* – the natural healing force in the universe – within the body. A moving form of meditation, students of the art learn a basic form or sequence of movements, resulting in a buildup of inner power within a flexible and responsive body. *T'ai chi* can be used to rejuvenate the individual, to heal and prevent illness and injuries, and also to lead to personal spiritual enlightenment.

YOGA

There are many different forms of this very ancient philosophy and practice which use physical positions or postures, breathing and breath control, and meditation to promote health and well-being. It is used as an effective means of encouraging relaxation, normalizing high blood pressure, helping to stave off anxiety, and to deal with stress, as well as to treat specific problems such as backache, arthritis, and rheumatism, or to speed healing or recovery from illness or injury.

THE MAJOR MEDICINE GROUPS

ACE INHIBITOR

(angiotensin-converting enzyme)

These drugs are used to treat kidney disease by acting as a diuretic and reducing body fluid, and in some heart conditions they can strengthen heartbeat and lower resistance in the arteries. This improves the body's blood flow and helps to reduce high blood pressure.

ALCOHOL

This is a drug produced from the fermentation or distillation of a wide range of organic substances, such as hops, grapes, and various grains. It is used to fortify wines such as sherry and port, which gives them a higher alcoholic content than red or white wine. Simple fermentation produces a solution containing not more than 11 percent alcohol – this includes beers and unfortified wines. More concentrated solutions such as gin, whiskey, brandy, and vodka are prepared by distillation.

In its simplest form, alcohol can be extremely dangerous. For instance, spirit distilled from wood is highly poisonous and can lead to blindness and death.

Alcohol is not a stimulant and acts as a tranquillizer or relaxant. It is used as an appetizer because it increases the flow of digestive juices, and used socially because it effectively reduces nervous tension and overcomes inhibitions.

Long-term drinking affects the central nervous system, impairing memory, concentration, judgment, and coordination. It can lead to inflammation of the stomach lining and cirrhosis of the liver, a condition in which the liver can no longer process the body's nutrients. Because alcohol also acts as a vasodilator, enlarging the blood vessels near the skin's surface, excessive drinking can lead to loss of body heat which can cause hypothermia.

ANESTHETICS

Local anesthetic: The application of a topical cream or an injection blocks the transmission of nerve impulses in the area where they are applied, and deadens sensation so that localized pain is "frozen" temporarily. An epidural is an anesthetic drug given between contractions during childbirth and is injected between the vertebrae of the spine. This deadens sensation in the lower part of the body. It is also used in general surgical procedures.

LEFT **Alcohol is a powerful drug that acts as a tranquillizer or relaxant. Excessive drinking can cause mental impairment and can lead to liver disease.**

General anesthetic: This is usually a combination of drugs that is injected, often some time after a relaxant "pre-med" drug has been administered. A general anesthetic means a total loss of consciousness because the drugs depress the activity of the central nervous system and relax the muscles, enabling a surgeon to carry out a procedure with no awareness on the part of the patient (see Barbiturates).

ANALGESICS

This drug group includes aspirin (acetylsalicylic acid), phenacetin (paracetamol) (UK only), acetaminophen (Excedrin and Tylenol in the US), and ibuprofen (Advil in the US). Aspirin is the best known of this drug group and probably the most commonly used drug today. It provides temporary relief from mild pain and reduces fever. It is also a short-term treatment for rheumatism and arthritis, reducing painful stiffness and swelling in the joints. Aspirin also minimizes the risk of heart attacks and strokes by preventing platelets (small blood cells) from forming clusters. These are small blood cells, also known as thrombocytes, which help to clot the blood and prevent bleeding.

Phenacetin, popularly known as paracetamol, is primarily used to provide temporary relief for mild pain and fever, and is less likely to cause gastric irritation than aspirin. In large doses, it causes irreparable liver damage. It is also given to those who have an allergic reaction to aspirin.

ANDROGENS

These are male hormones, either natural or synthetically produced, that correct male hormone deficiencies. They can stimulate the growth of red blood cells and correct undescended testicles in male children. They are also used to block growth of breast cancer cells in females by suppressing the production of estrogen.

ANDROGENS AND ESTROGENS

These are hormones that are given to replace deficiencies in male and female hormone levels (see Progesterones).

ANTACIDS

These are available from most drug stores without a prescription. They relieve heartburn and acid indigestion by neutralizing the hydrochloric acid in gastric juices which causes dyspepsia, or indigestion. There are several different antacids available but the combination of aluminum hydroxide and magnesium trisilicate is the most widely used preparation, since it relieves the symptoms without forming excessive quantities of air that in turn can produce flatulence.

ANTIANGINAL

These drugs are used to treat angina pectoris, the intermittent chest pain that comes from coronary heart disease. They can also be used to treat congestive heart failure. They work by increasing the blood flow to the heart muscle by relaxing the blood vessels. This limits the severity and frequency of angina attacks.

ANTIARRHYTHMIC

This group of drugs treats and prevents heartbeat irregularities in a condition called arrhythmia, a disorder of the cardiac rhythm that affects the heart's functional efficiency.

ANTIASTHMATICS

These drugs come in pills and liquid form but are mainly prescribed in aerosols so that they can be inhaled directly into the bronchial tubes rather than through the bloodstream. They reduce inflammation in the lungs and breathing passages.

ANTIBIOTICS

This group of drugs is used to combat all kinds of bacterial infections. There is a range of broad spectrum antibiotics that target a wide range of bacteria that affect the respiratory tract, sinuses, ears, and eyes. They are also used to treat urinary infections, gastrointestinal disorders, and inflammation of the heart valves and muscle. Others are more specific. Over-use and inappropriate use has led to a degree of immunity. These drugs do not have any effect on viruses and will not destroy fungi or parasites. The following types of drug fall into the antibiotics group.

Antibacterials: These combat bacterial infections by inhibiting the growth of bacteria. They can cause at least two problems. Firstly, they can eventually lead to the creation of resistant strains of the particular bacterium that has been targeted. Secondly, they can cause the sterilization of the intestine, which allows the overgrowth of yeast.

Antifungals: These are used in a variety of fungus infections, particularly in immunosuppressed patients susceptible to fungal mouth infections, as well as conditions such as athlete's foot, ringworm, and thrush.

Antivirals: These prevent and treat severe herpes infections such as shingles and chicken pox, and they also treat herpes simplex of the eye. They work by blocking the penetration of tissue cells and may relieve certain symptoms of Parkinson's disease. They are also used to block the HIV virus from replicating itself.

ANTICHOLINERGIC

This group of drugs is mainly used in the treatment of bronchial spasms but also reduces spasms in the digestive system, bladder, and urethra.

ANTICOAGULANTS

These drugs block the action of vitamin K, which is essential for blood clotting, and they also slow the rate of blood coagulation, which helps prevent the formation of abnormal blood clots.

ANTICONVULSANTS

These drugs treat bipolar disorders as well as petit mal and more major epileptic attacks. They work by inhibiting nerve transmissions in certain parts of the brain, which in turn reduces excitability. In children, anticonvulsants decrease seizure activity and lead to a significant improvement in quality of life.

ANTIDEPRESSANTS

Tricyclic: These treat many forms of depression by influencing the signals between the brain and nerve cells.

Monoamine-Oxidase Inhibitors (MAOIs): These destroy an enzyme called monoamine-oxidase, which is believed to be produced in excess during depression. They work by blocking the nerve transmissions in the brain.

Serotonin Inhibitors: This group alters the brain chemistry by inhibiting the uptake of serotonin in the central nervous system.

ANTIDIABETIC

Antihyperglycemic: These are used to control excess sugar levels in the blood, mainly in noninsulin dependent diabetics.

Sulfonylurea: These work by increasing insulin production through the pancreas, which stimulates cells to use sugar in blood (see Insulin).

ANTIDYSKINETICS

These drugs help to balance the brain chemistry, which improves the control of muscles in Parkinson's disease and Tourette's syndrome.

ANTIEMETICS

These drugs mainly work by blocking the messages between the sensitive nerves inside the inner ear and the part of the brain that controls vomiting, helping to prevent motion sickness. Some of them also inhibit the smooth muscle of the stomach from contracting which helps to prevent vomiting, and some are chemically very similar to marijuana. They are also used to combat the nausea and vomiting that can accompany chemotherapy.

ANTIGLAUCOMA

These drugs treat glaucoma by reducing the pressure in the eye and increasing the movement of fluid inside the eye. They are given in eye drops, pill form, or through injection.

ANTIHISTAMINE

These drugs block the action of histamines that are normally released by an allergic reaction and which cause a variety of symptoms including excessive sneezing, itching, watery eyes, and runny nose, as well as breathing problems. They are occasionally used to treat travel sickness.

ANTIHYPERTENSIVES

This group of drugs is used to treat high blood pressure, usually in combination with other drugs. They work best if accompanied by a low-salt, low-fat diet and a sensible exercise program.

ANTI-INFLAMMATORY

Nonsteroidal: Reduces the effect of prostaglandins, the hormones that cause inflammation and pain in rheumatic conditions.

Steroidal: Cortisone drugs are hormonal preparations used in the treatment of serious problems such as malignancies, kidney disease, and blood disorders and are also used to compensate where there is a deficiency of natural hormones. They are very powerful drugs and will effectively reduce irritation and inflammation. They may suppress resistance to infection and are believed to stunt growth in children.

Discontinuing these drugs should always be gradual. Adrenocorticoid drugs are used to treat noninfectious conditions, and are also used as a preventative for bronchial asthma and to relieve swelling from insect bites, allergic skin rashes, and many other skin conditions, such as eczema. Steroidal therapy produces serious side effects with long-term use, including diabetes and osteoporosis.

ANTIPROTOZOALS

As a malaria treatment, these drugs prevent parasites reproducing. As a treatment for certain kinds of arthritis, they can reduce inflammation.

ANTIPSYCHOTICS

These drugs are mainly used to treat conditions such as schizophrenia and manic depression by altering the chemical action of dopamine in the brain. Dopamine acts as a neurotransmitter in the brain and is essential to the functioning of the nervous system.

ANTIUROLITHICS

These drugs combine with calcium to inhibit its absorption in order to prevent the formation of kidney stones.

AMPHETAMINES

These drugs were developed originally to reduce uncontrollable bouts of sleep in narcoleptics by acting as a stimulant on the central nervous system. There is some controversy surrounding their use in children with attention deficit syndrome (ADHD), in which they work by subduing overactivity.

BARBITURATES

These are powerful drugs that work by limiting the connections between nerve impulses and nerve cells to depress brain activity and reduce anxiety. They are used to prevent mild epileptic seizures and as a sedative for short-term insomnia. These organic compounds are derived from barbituric acid and can be given intravenously for a short-term anaesthetic, such as in dental or minor surgical procedures. In small doses, they act as a tranquillizer or muscle relaxant to decrease anxiety. In larger doses, they act as an hypnotic and induce sleep (see Anaesthetics, Hypnotics, and Tranquillizers).

BENZODIAZEPINES

These are tranquillizers that reduce nervous tension, anxiety, and muscle spasm by affecting the limbic system, which is the part of the brain that controls emotion. They also act as muscle relaxants. Their use is more limited now because of their habit-forming potential and also because of the side effects they produce, which can mimic the symptoms for which they were prescribed. They are frequently used intravenously for "conscious" anesthesia in dentistry or minor surgery (see Anesthetics).

BETA-ADRENERGIC BLOCKING AGENTS
(beta-blockers)

These drugs literally block a range of

LEFT **The high caffeine content found in tea would explain its popularity as a pick-me-up.**

mechanisms to minimize the symptoms that have led to particular conditions. They can lower heart rate, blood pressure, fluid pressure in the eye, fluid retention, and reduce pain in migraine headaches.

BISPHOSPHONATES

These drugs are used to treat, not prevent, osteoporosis, a bone condition in which the rate of bone loss progresses faster than new bone is formed. These drugs increase bone mass while slowing the loss of bone tissue. They are also used to treat Paget's Disease. They can be taken in tablet or liquid form as well as through a nasal spray (for the prevention of osteoporosis, see Hormone Replacement Therapy).

BRONCHODILATORS

These can be taken in tablet form, syrup, nose drops, or through an inhaler. They work in several ways, depending on the strength of the drug prescribed, and can suppress an allergic reaction, act as a decongestant on the breathing passages in bronchial asthma, relax and expand the bronchial tubes, and reduce the severity of chronic bronchitis and emphysema.

CAFFEINE

This is a drug that acts as a stimulant on the central nervous system and is found in tea, coffee, and chocolate as well as in a great

many soft drinks. It is used as a component in various medicines. For example, it combines with ergot to treat migraine by constricting the blood vessels and reducing pain. It is also a diuretic and can be beneficial in some cases of asthma. Its stimulant properties help to combat fatigue and drowsiness.

CALCIUM CHANNEL BLOCKERS

These drugs act as stabilizers and are used to prevent angina, normalize an irregular heartbeat, and correct high blood pressure.

CALCIUM SUPPLEMENTS

These do exactly that, providing additional calcium to aid the prevention of osteoporosis.

CHEMOTHERAPY

This means chemical therapy, or treatment in which chemicals are used to kill organisms that are causing infections, but tends to be associated primarily with the treatment of cancer. Some of the chemicals, or drugs, used are called cytotoxic drugs. Toxic means poisonous, and these drugs have the capacity to damage and destroy cancerous cells, often by inhibiting cell division which prevents them from multiplying. While this cytotoxic action is desirable for attacking cancerous cells, there is a risk of destroying healthy cells at the same time. When this happens, damage

to the bone marrow occurs, which prevents the production of blood cells and can lead to anaemia. It also increases the patient's susceptibility to infection. For this reason, patients undergoing a course of such drugs have their blood counts measured on a regular basis.

CITRATES

This group of drugs is given to prevent and treat some forms of kidney stone. They work by increasing the excretion of bicarbonate ions, which has the effect of increasing the alkaline content of urine.

CYTOTOXICS

This is a powerful group of drugs that works by damaging or destroying cells. They are used as a treatment for venereal warts and in the treatment of various forms of cancer. They have to be administered with great care since they can also destroy normal cells and are individually regulated to suit each patient's needs. They are sometimes combined with radiotherapy (see Radiotherapy and Chemotherapy).

DECONGESTANTS

These drugs work by shrinking the swollen membranes lining the nose, which opens up the nasal passages and relieves congestion.

DIGITALIS

This derives from the foxglove and is used in different forms and combinations as a medicine to make the heartbeat stronger, as well as to strengthen the heart muscle and prevent congestive heart failure.

DIURETICS

Blood pressure is lowered and fluid retention reduced by increasing the levels of sodium and water eliminated from the body. Potassium-sparing diuretics alter chemicals in the kidneys so that only sodium and water are excreted, conserving potassium (salt).

GOLD TREATMENTS

Medicines containing gold compounds or gold salts are used in the treatment of rheumatoid arthritis, particularly in cases of juvenile arthritis. These salts are believed to modify the disease's activity through mechanisms that are not fully understood but probably act as a general stimulus to the body's immune mechanism.

HORMONE-REPLACEMENT THERAPY (HRT)

A combination of hormone medications, either oestrogen and progesterone or oestrogen and androgen, that replace deficient levels of naturally occurring hormones in the body. Hormones are chemical substances that regulate various body functions. Hormone Replacement Therapy is used to combat symptoms produced by declining estrogen levels just before, during, and after the menopause as well as to protect against other conditions affecting women in later years.

HYPNOTICS

This is a group of drugs that is used to treat insomnia and anxiety by directly impacting on the part of the brain that controls alertness.

IMMUNOSUPPRESSANTS

These powerful drugs limit the body's immune response following transplant surgery and are used in a variety of immune disorders. They are also used to treat cancer because they inhibit normal cell production.

INSULIN

Naturally occurring insulin comes from the pancreas and facilitates the breakdown of sugar into energy. Diabetes is a complex metabolic disorder in which the body either does not make sufficient insulin or makes none at all, which leads to high levels of glucose in the blood. Some forms of diabetes can be controlled by diet but others depend on insulin because the body cannot use glucose for energy without it and substitutes fat for energy. This can lead to a diabetic coma.

Insulin cannot be taken by mouth in tablet form because the body's digestive juices would destroy it before the substance had a chance to be absorbed into the blood stream.

LAXATIVES

These medicines are mainly derived from castor oil and senna, and treat the symptoms of constipation rather than the cause, working in different ways. Emollient laxatives act as lubricants to soften and ease the passage through the intestines. Bulk-forming laxatives add dietary fibre. Osmotic laxatives work by drawing water into the bowel to increase the bowel action. Stimulants are purgatives and literally stimulate muscular contractions in the intestines which produces a vigorous bowel action within three to six hours.

MALE HORMONE REPLACEMENTS

(see Androgens)

MINERAL SUPPLEMENTS

These are added to a diet to prevent or treat a deficiency, and include iron, magnesium, copper, calcium, and zinc. Ideally, a diet should provide the essential vitamins and minerals that constitute our daily requirements (see Vitamins).

MINOXIDIL

This is the only known substance which actually stimulates hair growth. It has been shown to work on some people but not others, for no particular reason. It works by dilating the blood capillaries which sends more blood to the hair follicles and stimulates hair growth, and was originally developed to relieve high blood pressure. It will not work where there is total baldness but is effective where hair is thinning or partially bald. It has to be applied daily, and if the application stops, the hair growth will also stop. Anyone using this drug to treat hair loss should always check that they are able to tolerate the predicted side effects beforehand. If there is no improvement in hair growth after approximately four to five months, it must be assumed that this medication is not going to work.

RIGHT **Diabetes sufferers can use a special kit containing a device for taking a sample of their blood and an instrument to test it for blood-sugar levels, to determine the amount of insulin required.**

MUSCLE RELAXANTS

These drugs work by interrupting the pain messages to the brain, and effectively alleviate muscle spasms. They are often used alongside analgesics and have a sedative effect (see Benzodiazepines).

NARCOTIC ANALGESIC and ACETAMINPHEN

This combination effectively blocks pain signals through the central nervous system. It can become habit-forming (see Narcotics).

NARCOTIC ANALGESIC and ASPIRIN

This is a strong combination that effectively reduces fever and inflammation and blocks pain. It does this by preventing the small blood vessels from dilating and stops platelets (small blood cells) from forming clusters (see Narcotics).

NARCOTIC ANALGESIC and CODEINE

Codeine is derived from the opium poppy just as morphine is but does not have its addictive properties. It is often combined with aspirin or paracetamol as a slightly stronger pain reliever in cough mixtures to minimize coughing. It is known to cause drowsiness (see Narcotics).

NARCOTIC ANALGESICS

This combination of drugs blocks the pain messages in the central nervous system and serves as a stronger pain reliever (see Narcotics).

NARCOTICS

Opiates, as they are also known, are either derived from opium or manufactured synthetically and include morphine, heroin, methadone, and pethidine. They are all extremely strong, highly addictive substances, prescribed to relieve severe pain. They slow breathing, dull consciousness, and induce a dreamlike state or sleep. Their characteristics vary, as does their specific application.

NIACIN (Nicotinic Acid)

This is a vitamin supplement and vasodilator that lowers cholesterol and helps to correct vertigo. It is also effective on pellagra, a wasting disease that stems from a deficiency of this vitamin.

NICOTINE

The smoke from nicotine in cigarettes weakens the efficiency of the immune defense system and contains nicotine, carbon monoxide, ammonia, and several different carcinogenic, or cancer-producing, tars.

NITROUS OXIDE and OXYGEN

These are traditionally known as "gas and air" and are used mainly in childbirth when they are inhaled 20 seconds prior to a contraction during labor. They induce a state of drowsiness.

ORPHENADRINE ASPIRIN and CAFFEINE

This strong combination is a non-steroidal, potentially habit-forming drug that works by interrupting the body's pain signals, reducing muscle spasm and pain, and regulating the body's temperature. It also has a stimulating effect on the central nervous system.

PAIN RELIEF

(see Analgesics)

PHENOTHIAZINES

These are tranquillizers that reduce activity in the part of the brain that affects emotions and behavior. They are mainly used in the treatment of mental, nervous, or emotional conditions.

PHOTOSENSITIZING MEDICATIONS

These are medications that cause abnormal skin reactions to sunlight and ultraviolet light. A great many medications do this, so it is always worth checking with your doctor or pharmacist, although you should be advised of the risk of photo-sensitivity automatically at the time of dispensing.

PROGESTERONES

These are female sex hormones used in menstrual and uterine disorders and to correct hormone imbalances. They are often combined with estrogens in the contraceptive pill and sometimes used to treat breast and uterine cancers.

PROTEASE INHIBITOR

This combines with other drugs in advanced cases of HIV. It blocks a replicating enzyme, so that when the virus produces new cells, these cannot become infected. It does not cure HIV (see Immunosuppressants).

RADIOLOGY

Radiation has the capacity to destroy malignant cells, and a range of radioactive drugs is used in the treatment of different kinds of cancer. These can be either artificial radioactive isotopes, which are given by injection, a combination of rays (beta, gamma, and x-rays), or with other substances added.

Diagnostic use: Minute amounts of a radioactive substance are either injected or taken orally, and their concentration in different parts of the body acts as a "tracer" in the diagnosis of a wide variety of conditions. A large amount of liquids is given to stimulate urination afterward to minimize the risk of radiation affecting the patient. Because the waste products may be radioactive, special measures are taken for their disposal.

Therapeutic use: Radioactive isotopes of elements, for example iodine in overactive thyroid conditions, are used in measured doses to normalize function by reducing the number of functioning cells. Radiation in larger doses is administered externally to kill cancerous cells. The inherent risk in this therapy is that a certain number of normal cells will also die.

RETINOIDS

These synthetically produced compounds are similar to vitamin A and are used to treat skin conditions such as acne by reducing the activity of the sebaceous gland. Retin-A is often included in many cosmetic preparations for the skin because it has been found to repair the aging lines and wrinkles that are the result of sun damage. It will not have any effect on skin changes that are part of the normal aging process.

SALICYLATES

Salts of salicylic acid reduce temperature by promoting sweating as well as reducing pain (see Aspirin under Analgesics).

SEDATIVES

These drugs reduce overactivity of the nervous system, which lessens excitement, anxiety, and emotional stress. They are sometimes used to reduce pain and induce sleep. Tranquillizers are intended to calm, and hypnotics are aimed at inducing sleep, so sedatives fall between the two categories. In larger doses, bromides and barbiturates are also sedatives.

THROMBOLYTIC AGENTS

These drugs are used to dissolve blood clots and slow the rate of blood clotting to prevent thrombosis (see Anticoagulants).

THYROID HORMONES

The thyroid is an important endocrine gland rich in iodine and regulates the body's metabolism and growth. An excess of thyroid hormone leads to Graves disease; a deficiency causes myxoedema. Both are treatable with either the appropriate quantities of replacement thyroid hormone or with a blocking agent to prevent excessive production.

VASOCONSTRICTORS

These drugs are used to prevent vascular headaches such as migraine by blocking serotonin, which normally constricts blood vessels.

VITAMINS

These are organic compounds that are essential in small amounts in the diet to maintain good health. Deficiencies in any one vitamin can lead to specific diseases. There are two main groups: Those that are fat-soluble, which includes vitamins A, D, E, and K, and those that are water-soluble, which includes vitamins C and B. Most normal diets provide adequate quantities of vitamins, but it may be necessary to use vitamin supplements during pregnancy and lactation or in cases of acute illness.

Many people add vitamins to their daily diet. Ideally, all food should produce enough for people's needs, but many foods in fact contain far less than expected. Vitamin C does not travel well, and if, for example, oranges are transported over long distances before they go on sale, the amount of vitamin C they contain will be greatly reduced in the process. Most cartons of orange juice reveal the gradual depletion of vitamin C content after opening. This principle should be applied to other foods providing other vitamins to make sure excessive vitamin supplements are not added, but essential ones are topped up where necessary. An excess of certain vitamins can be as damaging as a deficiency.

ABOVE **Some vitamin supplements can be harmful when taken in large amounts, because they can build up to dangerous levels in body tissues. However, this is rare with vitamins B and C because any excess is excreted in the urine.**

WHAT SCIENTISTS SAY ABOUT URI GELLER

"I was in scientific laboratories at Stanford Research Institute investigating a rather amazing individual, Uri Geller. Uri's ability to perform amazing feats of mental wizardry is known the world over. We in science are just now catching up and understanding what you can do with exercise and proper practice. Uri is not a magician. He is using capabilities that we all have and can develop with exercise and practice.

"After the Geller work, I was asked to brief the director of the CIA, Ambassador George Bush (later to become President of the United States), on our activities and the results. In later years during the Brezhnev period, I met with several Russian scientists who not only had documented results similar to ours, but were actively using 'psychic' techniques against the US and its allies."

DR. EDGAR D. MITCHELL SCD
Apollo 14 astronaut and the sixth man to walk on the moon

"Geller has bent my ring in the palm of my hand without ever touching it. Personally, I have no scientific explanation for the phenomena."

DR. WERNHER VON BRAUN
NASA scientist and father of the rocket, United States

"The evidence based on metallurgical analysis of fractured surfaces (produced by Geller) indicates that a paranormal influence must have been operative in the formation of the fractures."

DR. WILBUR FRANKLIN
Physics Department, Kent State University, Ohio, United States

"We have observed certain phenomena with the subjects (including Uri Geller) for which we have no scientific explanation.

"As a result of Geller's success in this experimental period, we consider he has demonstrated his paranormal, perceptual ability in a convincing and unambiguous manner."

(The results of these experiments were published in the respected British journal Nature, Vol 251, No 5.)

DR. HAROLD PUTHOFF AND RUSSELL TARG
Stanford Research Institute, California, United States

"Laser physicists Russell Targ and Harold Puthoff of Menlo Park's Stanford Research Institute admit their kind of research invites chicanery and trickery. They took special precautions, they said, to conduct the Stanford Research experiments under doubly strict laboratory conditions. 'Under these conditions,' they said, 'no magician has been able to duplicate through trickery the psychic feat performed by Uri Geller and others. Some won't even try.'"

LOS ANGELES TIMES
Monday July 28, 1975

"Based on preliminary investigations of Uri Geller, I cannot establish fraud. The powers of this man are a phenomenon which theoretical physics cannot yet explain."

DR. FRIEDBERT KARGER
Max Planck Institute for Plasma Physics, Munich, Germany

"The bends in metal objects (made by Geller) could not have been made by ordinary manual means."

DR. ALBERT DUCROCQ
Telemetry Laboratory, Foch Hospital Suren, France

"The Geller method of breaking is unlike anything described in the (metallurgical) literature, from fatigue fractures at -195° C to brittle fractures at +600° C. Why is metal bending important? Simply because we do not understand it. We feel that if similar tests are made later, enough substances of this kind will probably accumulate, so that there will be no room for reasonable doubt that some new process is involved here, which cannot be accounted for or explained in terms of the present known laws of physics. Indeed, we already feel that we have gone some distance toward this point."

PROFESSOR DAVID BOHM AND PROFESSOR JOHN HASTED
Professors of Physics, Birkbeck College, University of London, England
(Professor Bohm is the author of Wholeness and the Implicate Order, *and worked with Albert Einstein)*

"Geller altered the lattice structure of a metal alloy in a way that cannot be duplicated. There is no present scientific explanation as to how he did this."

(This is the first research related to parapsychology conducted at an American government facility to have been released for publication by the US Department of Defense.)

ELDON BYRD
US Naval Surface Weapons Center, Maryland, United States

"Metal objects were bent or divided (by Geller) in circumstances such as to prove conclusively . . . that the phenomena were genuine and paranormal."

DR. A. R. G. OWEN
New Horizons Research Foundation, Toronto, Ontario, Canada

"There is no logical explanation for what Geller did here. But I don't think logic is what necessarily makes new inroads in science."

DR. THOMAS COOHILL
Western Kentucky University, Physics Department, Bowling Green, Kentucky, United States

'The Geller Effect is one of those 'para' phenomena that changed the world of physics. What the most outstanding physicists of the last decades of this century could grasp only as theoretical implication, Uri brought as fact into everyday life."

DR. WALTER A. FRANK
Bonn University, Germany

"I have conducted research on Mr. Uri Geller at Freiburg University's laboratory. The results substantiated and proved my conviction and belief in his powers of metal bending. I have written extensively about his psychokinetic powers in my book, *Our Sixth Sense*, in 1982."

PROFESSOR HANS BENDER
Freiburg University, Germany

"I tested Uri Geller myself under laboratory-controlled conditions and saw with my own eyes the bending of a key which was not touched by Geller at any time. There was a group of people present during the experiment who all witnessed the key bending in 11 seconds to an angle of 30 degrees. Afterward we tested the key in a scientific laboratory using devices such as electron microscopes and x-rays and found that there was no chemical, manual, or mechanical forces involved in the bending of the key."

PROFESSOR HELMUT HOFFMAN
Department of Electrical Engineering, Technical University of Vienna, Austria

"Through intense concentration, Uri was able to bend a ⅜-inch cold rolled steel bar under controlled conditions, as he rubbed the top of it with his forefinger. I was sitting very close to him during this experiment. On another occasion, a radish seed sprouted and grew ½ an inch as he held it in his hand. I watched this very closely as well."

JEAN MILLAY, PHD
Saybrook Institute, United States

"I have failed to conceive of any means of deception in the static PK tests with Geller, nor have magicians I have consulted."

WILLIAM E. COX
Institute of Parapsychology, Durham, North Carolina, United States

"Uri Geller is extraordinarily gifted in telepathy."

PROFESSOR ERICH MITTENNECKER
Professor of Psychology, University of Graz, Austria

"Uri Geller was tested in my laboratory at UCLA. During the experiments in Kirlian photography and after hundreds of trials, he produced three extraordinary photographs in which flashes of energy were clearly visible.

What wonderfully welcome sights they were! I have also tested Uri's watch-fixing and metal-bending abilities. He has demonstrated these to me under controlled scientific conditions in a most convincing manner."

DR. THELMA MOSS,
Professor of Psychology at UCLA, and one of the first U.S. researchers to experiment with Kirlian photography

"Uri bent a strong heat-treated alloy bar held by myself and my assistant at each end. There was absolutely no pressure exerted by Uri while the bar was bending. All the controlled experiments I conducted with Uri Geller have been described in *Sciences et Avenir*, No 345, pp 1108–1113."

PROFESSOR CHARLES CRUSSARD
Professor of Metallurgy, School of Mines, Paris, and Scientific Director of Pechency, France

"I put the spoon that Uri bent into my pocket and kept checking it every 3–4 minutes. It gradually bent to about 90 degrees in 15 minutes while in my own possession with no one around me. The spoon was later examined by electron beam scattering. In my opinion, shared by my physicist colleagues, the phenomenon cannot be induced by our present laboratory means. It cannot be explained with our present knowledge."

PROFESSOR GEORGE EGEYLY
Physicist, Hungarian Academy of Sciences Central Research Institute for Physics, Budapest, Hungary

"Your coming to the University of California, Berkeley, and conducting your demonstrations was instrumental in setting up the conditions for me to bring together the group of 40 physicists to start and conduct the Fundamental 'Fysiks' Laboratory that met weekly from 1974 to 1979. The purpose of the FFL was to explore the nature of reality and the use of physical models to explain the space-time attributes of consciousness and remote connection models of Bell's Theorem. The key is that psychokinesis and psi in general, related powers of the mind, can be studied with the scientific method and you have had a key influence on scientists in their research and knowledge of PK and you have been instrumental in getting people to explore the

power of the mind. The purpose of life and scientific exploration is to learn what is."

DR. ELIZABETH A. RAUSCHER
Theoretical Physicist, Lawrence Berkeley Laboratory, University of California, Berkeley, United States

"Science is at last recognizing that quantum mechanics and relativity do predict some form of information laws, which may go a long way toward explaining the effects surround Uri Geller, one of the most powerful men alive today."

D. ROBERTSON
Physicist and metal bending researcher, England

"Uri Geller, as a psychic genius, has been able to demonstrate the repeatability of controlled scientific psychic experiments. Thereby he has proved the reality of psychic phenomena (such as telekinesis, clairvoyance, and telepathy)."

PROFESSOR P. PLUM, M.D.
Emeritus Professor of Pediatrics, University of Copenhagen, former chairman of the Danish Medical Research Council, Denmark

"In our presence and in the presence of numerous eye witnesses, Uri Geller demonstrated the following telekinetic effects: He bent at our request metal keys and teaspoons, the spoons bending to an angle of 90 degrees over a period of 5 minutes after his influence had been exerted on them. Before the eyes of those present he germinated a radish seed to a small sprout in 8 minutes. He reproduced target pictures exactly to the nearest millimeter (square, triangle with a dot in the center, etc.), and also wiped the information from an IBM cassette. He also correctly described a dome-shaped building that formerly stood in the Moscow river basin, the destruction of which was linked to the name of Stalin."

PROFESSOR V. G. LUKES
Director of the Ministry of Health Protection of the Russian Federation Institute of Traditional Medicine, Moscow, Russia;

A. A. KARPEYEV
Deputy Director

R. YU VOLKOV
Department Head;

A. P. DUBROV
Chief Scientific Collaborator

"The telepathy experiment was conducted under the following conditions: There were six people in the laboratory: two engineers from the factory that makes thermography (they are both graduates of Tokyo Denki University), two student assistants, myself, and Mr. Geller. Under no circumstances could Mr. Geller have seen my drawing before the experiment was all over. Only after Mr. Geller drew the image that he received was my drawing revealed."

PROFESSOR YOSHIO MACHI
Department of Electronics, Tokyo Denki University, Japan

"I have had more than 50 years experience with psychics and would-be psychics. From having observed Uri Geller bend a volunteered latchkey under excellent conditions, and from having studied Mr. Geller's record of tests under various auspices, I have not the slightest doubt that his psychic abilities are genuine."

JULE EISENBUD M.D.
Associate Clinical Professor of Psychiatry, University of Colorado Health Sciences Center, United States

"The Yale key at no time left our sight from the moment it was removed from the key ring and placed on the typewriter frame to the time when the splined end had bent upward. Our attention was not distracted and the key was not altered in position, accidentally or otherwise. We were all looking carefully for magician's tricks and there were none. Everything occurred exactly as I have described. As a result of this personally witnessed experiment in clear unequivocal conditions, I am able to state with confidence my view that Mr. Geller has genuine psychic capability."

PROFESSOR ARTHUR ELLISON
Emeritus Professor of Electrical Engineering, City University, London, England

"I have personally witnessed and experienced on two occasions the metal bending abilities of Uri Geller. These experiments were conducted under rigorous laboratory conditions. In these two experiments, the thick steel rod I was holding and observing carefully bent, and continued to bend, in my own hand. One rod bent to 90 degrees during a period of approximately 6 minutes while I was holding it. The other steel rod bent after Uri Geller stroked it and continued bending on a glass table without anyone touching it. The steel rods were provided by myself. I consider the Geller effect to be a phenomenon which should be studied seriously by science."

DR. KIT PEDLER
Head of the Electron Microscopy Department, University of London, England

"I am a psychiatrist with 30 years clinical experience, a conjurer with a wide knowledge of 'magic,' and someone who has investigated paranormal phenomena and found them wanting in the past. Uri Geller gave me a demonstration of spoon bending. I could find no evidence of trickery, nor the use of gimmicks. The fact that the spoon continued bending after he had handed it to me, for my mind, puts the event beyond rational explanation be it scientific or a feat of conjuring. He also demonstrated two examples of thought transference, first accurately reproducing a geometric figure I had drawn, and second and perhaps more significantly transmitting to me a figure and a color. As a life-long skeptic, I must record my total astonishment at these feats and testify my witness to a truly inexplicable and unique phenomenon."

DR. LAWRENCE RATNA
Consultant Psychiatrist, England

"What I saw Geller do in the laboratory was a truly mind-blowing experience . . . He manifests an extreme case of some unusual power, capacity, or energy, which I believe is genuine.

"Personally, I can tell you that I consider what I saw with you as truly mind-blowing experiences, which cannot be overlooked and should certainly be made common knowledge once we have established it."

(These tests were conducted at the Weizmann Institute in Rehovot.)

ZVI BENTWICH M.D.
Background in the fields of medicine and immunology, Kaplan Hospital, affiliated to the Medical School of the Hebrew University and Hadassah, Jerusalem, Israel.

"Uri Geller knows the power of thought and has been both courageous and generous in demonstrating and sharing the fruits of that knowledge with millions around the world. His persistent light has brightened a dark era (thankfully now coming to a close) in which 'scientific' orthodoxy became so immersed in matter as to lose sight of mind."

NEVILLE HODGKINSON
Former social policy correspondent, The Times, *and medical and science correspondent,* The Sunday Times, London; *author of* Will To Be Well – The Real Alternative Medicine *(Hutchinson, 1984) and* AIDS: The Failure of Contemporary Science *(Fourth Estate, 1994)*

"I have always felt that you are able to perform the phenomena ascribed to you, at least under favorable conditions, and was happy with your success at the November conference in Seattle."

WILLIAM A. TILLER, PHD
Professor, Stanford University, Department of Materials Science and Engineering, United States

"Attempts made to replicate this type of fracture in conventional ways were unsuccessful."

ANTON WEST, PHD
Expert in fracture of materials, Department of Materials Science and Engineering, Stanford University, California, United States

BIBLIOGRAPHY

Majno, G., *The Healing Hand – Man and Wound in the Ancient World*, Harvard University Press, 1991

Barasch, M. I., *The Healing Path*, Penguin, 1993

Miles, M., *Homeopathy and Human Evolution*, Winter Press, 1996

Jung, C., *Man and His Symbols*, Penguin, 1964

Fordham, F., *An Introduction to Jung's Psychology*, Penguin, 1991

Porter, R., *The Greatest Benefit to Mankind*, HarperCollins, 1997

Dunning, A. J., *Extremes: Reflections on Human Behaviour*, Harcourt Brace Jovanovich, 1992

Horney, K., *Neurosis and Human Growth*, W. W. Norton & Company, 1950

Eysenck, H. J., *Sense and Nonsense in Psychology*, Penguin, 1964

Brown, J. A. C., *Freud and the Post-Freudians*, Penguin, 1987

Abse, D., *Medicine on Trial*, Aldus Books, 1967

Marcuse, F. L., *Hypnosis – Fact and Fiction*, Penguin, 1982

OTHER BOOKS BY URI GELLER

My Story, Praeger/Robson

Shawn, Goodyer Associates

The Geller Effect, Henry Holt/Jonathan Cape/Grafton

Uri Geller's Fortune Secrets, Sphere

Change Your Life In One Day, Marshall Cavendish

Uri Geller's Mind-Power Kit, Penguin/Virgin

Uri Geller's Little Book of Mind Power, Robson

Ella, Headline Feature

Dead Cold, Headline Feature

Uri Geller's ParaScience Pack, van der Meer

BOOKS ABOUT URI GELLER

Uri, Andrija Puharich, Doubleday

The Amazing Uri Geller, Martin Ebon, New American Library

Uri Geller: Fup Eller Fakta?, Leo Leslie, Samlerens Piccoloboger

The Strange Story of Uri Geller, Jim Colin, Raintree (for children)

In Search of Superman, John Wilhelm, Pocket Books

The Geller Papers, Charles Panati, Houghton Mifflin

The Geller Phenomenon, Colin Wilson, Aldus Books

Superminds, John G. Taylor, Macmillan/Picador

The Metal Benders, John Hasted, Routledge and Kegan Paul

Mysterious Powers, Orbis Books

Uri Geller El Descubierto, Ramos Perera, Sedmay Ediciones

Uri Geller Magician or Mystic, Jonathan Margolis, Orion

Most of Uri Geller's books, mind games, and lots of other fascinating information and pictures, relating to him and his work, including his biography, are available on his web-site:
www.uri-geller.com

You can write to Uri Geller at:
Element Books Ltd.
The Old School House
The Courtyard
Bell Street
Shaftesbury
Dorset SP7 8BP
England
or e-mail him at urigeller@compuserve.com

USEFUL ADDRESSES

United Kingdom
Institute for Complementary Medicine
PO Box 194, London SE16 1QZ
Telephone: 0171 237 5165

Powerwatch Update
Information about living with electricity can be obtained from their website:
www.powerwatch.org.uk

The National Institute of Medical Herbalists
56 Longbrook Street, Exeter EX4 6AH
Telephone: 01392 426022

The Royal Homeopathy Hospital
Great Ormond Street, London WC1 3HR
Telephone: 0171 837 8833

The School of Meditation
158 Holland Park Avenue, London W11 4UH
Telephone: 0171 603 6116

United States
American Holistic Medical Association
4101 Lake Boone Trail
Suite 201, Raleigh, North Carolina 27607

American Herb Association
PO Box 1673, Nevada City, California 95959

American Institute of Homeopathy
1585 Glencoe, Denver, Colorado 80220

Andrew Weil, M.D.
Website "Ask Dr. Weil"
www.drweil.com

The Chopra Center for Well Being
7630 Fay Avenue, La Jolla
California 92037
Telephone: (619) 551 7788
Website: www.chopra.com

FURTHER READING

Brennan, R., *Mind and Body Stress Relief with the Alexander Technique*, Thorsons, 1998

Carrington, P., *The Book of Meditation*, Element, 1998

Chang, S., *The Complete System of Chinese Self-healing*, Thorsons, 1998

Collinge, W., *Subtle Energy*, Thorsons, 1998

Dossey, L., *The Power of Prayer and the Practice of Medicine*, HarperCollins, 1993

Fontana, D., *The Elements of Meditation*, Element, 1991

Fontana, D., *The Meditator's Handbook*, Element, 1998

Harrod, J., *Bach Flower Remedies for Women*, C W Daniel Company Limited, 1994

Porter, R., Medicine – *A History of Healing*, Michael O'Mara, 1997

Robbins, A., *Awaken the Giant Within*, Simon and Schuster, 1991

Stein D., *Natural Remedy Book for Women*, The Crossing Press, 1995

ACKNOWLEDGMENTS

There are too many people to mention who have directly or indirectly contributed to Mind Medicine and they all deserve credit. I wish to express my profound gratitude to those kind friends as well as to my fantastic family – not forgetting our five dogs whose demands for long daily walks presented a perfect excuse to stretch my legs and stretch my mind, providing time and space to gather my thoughts and inspire many of the ideas contained in this book.

INDEX